CAMBRIDGE
UNIVERSITY PRESS

CAMBRIDGE ENGLISH
Language Assessment
Part of the University of Cambridge

C000131703

OFFICIAL
PREPARATION MATERIAL

Cambridge English

FUN for Starters

TEACHER'S BOOK

Anne Robinson
Karen Saxby

4th edition

Cambridge University Press
www.cambridge.org/elt

Cambridge Assessment English
www.cambridgeenglish.org

Information on this title: www.cambridge.org/9781316617496

© Cambridge University Press & Assessment 2016

First published 2006
Second edition 2010
Third edition 2015
Fourth edition 2016

20 19 18 17 16 15 14

Printed in Malaysia by Vivar Printing

A catalogue record for this publication is available from the British Library

ISBN 978-1-316-61746-5 Student's Book with online activities with audio and Home Fun Booklet
ISBN 978-1-316-63191-1 Student's Book with online activities with audio
ISBN 978-1-316-61749-6 Teacher's Book with downloadable audio
ISBN 978-1-108-72816-4 Presentation Plus

Contents

The authors and publishers would like to thank the ELT professionals who commented on the material at different stages of its development.

The authors are grateful to: Niki Donnelly of Cambridge University Press.

Anne Robinson would like to give special thanks to Adam Evans and her parents Margaret and Jim and to many, many teachers and students who have inspired her along the way. Special thanks to Cristina and Victoria for their help, patience and enthusiasm. And in memory of her brother Dave.

Karen Saxby would like to give special thanks to everyone she has worked with at Cambridge Assessment since the birth of YLE! She would particularly like to mention Frances, Felicity and Ann Kelly. She would also like to acknowledge the enthusiasm of all the teachers she has met through her work in this field. And lastly, Karen would like to say a big thank you to her sons, Tom and William, for bringing constant FUN and creative thinking to her life and work.

Freelance editorial services by Christine Barton

Design and typeset by Wild Apple Design.

Cover design by Chris Saunders (Astound).

Sound recordings by dsound Recording Studios, London

The authors and publishers acknowledge the following sources of copyright material and are grateful for the permissions granted. While every effort has been made, it has not always been possible to identify the sources of all the material used, or to trace all copyright holders. If any omissions are brought to our notice, we will be happy to include the appropriate acknowledgements on reprinting and in the next update to the digital edition, as applicable.

The authors and publishers are grateful to the following illustrators:

T = Top, B = Below, L = Left, R = Right, C = Centre, B/G = Background

Stephen Dew pp. 109, 115; Andrew Elkerton (Sylvie Poggio Artists Agency) p. 108; Nigel Kitching p. 107; Ray & Corinne Burrows @Beehive pp122, 124(b), 125(m), 129(m,b), 130(m), 131, 133(legs of dog), 140(bottom four images) Pip Sampson pp. 126, 131, 139; Melanie Sharp (Sylvie Poggio Artists Agency) pp. 123, 134, 135; Sue Woollatt (Graham-Cameron Illustration) pp. 113, 114, 122, 124, 125, 129, 130, 132, 133, 140.

Introduction

Welcome to *Fun for Starters Fourth edition*

Fun for Starters Fourth edition is the first in a series of three books written for learners aged between 7 and 13 years old. *Fun for Movers Fourth edition* is the second book in the series and *Fun for Flyers Fourth edition* is the third.

Who is *Fun for Starters Fourth edition* for?

Fun for Starters is suitable for:

o learners who need comprehensive preparation for the *Cambridge English: Starters (YLE Starters)*, in addition to their general English course

o mixed classes where some of the learners are preparing to take the *Cambridge English: Starters* test, and who need motivating and fun English lessons

o small and large groups of learners

o monolingual and multilingual classes

Fun for Starters supports the development of good learning habits and language practice in meaningful, fun, creative and interactive ways. It is ideal for learners who have been studying English for between one and three years, and who need to consolidate their language and skills.

The key features include:

o complete coverage of the vocabulary and grammar on the *Cambridge English: Starters* syllabus

o thorough preparation for all parts of the *Cambridge English: Starters* test

o a focus on all four skills, with an emphasis on those areas most likely to cause problems for young learners at this level

o recycling of language and topics

o fun activities that practise English in a meaningful way

o opportunities for learners to personalise the language and make the tasks relevant to them

Cambridge English: Young Learners

For more information on *Cambridge English: Young Learners*, please visit https://www.cambridgeenglish.org/exams-and-tests/. From here, you can download the handbook for teachers, which includes information about each level of the Young Learners exams. You can also find information for candidates and their parents, including links to videos of the Speaking test at each level. There are also sample test papers, as well as games, and links to the Teaching Support website.

Course components
Student's Book with downloadable class audio and online activities

The Student's Book has been updated to include:

o even more opportunities for test practice. In most units, there will be at least one authentic test-style task. The instructions for these tasks are shown in (blue lozenge), while instructions for tasks which provide more general test practice are shown in black.

o new illustrations, designed to stimulate learner engagement

o a variety of fun activities, such as games, puzzles, drawing and colouring, to ensure your learners are involved in, and enjoy, their English lessons

o recordings for the listening tasks, which are available via the access code at the front of the book, so that learners can practise at home.

o online activities, available via the access code at the front of the book, which provide further practice of the grammar and vocabulary featured in the Student's Book as well as exam preparation activities

o projects that encourage learners to explore topics in more depth and produce work more independently

Teacher's Book with downloadable class audio

In the fourth edition of the Teacher's Book, you can find:

o clear signalling of *Cambridge English: Starters* test practice tasks and authentic test-style tasks that appear in each unit. These are listed in the information boxes at the start of each unit, under **Starters practice** or **Starters test**. In the unit notes, an icon like this Listening **2** indicates the part of *Cambridge English: Starters* that an authentic test-style task replicates.

o useful tips to guide and support learners in their preparation for each part of the test.

o materials and equipment needed to teach each unit. This means less preparation is needed, as you can see at a glance the audio resources or numbers of photocopies you need for each lesson.

o suggested wording of classroom language at the learners' level of English

o support for teaching pronunciation activities in a fun and motivating way for learners of this age

o ideas for maximising the involvement of learners in their learning process

o ideas for extending activities into simple, fun projects that give learners the chance to explore topics more independently and consolidate their English in creative ways

o additional resources, visuals and lesson ideas for teachers, and interactive games and activities to accompany *Fun for Starters*.

Online audio

The audio is available to download by following the instructions and using the access code at the front of the Student's Book.

Presentation plus

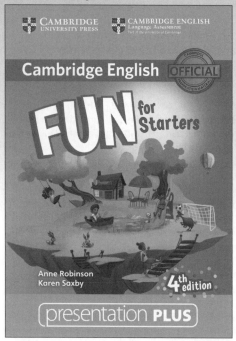

Presentation plus is a digital version of the Student's Book and all the audio to complete the listening tasks. The integrated tools enable you to make notes, highlight activities and turn the Student's Book into an interactive experience for your learners. The Presentation plus includes:

O   all the Student's Book pages

O   all the audio for the Student's Book

O   pdfs of the Teacher's Book, including a complete practice test with the Listening audio

O   unit tests – one per unit, testing the key language covered in each unit

An app for mobile phones and tablets

For further practice of the list of vocabulary for *Cambridge English: Starters*, download our new app and encourage your learners to practise their vocabulary while having fun!

Online activities

The online activities provide students with extra practice in grammar, vocabulary and exam tasks. All of the students' online work can be tracked and reviewed by the teacher.

For access to Fun for Starters online content, contact your local Cambridge representative.

How is the Student's Book organised?

Contents

This lists the Student's Book unit numbers and titles.

45 units

Each unit is topic-based and designed to provide between 75 and 90 minutes of class time. Language is presented and practised throughout the unit and the final activity usually provides freer, fun practice of the unit's key content language.

Ideas for project work on topic are included in many units and signalled by a 🗂 icon, as are fun activities to practise specific phonemes or other key aspects of pronunciation.

Pairwork activities pages (pages 96–100)

Learners will use these in specific unit tasks.

Unit wordlist (pages 101–111)

This is a list of the key words which appear in each unit (organised by topic or word class). There is space for learners to make notes or to write translations for each word.

How is the Teacher's Book organised?

Contents

This shows where to find each section of the Teacher's Book.

Introduction

This will help you use *Fun for Starters Fourth edition*. It includes:

O   a **quick guide** to how units in the Teacher's books are organised (page 7)

O   suggestions for **games and activities** (page 7)

O   suggestions for how to use **pictures in the Student's Book** (page 8)

O   suggestions for **using small pictures or word cards** (pages 8)

Checklist for Cambridge English: Starters preparation (page 9)

O   a quick guide to what learners have to do in each part of the Starters test and units where each part is covered in the Student's Book. 'Test' indicates those activities that reflect the format of the Starters Listening, Reading and Writing or Speaking test. 'Practice' indicates activities that prepare for a particular part of the Starters, but do not reflect the identical format of the test.

Map of the Student's Book (pages 10–13)

O   an overview of the content and organisation of all the units in the Student's Book.

Topics and grammar indexes (pages 14–15)

Unit guides / Teacher's notes

O   the teacher's notes for each of the 45 units. See below for a detailed guide to these.

Photocopiable activities (pages 106–121)

O   these relate to specific units as indicated in the teacher's notes.

Starters photocopiable practice test (pages 122–140)

O   a complete Starters Practice Test (Listening, Reading and Writing, Speaking) to photocopy and use with learners. Audioscripts and a key are also provided.

How is each unit organised?

Topics, non-Starters words
This is a list of all the topics covered in the unit. Any words that appear in the unit but not in the Starters wordlist are also listed below.

Equipment needed
This lists any equipment, for example: audio resources and/or material needed for the unit, including the number of photocopies needed for any activities. Pages to be photocopied are found at the back of the Teacher's Book.

Instructions
These are usually labelled A, B, C, etc. and correspond to the different activities which appear in the Student's Book.

There are some activities that appear only in the teacher's notes and are not labelled A, B, C, etc.

Audioscripts
The audioscripts for each Listening are at the end of the activity where they are used.

Project work
There are a number of suggestions for projects. The instructions for these generally appear at the ends of units.

Listening tasks

There is a listening icon at the beginning of each listening task. In the Starters **test practice** tasks, the lengths of the pauses in the audio are the same as in the Young Learners English Tests the first time they are played.

When the audio is heard the second time in the Cambridge English: YLE Tests, the pauses are slightly shorter, allowing time to add any missing answers and/or to check answers.

For all other Listening tasks in this book, the lengths of pauses are approximate. You may want to re-start or stop the audio to allow your learners less or more time in which to complete tasks.

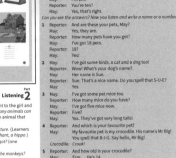

Fun and games

The following games and activities can be done in class to practise or revise a wide range of vocabulary or grammar.

Bingo
Learners make a grid of six or nine squares, in two or three rows of three. They write a word in each square. Read out words, one by one. If learners have the word, they cross it out or cover it with a small piece of paper.

The first learner to cross out or cover all their words is the winner. Check that learners have heard the right words by asking them to say the words and comparing them with your list of words.

Seven lives ('Hangman')
Draw (or stick) seven body outlines on the board.

 XXXXXXX

Choose a word. Draw one line on the board for each letter in the word, for example: _ _ _ _ _ . (dress) Learners put up their hands to say letters. If the letter is in the word, you write it on the line. If the letter is not in the word, you remove one of the bodies from the board. The game finishes when the learners complete the word or they lose all seven lives. Learners then play in groups, drawing lines for their own words.

The long sentence
Choose a simple sentence which can grow if words are added to the end of it.
For example:
Teacher: In my bedroom, there's a bed.
Learner 1: In my bedroom, there's a bed and a table.
Continue round the class, with each learner repeating the sentence and all the words which have been added, before then adding another word. The winner is the person who remembers all the words in the correct order when everyone else has been eliminated.

Change places
Learners sit in a circle. Say sentences starting with the words: Change places if ... For example: Change places if you got up at 8 o'clock today. All the learners who got up at 8 o'clock have to stand up and move to sit in a different place.

Spell it!
Choose a group of words (from a particular topic, like body or animals, or the words could be unrelated). Tell learners to listen and write the letters as you say them to spell the word. For example, P-E- If learners think they know the word, they say Stop! and say the remaining letters, for example: A-R and the word (pear). If they are right, they get a point for each letter they gave. If they are not right, continue to spell out the word, letter by letter.

Guess what I'm drawing
One learner chooses a word and draws a picture of it on the board, one line at a time. After each line, the learner asks: What's this? The other learners try to guess what it is. The learner who guesses correctly then draws on the board. The game can be played in groups with learners drawing lines on paper.

Group or order the words
Take any group of words (related or not) and ask learners to group or order them:

○ **from longest to shortest.**
Learners either write the words in order according to the number of letters they have, or learners write the words in order according to the number of vowels they have.

○ **from smallest to biggest.**
Learners write the words starting with the smallest thing / animal / food, etc.

○ **in alphabetical order.**
Learners write the words in alphabetical order.

- o **in colour groups.**
   Learners write words in groups according to their colour.
- o **in sound groups.**
   Learners write words in groups according to pronunciation similarities (stress patterns, vowel sounds, etc).

Backs to the board

- o Make teams of 4–8 learners, depending on the size of the class.
- o Put one chair for each team at the front of the class. A learner from each team comes and sits on a chair, with their back to the board.
- o Write up a word on the board (for example: *page*). One team gives clues to the learners on the chairs so that they can guess the word.
- o The first learner from the chairs at the front to stand up gives an answer. If they are right, they get a point for their team. If they are wrong, they sit down and another team gives a clue. Again the first person to stand up gives an answer. Teams get a point for every correct answer.
- o When the word has been guessed, different learners from each team come to the front of the class and sit down and the activity is repeated.

Fun with pictures

You can use the pictures in the Student's Book in many different ways to revise and practise language. Here are some suggestions.

Which picture?

In pairs or small groups, one learner chooses a picture from any page in *Fun for Starters Fourth edition*. The other learner(s) have to ask questions to discover which picture. For example: *Can you see some people? Is it in a house/park, etc?* Once the other learner(s) have found the picture, they choose a picture and are asked questions.

Yes or no?

In small groups, learners write sentences about a picture in the Student's Book. Some sentences should be true for the picture and some should be false. They either pass their sentences on to another group or they say the sentences to the other group. The other group has to say or write *yes* for the true sentences and *no* for the false ones.

Listen and draw

Learners work in pairs or small groups. One learner looks at one of the pictures in the Student's Book. This person describes the picture to the other learner(s), who has/have to draw the picture.

Where am I?

A learner 'hides' somewhere in the picture. Learners have to find out where they are by asking questions. For example: page 21 (Unit 8) *Are you on the armchair?* (No) *Are you on the table?* (Yes!)

Say something more!

- o Divide the class into groups of 6–8 and ask them to sit in circles. All learners look at the same picture in the Student's Book (for example: page 62 , Unit 29, Picture 1). One learner starts and says a sentence about the picture. For example: *The people are in a toy shop.* The learner next to that learner says another sentence about the picture. For example: *A man is cleaning the floor.*
- o Continue round the circle. If a learner repeats a sentence that someone else has said, they are eliminated (or lose a point).
   Variation: Each learner has to repeat the previous sentences and then add a new one.

How many words?

Teams look at a picture and write as many different words as they can for things they can see. For example: Page 68, A, Unit 32. *Sausages, burgers, plates, balloons, table, etc.* The winners are the team with the most number of correctly spelt words.

Fun with small pictures or word cards

Which one is missing?

Divide the class into groups of 4–5 learners. Each group puts 10–12 picture cards (such as the ones on pages 108, 109, 113 or 114 of the Teacher's Book) face up on a table in the middle of the group. Everyone except one learner closes their eyes. This learner takes one of the cards off the table. The other learners in the group open their eyes and look at the cards on the table. The first person to say which picture card is missing then takes the next card from the table.

Make pairs

Divide the class into groups of 4–5 learners. You need two sets of picture or word cards for each group. The cards are dealt out to all the learners in the group. Each learner looks at their cards. If they have a 'pair' (two cards with the same picture or word), they put the cards face up in front of them.

Learners take it in turn to ask a learner in the group for a certain card, for example: *Marga, have you got 'children'?* If the other learner has that card, they must give it to the asking learner, who can then put the pair of two cards on the table. The winner is the learner with most pairs of cards.

Tell me more about these people

Learners work in pairs to imagine and talk or write about the people in the picture.

For example: page 15, Unit 5: *What are these children's names? How old is the girl? What does she like doing? What's her favourite animal/game/colour? etc.*

What are they saying?

Pairs decide what different animals or people could be saying to each other in the picture. For example: page 54, Unit 25: *What's the fish saying to the tiger? What's the monkey saying to the hippo? What's the bird saying to the giraffe?*

Checklist for Cambridge English: Starters preparation

Paper	Part	Task	Unit
Listening 20 minutes	1	Draw lines between names outside and people inside a scene picture.	*Practice*: 11, 14, 15, 18 *Test*: 5, 17, 33
	2	Write numbers and names.	*Practice*: 1, 3, 5, 11, 19, 20, 25, 29, 30, 44 *Test*: 2, 23, 26, 40
	3	Multiple choice. Tick the correct picture.	*Practice*: 5, 6, 8, 17, 36, 37, 40, 44 *Test*: 13, 21, 27, 37, 41
	4	Follow instructions and colour objects.	*Practice*: 2, 4, 5, 9, 19, 24, 27, 30, 31, 34, 35, 39, 42, 43 *Test*: 20, 25, 32, 36, 42
Reading and Writing 20 minutes	1	Put a tick or a cross to indicate whether the sentence is correct or not for the picture.	*Practice*: 4, 5, 10, 11, 17, 23, 32, 45 *Test*: 20, 37, 39
	2	Write *yes* or *no* beside each sentence about a scene picture.	*Practice*: 4, 5, 9, 12, 13, 20, 21, 24, 30, 35, 36, 39, 41, 43 *Test*: 5, 14, 23, 26, 29
	3	Write the words beside the pictures.	*Practice*: 2, 3, 4, 5, 8, 12, 14, 15, 16, 17, 19, 21, 23, 25, 27, 32, 33, 39, 40, 41, 42, 45 *Test*: 1, 7, 31, 36
	4	Picture gap fill. Write one word in each gap.	*Practice*: 5, 7, 8, 15, 16, 19, 20, 23, 25, 32, 33, 36, 37, 38, 42, 45 *Test*: 6, 18, 22, 28, 31
	5	Write one-word answers to questions about three scene pictures.	*Practice*: 2, 5, 6, 8, 14, 15, 18, 21, 22, 24, 28, 30, 33, 34, 35, 37, 39 *Test*: 12, 29, 41
Speaking 3–5 minutes	1 Scene picture and object cards	Point to the correct part of the picture. Place the card in the correct place.	*Practice*: 4, 11, 14, 16, 17, 18, 19, 21, 25, 27, 28, 32, 35, 42, 43 *Test*: 15, 17, 30, 31, 33, 39, 41, 42
	2 Scene picture	Answer questions about the picture.	*Practice*: 4, 9, 10, 14, 16, 18, 19, 24, 26, 27, 28, 34, 35, 36, 43 *Test*: 15, 17, 30, 31, 33, 39, 41
	3 and 4 Object cards and personal questions	Answer questions about the cards and answer personal questions.	*Practice*: 4, 6, 12, 14, 18, 21, 32, 35, 36, 43 *Test*: 15, 17, 30

Map of the Student's Book

1 Say hello!	letters, animals, colours	questions, *this/these*	Listening Part 2 Test: Reading and Writing Part 3
2 Numbers, numbers, numbers	numbers, colours	questions, *there is/are*, present simple, prepositions, possessives	Listening Part 4, Reading and Writing Parts 3 and 5, Speaking Part 3 Test: Listening Part 2
3 What's your name?	names, family and friends	*to be*, questions	Listening Part 2, Reading and Writing Part 3, Speaking Part 3
4 Red, blue and yellow	body and face, colours, the world around us	questions, *there is/are*, prepositions, present continuous, *to be, this/that*	Reading and Writing Parts 1, 2 and 3, Speaking Parts 1 and 3 Listening Part 4
5 Answering questions	school	imperatives, *there is/are*, *have got*, present continuous, prepositions	Listening and Reading and Writing (all parts) Test: Listening Part 1, Reading and Writing Part 2
6 Animals and aliens	body and face, animals, food and drink	*this/that*, pronouns, possessives	Listening Part 3, Reading and Writing Part 5, Speaking Part 3 Test: Reading and Writing Part 4
7 Look, listen, smile, draw	body and face, numbers, sports and leisure	plurals, possessives, *have got*, present simple, *can ...*	Reading and Writing Part 4 Test: Reading and Writing Part 3
8 In my clothes cupboard	clothes, family and friends, the home	plurals, *this/these*, questions, present simple and continuous, *there is/are*	Listening Part 3, Reading and Writing Parts 3, 4 and 5
9 Funny monsters	body and face, colours	*have got*, present continuous, questions	Listening Part 4, Reading and Writing Part 2, Speaking Part 2
10 Our families	family, names, animals	questions, pronouns, present simple, *have got, this/these*	Reading and Writing Part 1, Speaking Parts 2 and 3
11 Whose is it?	names, sports and leisure	possessives, questions and short answers, prepositions, *have got*	Listening Part 2, Speaking Parts 1 and 3 Test: Reading and Writing Part 1
12 Who's got the red balloon?	family and friends, the home, colours	*have got*, plurals, questions with present simple and continuous	Reading and Writing Parts 2 and 3, Speaking Part 3 Test: Reading and Writing Part 5
13 Who can do this?	sports and leisure, names	*can/can't*, present continuous, *have got*, conjunctions	Reading and Writing Part 2, Speaking Part 3 Test: Listening Part 3

Unit	Topic	Grammar	Exam Practice
14 Big, small, happy or sad?	the world around us	adjectives, prepositions, articles, questions, present continuous, *this/these*, *have got*	Reading and Writing Parts 3 and 5, Speaking Parts 1, 2 and 3 Test: Reading and Writing Part 2
15 One, two, three animals	animals	questions, adjectives, prepositions, *can*	Listening Part 1, Reading and Writing Parts 3, 4 and 5 Test: Speaking Parts 1, 2 and 3
16 What's your favourite fruit?	food and drink, colours, family and friends	present simple and continuous, plurals, questions	Reading and Writing Parts 3 and 4, Speaking parts 1 and 2
17 What's on the menu?	food and drink, colours, the home	questions, *can*, present simple, *would like …* , prepositions	Listening Part 3, Reading and Writing Parts 1 and 3, Speaking Parts 1, 2 and 3 Test: Listening Part 1
18 A colourful house	the home	*there is/are*, questions, prepositions, present simple	Reading and Writing Part 5, Speaking Parts 1, 2 and 3 Test: Reading and Writing Part 4
19 What's in your bedroom?	colours, the home	adjectives, prepositions, questions, *there is/are*	Listening Parts 2 and 4, Reading and Writing Parts 3 and 4, Speaking Parts 1, 2 and 3
20 Ben and Kim live here!	the home, places, family and friends	*there is/are*, … possessives, questions, prepositions, *no*, *or*	Listening Part 2, Reading and Writing Parts 2 and 4, Speaking Part 3 Test: Listening Part 4, Reading and Writing Part 1
21 Play with us!	transport, toys, names	present continuous, *would like …* , prepositions, possessives, questions	Reading and Writing Parts 2, 3 and 5, Speaking Parts 1, 2 and 3 Test: Listening Part 3
22 In our bags and in our school	school	present simple and continuous, articles, plurals, prepositions	Reading and Writing Part 5 Test: Reading and Writing Part 4
23 At our school	school, numbers, names	possessives, questions, present simple, prepositions	Listening Part 1, Reading and Writing Parts 1 and 4, Speaking Part 3 Test: Listening Part 2
24 What's the class doing?	school, names	present continuous, questions	Listening Part 4, Reading and Writing Parts 2 and 5, Speaking Part 2

Unit	Topic	Grammar	Exam Practice
25 Animal challenge	animals, body and face	*can/can't*, prepositions, possessives	Listening Part 2, Reading and Writing Parts 3 and 4, Speaking Part 1 Test: Listening Part 4
26 How many pets?	animals, the home, names, numbers	plurals, present simple and continuous, questions, *there is/are*, *this/these*, *have (got)*	Speaking Parts 2 and 3 Test: Listening Part 2, Reading and Writing Part 2
27 Food I really like!	food and drink	questions, *can/can't*, *like + ing*	Listening Part 4, Reading and Writing Part 3, Speaking Parts 1 and 2 Test: Listening Part 3
28 My favourite food day	food and drink	present simple questions, *would like* + noun	Reading and Writing Part 5, Speaking Parts 1, 2 and 3 Test: Reading and Writing Part 4
29 We're in the toy shop today	places, toys, colours, numbers	questions, prepositions, present continuous, *would like ...*, imperatives	Listening Parts 1 and 2, Speaking Part 3 Test: Reading and Writing Parts 2 and 5
30 Monsters in the park	the home, colours, names	questions, prepositions, present continuous, imperatives	Listening Parts 2 and 4, Reading and Writing Parts 2 and 5 Test: Speaking Parts 1, 2 and 3
31 Coming and going	transport, colours	prepositions, present simple and continuous, *have* + object + infinitive	Listening Part 4, Speaking Part 3 Test: Reading and Writing Parts 3 and 4, Speaking Parts 1 and 2
32 Happy Birthday!	food and drink, clothes, colours	questions, prepositions, present simple and continuous, pronouns, possessives	Listening Part 1, Reading and Writing Parts 1, 3 and 4, Speaking Parts 1 and 3 Test: Listening Part 4
33 On the beach	the world around us, numbers, colours	present simple and continuous, *like + -ing*, questions	Reading and Writing Parts 3, 4 and 5 Test: Listening Part 1, Speaking Parts 1 and 2
34 Let's go to the park	animals, colours, sports and leisure	questions, present continuous, prepositions, articles	Listening Part 4, Reading and Writing Part 5, Speaking Parts 2 and 3
35 What, who and where?	the home, possessions, colours	prepositions, present continuous, *this/these*, *there is/are*	Listening Part 4, Reading and Writing Parts 2 and 5, Speaking Parts 1, 2 and 3

Unit	Topic	Grammar	Exam Practice
36 Great games, great hobbies!	sports and leisure, colours	present simple and continuous pronouns, questions, *like + -ing*, prepositions	Listening Part 3, Reading and Writing Parts 2 and 4, Speaking Parts 2 and 3 Test: Listening Part 4, Reading and Writing Part 3
37 Let's play	sports and leisure, places	questions, present simple and continuous, *Let's* + infinitive, *would like*, *like + -ing*	Listening Part 3, Reading and Writing Parts 4 and 5, Speaking Part 3 Test: Listening Part 3, Reading and Writing Part 1
38 My favourites	general revision	questions, conjunctions, pronouns, possessives, present simple	Reading and Writing Part 4, Speaking Part 4
39 One foot, two feet	numbers, people, the world around us	plurals, *there is/are*, present continuous, prepositions, questions	Listening Part 4, Reading and Writing Parts 2, 3 and 5, Speaking Parts 2 and 3 Test: Reading and Writing Part 1, Speaking Parts 1 and 2
40 Night and day	time, numbers	prepositions, present simple and continuous	Listening Part 3, Speaking Part 3 Test: Listening Part 2
41 Trains, boats and planes	transport, sports and leisure, the world around us	questions, present simple and present continuous	Reading and Writing Parts 2 and 3, Speaking Part 3 Test: Listening Part 3, Reading and Writing Part 5, Speaking Parts 1 and 2
42 About a phone	places, the home	present simple and continuous, prepositions, plurals, *there is/are*, *this/these*	Listening Parts 1 and 4, Reading and Writing Parts 3 and 4, Speaking Part 1 Test: Listening Part 4, Speaking Part 1
43 What are they saying?	clothes, family and friends	possessive, adjectives, questions, present continuous, *have (got)*	Listening Part 4, Reading and Writing Part 2, Speaking Parts 1, 2 and 3
44 About us	general revision	pronouns, possessives, *have (got)*, *love / like / enjoy + -ing*	Listening Parts 2 and 3, Speaking Part 4
45 Happy ending!	general revision	adjectives, verbs, nouns, present simple, *like + -ing*	Reading and Writing Parts 1, 3 and 4, Speaking Part 4

Fun for Starters topic index

Topics	Units
Numbers, names and colours	1 Say hello! 2 Numbers, numbers, numbers 3 What's your name? 4 Red, blue and yellow
School	5 Answering questions
Animals, family and friends, body and face	6 Animals and aliens 7 Look, listen, smile, draw 8 In my clothes cupboard 9 Funny monsters 10 Our families
Sports and leisure, the home	11 Whose is it? 12 Who's got the red balloon? 13 Who can do this? 14 Big, small, happy or sad? 15 One, two, three animals
Food and drink, colours, the home	16 What's your favourite fruit? 17 What's on the menu? 18 A colourful house 19 What's in your bedroom? 20 Ben and Kim live here!
Transport, toys and school	21 Play with us 22 In our bags and in our school 23 At our school 24 What's the class doing?
Animals	25 Animal challenge 26 How many pets?
Food and drink	27 Food I really like! 28 My favourite food day
Toys, transport, the world around us	29 We're in the toy shop today 30 Monsters in the park 31 Coming and going 32 Happy Birthday! 33 On the beach
Sports and leisure	34 Let's go to the park 35 What, who and where? 36 Great games, great hobbies! 37 Let's play
Numbers, time and transport	38 My favourites 39 One foot, two feet 40 Night and day 41 Trains, boats and places
Places, clothes, the home	42 About a phone 43 What are they saying? 44 About us 45 Happy ending!

Fun for Starters grammar index

Grammar	Units
adjectives	14, 15, 19, 43, 45
articles	22, 34,
can/can't	7, 13, 15, 17, 25, 27
conjunctions	13, 20, 38
have (got)	5, 7, 9, 10, 11, 12, 14, 26, 31, 43
imperatives	5, 29, 30
let's	37
like + ing	27, 36, 37, 44, 45
plurals	7, 8, 12, 16, 22, 26, 33, 39, 42
possessives	2, 6, 7, 11, 20, 21, 23, 25, 32, 38, 43, 44
prepositions	2, 4, 5, 11, 14, 15, 17, 18, 19, 20, 21, 22, 23, 25, 29, 30, 31, 32, 34, 35, 40, 42
present continuous	4, 5, 8, 9, 12, 13, 14, 16, 21, 22, 24, 26, 29, 30, 31, 32, 33, 34, 35, 36, 37, 39, 40, 41, 42, 43
present simple	2, 7, 8, 10, 12, 16, 17, 18, 22, 23, 26, 28, 31, 32, 33, 36, 37, 38, 40, 41, 42, 45
pronouns	6, 10, 14, 32, 36, 38, 44
questions	1, 2, 3, 4, 8, 9, 10, 11, 12, 15, 16, 17, 18, 19, 20, 21, 23, 24, 26, 27, 28, 29, 30, 32, 33, 34, 37, 38, 39, 41, 43
short answers	11, 20
there is/are	2, 4, 5, 8, 18, 19, 20, 26, 35, 39, 42
this/that/these	1, 4, 6, 8, 10, 14, 26, 35, 42
to be	3, 4
would like …	17, 21, 28, 29, 37

1 Say hello!

Topics letters, animals, colours

Equipment needed

- Starters audio 1B, 1D, 1F.
- Colouring pencils or pens.
- A card for each letter of the alphabet, handmade or printed and cut out See G.

Ⓐ Hello! Say, spell and write names.

- Introduce yourself. Say: *Hello, my name is (Linda).* Spell your name as you write it on the board. Ask 3–4 different learners: *What's your name?* Learners answer: (*Matilde, Suzy, Lee*). Ask the class: *How do you spell (Matilde)'s name?* Learners spell the names as you write them on the board.
- In pairs, learners ask and answer: *My name is … . What's your name?* They write their name and their partner's name on the lines. Learners can write their names in a decorative way and use pencils or pens to add colour if they want. For example:

Ⓑ ▶ Know your letters!

> **Starters tip**
> Practise saying and writing the letters of the alphabet which cause problems for your learners. When spelling words, make sure that learners know the sounds for naming vowels and difficult consonants ('r', 'w', 'y', etc). Also practise pairs of consonants that your learners might confuse ('g' and 'j', 'n' and 'm', 's' and 'c', 'p' and 'b', etc).

Note: If your class needs longer to learn the alphabet, you might prefer to teach only the letters needed for 2–3 of the learners' names (mentioned in **A**) to begin with. Give learners practice saying and writing these letters and then introduce and practise saying and writing the remaining letters.

- Write the following letters on the board. Each line represents a missing letter in the alphabet.

  a b _ d e f _ h i j _ l m _ o

  p q _ s t u _ w x _ z

- Point to the missing letters and ask: *What's this letter?* (c, g, k, n, r, v, y). Add the missing letters to the board. As you write each one, practise its pronunciation by asking 4–5 learners: *What's this letter?*

- Group letters on the board. In a circle write: *a h j k*
  Say the letters. Learners listen and repeat. Show learners that these letters all share an /eɪ/ sound.
- Do the same with *b c d e g p t v*. These letters all share an /i/ sound.
- Do the same with *f l m n s x*. These share an /e/ sound.
- Do the same with *q u w*. These share a /juː/ sound.
- Do the same with *i y*. These share an /aɪ/ sound.
  Note: 'o', 'r' and 'z' are the only letters that do not fit into these phonemic groups.
- Learners look at the letter pond in **B**. Say: *Find the letters in your name.* Learners use a coloured pen or pencil to draw a small circle around the letters they need to write their own first name. If learners know how to spell their surnames, they could use a different colour to also circle those letters.
- Make sure learners have grey, green, red and blue colouring pencils among others. Say: *Listen to the letters now.* Play the audio, stopping at the first pause. Learners find 'a', 'h', 'j' and 'k' in **B**, find their grey pencil and colour in their leaf shapes.
- Play the other groups pausing between each one while learners find letters and colour them again. Repeat audio.
- At the end of the audio, ask: *Which letters have no colour?* ('o', 'r' and 'z')
- Learners show each other their coloured letters. Ask 2–3 learners: *What colour is your h? t? s? u?* Learners answer. (grey, green, red, blue)
- In pairs, learners ask and answer: *What colour is your … ?* questions.
- Ask questions about sound groups, for example: *Which letter sounds like 'i'?* (y); *Which sound like 'q'?* (u, w); *Which letter sounds like 'k'?* (a, h, j)

Audioscript

Listen and say the letters.	
One:	a h j k
	a h j and k are grey!
	Find your grey pencil. They're grey!
Two:	b c d e g p t v
	b c d e g p t and v are green!
	Listen again! They're green!
Three:	f l m n s x z
	f l m n s x and z are red!
	They're red! They're red!
Four:	q u w
	q u and w are blue! Yes! They're blue!
Five:	Now i and y
	i and y are … You choose the colour!
	You choose!

Ⓒ Draw a red line (a–z) from the baby spider to its dad!

- The whole class says the alphabet again.
- Point to the animals in **C** and ask: *Where's the baby spider? Where's its dad?* Learners find the two spiders. Ask: *Where's the letter 'a'? And 'b'? And 'c'?* Learners point to the letters a, b and c.
- Make sure learners have red pencils. Say: *Draw a red alphabet line!* Learners draw a red line to link the 26 letters (a–z) across the box.

D ▶ Listen! Draw a line from the baby frog to its mum!

○ Make sure learners have green pencils. Say: *Let's draw a green line from the baby frog to its mum now. Listen!* Play the audio. Learners listen and draw a green line to help the baby frog find its mum. Play again as necessary.

Optional extension:

Divide learners into A and B pairs. Pairs choose a parent and baby animal (for example a cat and a kitten) and draw these either side of the letter box. Without showing each other, A learners draw a purple line between the letters in the letter box from the baby animal to its parent. B learners draw a brown line between the letters in the letter box from the parent to its baby.

A learners then say the letters in their purple line and B learners listen and draw their own purple line. B learners then say the letters in their brown line and A learners listen and draw their own brown line.

Pairs then compare their letter boxes.

Audioscript

q-g-r-b-g-h-z-s-c-v-i-y-w-o-n-a-e-f-x

E What's this? Write the word.

Reading & Writing Part 3

○ Learners look at the picture. Ask: *How many animals can you see?* (six)
  Ask: *Where's the fish?* Learners point to the fish. Ask about the other animals. *Where's the frog / goat / duck / spider / sheep?*

○ Check the animal words again. Point to the fish and ask: *What's this?* ([It's] a fish) Continue in the same way pointing and asking *What's this?* questions about the frog, goat, duck, spider and sheep. Learners look at the picture and answer.

○ Point at the six puddles. Say: *Look! The letters for the animal words are in the water.* Point to the example and the answer 'fish' on the line.

○ In pairs, learners look at the numbers and find the right puddle for each animal. Crossing off the letters as they use them to spell the animal words, learners write the answers on the lines.

○ Check answers by asking different pairs:
  How do you spell duck / sheep / frog / goat / spider?
  Learners say the letters to spell the words.

> **Check answers:**
> 1 duck 2 sheep 3 frog 4 goat 5 spider

○ Ask what noises a fish / frog / goat / duck / sheep makes. Demonstrate if necessary!

○ Learners work in pairs. They take it in turns to ask: *What's this?* and then make animal noises. Partners say which animal it is. Extend this if learners know more animals.

Note: The picture could also be used to ask: *What colour is the … ?* questions. (The fish is red. The frog is green. The goat is brown. The duck is yellow. The sheep is black and white. The spider is black and grey.)

F ▶ What's the animal?

○ Learners look at the animal words (1–5 only) to complete. Point to the example answer, 'goat'. Point to each vowel that is already on a line and ask: *What's this letter?* (a, e, i, o, u). Check pronunciation and drill if necessary.

○ In pairs, learners complete the words. If they need help, they can find all the words in **E**.

> **Check answers:**
> 2 sheep 3 spider 4 frog 5 duck

○ Point to the cat, dog and snake in the star. Ask: *Do you know these animals too?* Learners complete the words 'cat', 'dog' and 'snake' in the star. Ask learners what noises these three animals make.

○ Play the audio. Pause after each animal noise for learners to answer. (It's a sheep / cat / snake / duck / dog / frog!)

○ Pairs choose names for this cat, dog and snake and write them on the lines. Ask 3–4 pairs: *What's your name for this cat / dog / snake?* Learners answer. Ask: *How do you spell their names?*

Audioscript

> What's this?
> *(sheep noise)*
> And what's this?
> *(cat noise)*
> Now, what's this?
> *(snake noise)*
> And this?
> *(duck noise)*
> Now, what's this?
> *(dog noise)*
> And what's this?
> *(frog noise)*

G Play the game! Can you make a word?

○ Say these letters, one by one: q-o-r-t-s-g-i-u-y-a-c-f-h-s-l-m-i-b-e-w-z-f-p-d-h

○ Learners listen and write the letters. In pairs, they then compare the letters they have written to check they are the same.

○ Learners circle the letters that they hear more than once. (s, i, f, h)

○ Learners make a word with these letters. (fish)

○ Now say these letters, one by one:
  n-q-o-e-r-t-g-i-u-y-a-c-k-s-k-l-m-i-b-e-w-z-a-n-f-p-d-s

○ Learners listen and again write the letters, circling the letters that they hear twice, (k, e, a, n, s) Pairs find the animal word for these letters. (snake)
  If learners enjoy letter puzzles, dictate d-g-d-n-c-o-a-t-o for learners to find three words. (cat, goat and dog)

2   Numbers, numbers, numbers

Topics numbers, colours

Movers word: *thing*

Equipment needed

o   Starters audio 2D.

o   Eight large letter cards showing *f o o t b a l l*. See B.

o   Colouring pens or pencils. See E.

Get into groups.

o   Learners stand up. Ask three learners to stand together in a group. Say: *Look! Three children!* Ask one learner to sit down again. Point to the two remaining learners and say *Look! Two children!*

    Ask everyone to join in. Say: *Three!* All learners get into groups of three.

o   Repeat the game using different numbers between two and six. Learners form groups of between two and six.

    After a few turns, say: *Now you!* Learners then take turns to say a number. Other learners form the groups.

Ⓐ Write the numbers.

> **Starters tip:**
>
> In some Reading and Writing and Listening parts, learners will have to write numbers. Teach learners that in answers for the tests, they only need to write numbers as digits (1, 2) and not as words (one, two). They will be less likely to make mistakes or lose marks. It's quicker too!

o   Learners look at the numbers. Look at the example. Say: *Look at the words and write the numbers on the lines.*

o   Write on the board numbers 1 and 20, adding lines for the missing numbers 2–19:

    1_ _ _ _ _ _ _ _ _ _ _ _ _ _ _ _ _ _20

o   Point at the lines and ask: *What are these numbers?* Learners answer. Write numbers 2–19 on the lines.

o   Point to **A** and ask learners which numbers between 1 and 20 are not on their page (1, 3, 4, 6, 14, 16, 17, 18, 19). Check pronunciation of the 'teen' syllable /tiːn/.

Optional extension:

Learners could work in pairs to try to write numbers 1–20 in words as quickly as possible. Walk round and help with numbers that are more difficult to spell, for example: eight, twelve, thirteen and fifteen.

Ⓑ Look at the letters. Write words for six things in the picture.

o   Learners look at the picture. Say: *Look at the example and its line.* Point to the car and ask: *What's this?* (a car) Show learners that the three big letters to make the word 'car' are jumbled. Point to the answer and ask: *How do you spell car?* (c-a-r)

    In pairs, learners look at the words and lines and write the words for 1–5.

> **Check answers:**
> **1** bed   **2** sock   **3** shoe   **4** book   **5** cat

o   Point to the line from 6 in the picture and ask: *What's this?* (a football)

    Ask eight learners to come to the class and stand in a line. Give them the football letter cards in random order (for example learner 1 has an 'l', learner 2 an 'o', learner 3 the 'f', etc). Learners hold up the letters. Ask learners to reorder themselves to make the word 'football'! Ask the class: *Is that correct?*

    Learners write *football* on the line.

    Teach/revise: 'on'

    Ask: *Is there a shoe on the bed?* (no) *Are there cats on the bed?* (yes) *Is there a sock on the bed?* (yes) *Are there apples on the bed?* (yes) *Are there socks, cats, apples, balls and books on <u>your</u> bed at home?* (no!)

Ⓒ Let's count! How many can you see? Answer the questions.

o   Learners look at the picture. Point to question 1 and ask: *How many cats are there in the picture? Let's count the cats … one, two, three! There are three cats!*

o   Ask learners the following questions about the picture. They can answer with just a number. Alternatively teach learners how to answer in a full sentence, for example: *There are four cars.*

    1   *How many cars are there?* (four)

    2   *How many books are there?* (seven)

    3   *How many apples are there?* (six)

    4   *How many socks are there?* (two)

o   In pairs, learners read the two other 'How many' questions and write answers.

    Ask: *How many balls are there?* (eight) *How many shoes are there?* (five)

    Say: *Look at the picture again.* Give learners half a minute to look carefully at the picture then say: *Close your books, now.*

    Ask number questions about the picture. For example:

    How many apples / balls / cats / shoes / cars / books are there?

    Learners could then play the game in groups of 3–4, taking it in turns to ask and answer the 'How many' questions.

o   Ask learners questions about their classroom.

    Suggestions:

    How many shoes / books / boys / girls / teachers / chairs can you see?

Ⓓ ▶ Listen! Write a name or number.   Listening Part **2**

o   Write on the board:

    1   *What's your name?*

    2   *How old are you?*

    3   *What's your teacher's name?*

    4   *What's your favourite number?*

    5   *What's your friend's name?*

    6   *How many books have you got?*

    7   *How old is your friend?*

Ask different learners to read out the questions. Ask: *How many answers are names?* (three) *How many answers are numbers?* (four) Ask: *Which questions have name answers / number answers?*

> **Check answers:**
> Names: 1, 3, 5   Numbers: 2, 4, 6, 7

o Learners copy the questions into their notebooks and write their answers. Ask 3–4 learners different questions, for example: *What's your favourite name for a boy/girl, Mario? How many books have you got, Anna?*

o In pairs, learners interview each other by taking it in turns to ask and answer the seven questions.

o Learners look at the example questions in **D**. Ask: *What's the boy's name?* (Tom) *How old is he?* (nine).
   Learners look at questions 1–5. Ask: *How many answers are names?* (two) *How many answers are numbers?* (three).
   Say: *Listen! A girl is talking to her teacher. She's talking about Tom.*

o Play the audio twice. Learners listen and write answers.
   Note: Learners will see possessive 's' in the example and questions 2 and 4. You might want to explain the meaning of this.

> **Check answers:**
> **1** 6   **2** Lucy   **3** 5   **4** Park   **5** 10

Audioscript

Look at the picture. Listen and look. There are two examples.
   Man: Hello! What's this boy's name?
   Girl: His name's Tom.
   Man: Can you spell his name?
   Girl: Tom's name? Yes! T-O-M.
   Man: How old is he?
   Girl: He's nine.
   Man: Nine?
   Girl: Yes, that's right.
Can you see the answers? Now you listen and write a name or a number.
1 Man: How many toys has Tom got?
   Girl: He's got six toys!
   Man: Sorry?
   Girl: He's got six toys!
2 Man: I like his cat. What's his cat's name?
   Girl: His cat's name is Lucy!
   Man: Lucy? That's a nice name.
   Girl: Yes. You spell it L-U-C-Y.
3 Man: How many books has Tom got?
   Girl: He's got five books.
   Man: How many?
   Girl: He's got five books.
4 Man: What's the name of Tom's school?
   Girl: Tom goes to Park School.
   Man: Can you spell that?
   Girl: Park? OK. You spell it P-A-R-K.
5 Man: Which class is Tom in?
   Girl: He's in class 10.
   Man: Class 10. That's good!
   Girl: Yes. He really likes school.

E Listen and draw lines between the letters and numbers.

o Write on the board: *V   12*
   Say: *Look at the picture. Find the letter V.* (It's under the giraffe's head.)
   Say: *Now find the number 12.* (It's halfway down the giraffe's body at the front.)
   Say: *Draw a line between V and 12.* Make sure learners understand your instruction by drawing a line between the V and the number 12 on the board.

Tell learners you are going to say more letters and numbers. They draw lines between them to finish the picture.

o Say slowly: *12-Y-14-A-20–7-R-O-E-11-C-13-H-15-I-K-5–18-Q*

o Ask: *What can you see?* (a giraffe)

F Colour and draw.

o Make sure learners have brown, green and yellow colouring pencils or pens.
   Say: *Now colour the picture. Colour the Bs brown. Colour the Gs green.* Give learners time to finish their colouring.

o Draw a sun on the board. Ask: *What's this?* (the sun) Check that learners have understood the drawing instruction in **F**. Learners draw a sun and colour it yellow. They could also choose other colours for the flowers, the giraffe's eyes and background body colour if they want to. Ask: *What colour is the sun?* (yellow) *What colour are the flowers / the giraffe?* Learners answer.

G Play number games!

o Choose one of the following number games to suit your class.

I know your number!

o Demonstrate the game first with all the class. Tell one learner to think of a number between 1 and 20 and to write it in their notebook.
   Teacher: *I know your number. It's seven!*
   Learner: *No!*
   Teacher: *Then it's five!*
   Learner: *Yes!*
   Teacher: *Great! How do you spell five?*
   Learner: *F-I-V-E!*

o Play the game with the whole class a few times until you are sure that the learners understand what they have to do.
   Learners then play the game in groups of 3–4 to practise numbers 1–20.
   When a learner guesses and spells the number correctly, it's their turn to think of a different number and the other learners guess.

Listen and circle the number!

o Give each learner half a sheet of paper. Write the words for numbers 1–20 on the board, asking learners to help with spellings.
   Say: *Now write these number words on your paper.*
   Tell learners to write the words in big letters anywhere on the paper and not to write the words in the correct order. For example:

three   *eleven*   *fifteen*
        two   *nineteen*
twelve   *seven*   *five*
     eight   *fourteen*   *twenty*
              six   *ten*
        one   *sixteen*
eighteen   *four*
        nine   *thirteen*   *seventeen*

Divide learners into A and B pairs. Shout out any number between 1 and 20. Say: *Draw a circle round that number!*
Each learner hurries to find the correct number and draw a circle round it. The first learner in each A and B pair to correctly circle the number you called out, wins a point. Repeat with other numbers until all the numbers have been circled or until learners tire of the game. Pairs keep their own scores.

3   What's your name?

Topics names, family and friends

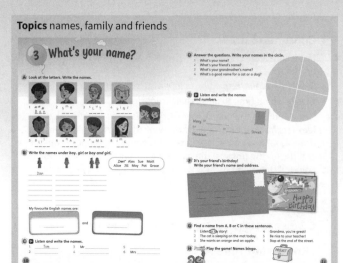

Movers words: *address, round, party*; Flyers word: *card*
Not in YLE wordlist: *bingo*

Equipment needed

o   Starters audio 3C, 3E.

A   Look at the letters. Write the names.

o   Point to the boy in picture 1 and say: *Look! This is Ben. That's B-E-N.* Point to the capital 'B' at the start of his name. Remind learners that the first letters of names are written with capital letters.

o   Say: *Here are pictures of ten people.* Explain that the names for the people in pictures 1–8 have been jumbled up. For 2–8, learners put the letters back in the correct order to spell the names and write them on the lines. The capital letters will help them do this!

> **Check answers:**
> **2** Sam   **3** Lucy   **4** Nick   **5** Bill   **6** Anna   **7** Mark   **8** Kim

o   Learners choose a name for the boy and the girl in 9. They jumble up the letters of the names and write them under picture 9 (for example *n n A a*). Under each jumbled name, learners draw the correct number of lines for each name (for example _ _ _ _).
In pairs, learners exchange books. They unjumble the letters and write the letters on the lines to write the names correctly spelt.

B   Write the names under *boy*, *girl* or *boy and girl*.

> **Starters tip**
>
> Make sure that your learners are familiar with the 20 first names that appear on the Starters wordlist (and in this unit). These names appear in many parts of Starters and some of them are tested in Listening Part 2 (they are always spelt out). Knowing if names are for boys or girls, or for both, is useful.

o   Say: *Dan is a nice name. Is 'Dan' a boy's name or a girl's name?* (boy's) *How do you spell 'Dan'?* (D-A-N)
Point to the name 'Dan' in the wordbox and on the line. Say: *Dan is a name for a boy or man. It's under 'boy' here.*
Point to the next name in the box (Alex). Say: *Alex is a nice name, too. Is 'Alex' a boy's name or a girl's name?* Explain that Alex is a name we can use for a boy or a girl. Ask: *How do you spell 'Alex'?* (A-L-E-X) *Write 'Alex' on the line under boy and girl, please!* Learners write *Alex* on the first line in the 'boy and girl' column.
Say: *Look at the names in the box.* Write the names under 'boy', 'girl' or 'boy and girl'.

> **Check answers:**
> boy: Matt   girl: Sue, Alice, Jill, May, Grace   boy and girl: Alex, Pat

o   Say: *Now look at the names in 1–8 in A. Which are boys' names? Which are girls' names? Which are boys' or girls' names? Write the names on the lines in B.*

> **Check answers:**
> boy: Ben, Nick, Bill, Mark   girl: Lucy, Anna
> boy and girl: Sam, Kim

o   Ask: *What are the boy's and girl's name in your picture 9 in A? Is the boy's name a girl's name too? Is the girl's name a boy's name too?* Learners talk about the names they wrote.
Note: Learners can check online to see if their names are for both boys and girls.
If relevant, you could talk about names that are for both girls and boys in your learners' country.

o   Say: *I like the names (George) and (Helen). What English names do you like? Write your favourite English names on the lines in the boxes in B.*

C   Listen and write the names.

o   Say: *Listen to the woman and girl. Which names do they say?* Play conversation 1 on the audio. Ask: *What's the girl's name?* (Lucy) *What name does Lucy say?* (Tom) Point to 'Tom' on line 1. The woman says *Lucy* and the girl says *Tom.* Learners listen to conversations 2–6 and write the names.

> **Check answers:**
> Ask different learners to spell the names and write them on the board:
> **2** Alex   **3** Ride   **4** May   **5** Happy   **6** Duck

o   Point to 'Mr' and 'Mrs' on the lines in 3 and 6 and ask: *Is 'Mr Ride' a man or a woman?* (a man) *Is 'Mrs Duck' a man or a woman?* (a woman) Explain that we can also use 'Miss' and 'Ms' for a woman.

o   Write on the board:
............is Lucy's brother.
Ask: *What's Lucy's brother's name?* (Tom) Write *Tom* in the gap in the sentence on the board.
Write on the board:
............is the girl's school friend.
............is a grandmother.
............is a dog.
............is an English teacher.
Learners complete the sentences with the names from **C**. Let them listen again if necessary.

> **Check answers:**
> school friend – Alex, grandmother – May, dog – Happy, English teacher – Mrs Duck

Audioscript

Listen and write the names.

1	Woman:	Hello, Lucy. Is that your brother?
	Girl:	Yes.
	Woman:	What's his name?
	Girl:	Tom.
	Woman:	Tom? Is that T-O-M?
	Girl:	Yes.
2	Man:	Have you got a good friend at school?
	Girl:	Yes.
	Man:	What's her name?
	Girl:	Alex.
	Man:	Alex? Do you spell that A-L-E-X?
	Girl:	Yes. She's very nice.

3 Woman: What's your teacher's name?
    Boy: Mr Ride. It's Mr Ride.
    Woman: How do you spell that?
    Boy: R-I-D-E.
    Woman: Oh yes, I know him.

4 Man: What's your grandmother's name?
    Boy: Her name's May.
    Man: Can you spell May?
    Boy: Yes. It's M-A-Y.

5 Woman: Is that your dog, Tom?
    Boy: Yes.
    Woman: What's her name?
    Boy: Her name's Happy.
    Woman: Happy? How do you spell that?
    Boy: H-A-P-P-Y.
    Woman: That's a good name for a dog.

6 Girl: Do you learn English at school, Ben?
    Boy: Yes. It's my favourite lesson.
    Girl: Who's your English teacher?
    Boy: Her name's Mrs Duck.
    Girl: How do you spell her family name?
    Boy: Duck? You spell it D-U-C-K.

Names, questions, circles …

o Tell the class to sit in a circle. (Large classes: make several circles.)

o Ask one learner: *What's your name?* This learner answers, for example: *My name's Jean*, and then turns to the learner on their **right** and asks them the same question: *What's your name?* This learner answers then turns to the learner on their **right** and asks the question. This continues round the circle until all the learners have asked and answered the name question.

o Learners do the same with the second question: *Can you spell your name?* But this time, they turn and ask the person on their **left**.

o Learners ask each other the third question: *What's your favourite name?* Changing direction in the circle again, they ask the learner on their **right**.
Note: Encourage learners to work quickly round the circle.

D Answer the questions. Write your names in the circle.

o Learners read questions 1–4 and write their answers in the four sections of the circle.

o Draw a circle on the board with a cross inside like the one in **D**. Write your answers to questions 1–4 in the sections. For example: *Mary, Lucky, Agnes, Anne.*

Explain that these are your answers to questions 1–4. Ask learners: *Who is Agnes?* They try to guess: *Your friend?* (no) *Your grandmother?* (yes) Learners find out which question the other names answer.

o Learners do the same in pairs. Learner A shows B their names circle. Learner B guesses who each name belongs to. Then Learner B shows their four names and Learner A guesses.

E ▶ Listen and write the names and numbers.

o Tell learners to look at the envelope in **E**. Show learners that some things are missing from the name and address. Ask learners to suggest which things are missing. Play the audio. Learners listen and say which things are mentioned. (Mary's family name, the number of her house and the name of her street)

o Play the audio again. Learners listen and write names or numbers.

Check answers:
1 Door **2** 17/seventeen **3** Lime

Audioscript

Listen and write.

1 Boy: Mum, can you help me?
    Woman: OK.
    Boy: Can you tell me Mary's family name?
    Woman: Yes. It's Door. D-O-O-R.
    Boy: D-O-O-R. Thanks.

2 Boy: And what's the number of Mary's house?
    Woman: 17. She lives at number 17.
    Boy: Oh yes!

3 Boy: And what's the name of the street?
    Woman: You know that! It's Lime Street!
    Boy: Do you spell that L-I-M-E?
    Woman: That's right: L-I-M-E.
    Boy: Great! Thanks, Mum!

F It's your friend's birthday! Write your friend's name and address.

o Explain to learners that this is a birthday card for their friend. Tell them to write their friend's name and address on the envelope.

o Ask different learners to read out their friend's name and address. Ask: *How do you spell your friend's name? How old is your friend?*

G Find a name from A, B or C in these sentences.

o Read out the example sentence: *Listen to my story!* Ask: *Can you see the name Tom here? T-O-M.* Say: *Now find a name in sentences 2–6!*

> **Check answers:**
> **2** Matt **3** Dan **4** May **5** Ben **6** Pat

Note: Remind learners that we write names with capital letters!

H Play the game! Names bingo.

o Learners close their books. Ask: *Can you say the 17 names from B?* Different learners come to the board and write a name: *Alex, Alice, Anna, Ben, Bill, Dan, Grace, Jill, Kim, Lucy, Mark, Matt, May, Nick, Pat, Sam, Sue.*

o Learners choose five names and write them on a piece of paper.

o Explain that you are going to say and spell out some of these names. Say or spell the different names on the board. Learners listen. If the name you spell is one of the five names that the learner has written, they cross it out. The winner is the first person to cross out all five names on their piece of paper.
Note: with bigger classes, play this in groups with one learner saying the names.

o To check the winning names, ask that learner to say and spell the names. Play the bingo name game a number of times to allow different learners to win and spell.

🗃 What does my name mean?

o Learners find out the origin and meaning of their name and/or of their favourite English name.

o They can also find out the most popular name for the year they were born / for this year in their country or in the world.

o Learners tell the class what they have found out (in their own language if necessary).

4   Red, blue and yellow

Topics body and face, colours, the world around us

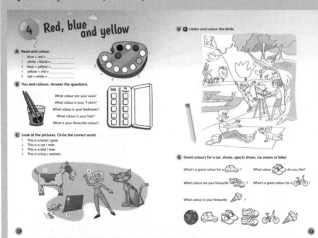

Movers word: *circle*; Flyers word: *missing*

Equipment needed

o   Starters audio 4D.

o   Colouring pencils or pens.

A Read and colour.

o   Point to the colour palette in **A** and say: *Look at these paints. Which colours can you see?* (red, black, white, blue, yellow) Point to 1 and say: *Blue and red make … What colour can I make with blue and red paints?* (purple) *Colour circle 1 purple please!*
Learners read 2–5 and colour the circles in the palette with the colour that these two colours make when they are mixed together.

o   Write on the board: .... *and* .... *make* ....
Check answers by asking different learners to add the colours to this sentence and also to point to the colours in the palette as they say them.

> **Check answers:**
> **2** grey   **3** green   **4** orange   **5** pink

o   Say: *We can't see a paint colour between green and grey. Which colour is this? Listen! Dogs and cats can be this colour. Part of a coconut is this colour (but you don't eat that part!) Lots of chairs, tables and floors are this colour. And chocolate too! Which colour is it?* (brown) Learners take their brown pencils and colour the circle between green and grey.

o   In pairs, learners choose five colours from the palette. They write the colours in their notebooks, adding three or four things that are that colour. (See suggestions below.)

Suggestions:

red	tomatoes, part of a watermelon, my watch
black	my computer, spiders, my pen
white	milk, part of a coconut, my shirt
blue	the sea, my trousers, my eyes
purple	grapes, the door, flowers
yellow	sand, lemons, bananas, the sun
grey	elephants, pencils, my phone
green	frogs, peas, limes, trees, aliens
orange	tigers, carrots, oranges
pink	my mouth, my T-shirt, my doll

o   Different pairs say their three or four objects. Other learners guess their chosen colour.

Optional extension:
Learners bring in pictures from magazines or draw and colour pictures of objects that are the same colour. Working in pairs, learners then stick their pictures on a large piece of paper to make a 'colour poster'. Some learners may prefer to download pictures and create their poster online.

B You and colours. Answer the questions.

o   Say: *Read and answer the questions in B. Colour the paints under 'Me'.* Make sure learners understand what to do by asking one learner: *What colour are your eyes? Are your eyes brown? Then take your brown pencil and colour!* Learners colour the five paintbox squares under 'Me'.

o   In pairs, learners ask and answer the questions. They use colours to show their partner's answers in the paintbox squares under 'My Friend'.

C Look at the pictures. Circle the correct word.

o   Say: *Look at the pictures and read sentences 1–4. Which word is correct?* For example: *Is 1 a boat or a goat?* (goat) Tell learners to draw a circle round the word 'goat' in sentence 1.

o   Learners draw a circle around the other correct words.

> **Check answers:**
> **2** cat   **3** kite   **4** woman

o   Ask learners to find the 'boat', 'mat', 'tree' and 'boy' in the picture in **D**. In pairs, learners point to each of these things and say: *This is a boat / mat / tree / boy.*
Learners choose colours and colour the boat, mat, one of the trees and the boy's face in **D**.
In small groups, they point to each of these things in their picture and say: *This a (green) boat. This is a (purple) mat,* etc.

D Listen and colour the birds.

o   Point to the picture in **D** and ask: *Where's the … ?* questions.
Where's the kite / girl / painting / baby / tree / boy / bag / woman?
To answer, learners point to the different things in the picture. Learners check with their partner to make sure that they are both pointing at the same thing. Move around the class and check learners are pointing at the correct parts of the picture.

o   Say: *Look at the picture. How many birds can you see?* (seven)
Say these sentences. If the sentence is correct for the picture, learners say *yes* and stand up. If it is not correct, they say *no* and sit down.

There's a bird in the tree.	(*Yes* – stand up)
There's a bird on the girl's T-shirt.	(*No* – sit down)
There's a bird on the kite.	(*Yes* – stand up)
There's a bird on the woman's bag.	(*No* – sit down)
There's a bird on the boy's T-shirt.	(*Yes* – stand up)
There's a bird on the boat.	(*Yes* – stand up)

> **Starters tip**
> In Listening Part 4, candidates need to focus on an object or thing that appears several times in different locations within the same picture (in this example, the bird). They should think about where each one is in the picture and the prepositions that will help find them, for example: *in, on, under.*

- Say: *Listen to a woman and a boy. They're talking about the picture.* Play the example on the audio. Ask: *Where is the yellow bird in the tree?* Learners point to this bird.
- Play the rest of the audio. Learners listen and colour. Play the recording twice.
- Learners swap books and check each other's colouring. Check answers by asking questions. Say: *Find the bird on the kite.* Ask: *What colour is that bird?* (blue) Do the same with the bird on the boat, the bird in the baby's hand, the bird in the girl's picture, the bird on the boy's T-shirt.

> **Check answers:**
> **1** the bird on the kite – blue.
> **2** the bird on the boat – orange.
> **3** the bird in the baby's hand – pink.
> **4** the bird in the girl's picture – red.
> **5** the bird on the boy's T-shirt – purple.

Note: In Listening Part 4, candidates will only hear each colour once. But in this listening task, learners will hear the colours twice to give them more support.

Audioscript

Look at the picture. Listen and look. There is one example.
Woman: Can you see the bird in the tree?
Boy: Yes.
Woman: Good. Colour it yellow, please.
Boy: Pardon?
Woman: Colour the bird in the tree. Colour it yellow.
Can you see the yellow bird in the tree? This is an example. Now you listen and colour.

1 Woman: Look at the bird on the kite.
Boy: Oh yes. Can I colour it?
Woman: Yes, colour it blue.
Boy: Great! The bird on the kite is blue now.

2 Woman: Find the bird on the boat.
Boy: Sorry? Which bird?
Woman: The bird on the boat. Colour it orange.
Boy: Orange. OK. I'm doing that now.

3 Woman: Can you see the baby?
Boy: Yes. She's holding a bird in her hand too.
Woman: That's right. Let's colour that bird pink.
Boy: OK. Now there's a pink bird in the baby's hand.

4 Woman: Can you see the girl? She's painting a picture.
Boy: Yes, I can. And there's a bird in her picture!
Woman: Yes, there is. Colour that bird red.
Boy: Red?
Woman: Yes, please.

5 Woman: Look at the boy's T-shirt.
Boy: It's got a bird on it too!
Woman: I know! Colour that bird purple.
Boy: Sorry?
Woman: Colour the bird on the boy's T-shirt purple.
Boy: OK.

E Great colours for a car, shoes, sports shoes, ice cream or bike!

- Ask 2–3 learners: *Does your family have a car? What colour is it? What's a good colour for a car?* Learners colour the car in the question their favourite colour for a car.
- Ask different learners: *What colour are your shoes? Are those your favourite shoes?*
  In pairs, learners take it in turns to read out one of the four questions. They both say their answer, then colour the shoes, the sports shoes, bike and ice cream their favourite colour for those things.
- Next, give each pair a question from **E**. They have to ask everyone in the class their question and find out how many learners chose different colours for that thing. For example, pair A ask: *What's a good colour for a car?* Six learners say *blue*, four say *red*, three say *grey*, two say *black* and one says *white*. Pairs count the number of learners who chose each colour. Everyone colours the car, shoes, sports shoes, bike and ice cream the most popular colour for the class.
- Ask learners to discuss in small groups which colour they think most people in the world choose when they buy cars, shoes, sports shoes, bikes and ice creams.

> **Answers:**
> cars – white, shoes – black, sports shoes – white, bike – red, ice cream – yellow

Learners colour the shoes black, the ice cream yellow, and the bike red. They don't colour the car or the sports shoes, because the world's favourite colour for these is white!

5 Answering questions

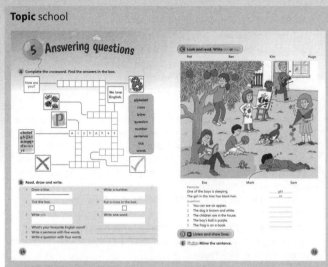

Movers word: *back*

Not in YLE wordlists: *crossword*

Equipment needed

o Starters audio 5D.

o Photocopies of the sentences on page 106 (one for each pair of teams), cut up. See E 'Mime the sentence'.

Ⓐ Complete the crossword. Find the answers in the box.

o Point to the picture of the alphabet and ask: *Can you see the word 'alphabet' in the crossword?* (yes) Point to the word 'alphabet' in the wordbox and say: *This is an example. Look at the pictures, find the words here in the box and write them in the crossword.* Remind learners to check that the number of letters in their answer is the same as the number of letters in the crossword. Learners write their answers in the crossword.

> **Check answers:**
>
> Across (top to bottom): question, words, tick, cross
>
> Down (left to right): letter, number, sentence

o Say: *In one of the boxes, there's a letter. Which letter is it?* (p) *And there's a number in one of the boxes. Which number is it?* (8) *Can you spell 8?* (e-i-g-h-t)

What are:

three, seven (numbers)

d, f, p, q (letters)

name, sock, listen (words)

I'm a teacher. You're learning English. (sentences)

How old are you? What's your name? (questions)

Ⓑ Read, draw and write.

> **Starters tip**
>
> Train learners to read and follow the instructions for each part of the Starters Test. In the test, they have to draw lines, colour things, put ticks or crosses or write names and numbers, 'yes' or 'no' or one-word answers. Practise drawing ticks and crosses. This may not be the usual way for learners in their country to show that something is right or wrong.

o Point to the first instruction. Ask learners what they have to do (draw a line). Point to the example line in the first box.

o Learners read 2–6 and write or draw the answers.

Check answers by asking different learners to write or draw their answers on the board (for 4 and 6 you could ask all learners to write a number or word on the board): **2** ✔ **3** yes **4** (eg) 7 **5** ✗ **6** (eg) beautiful

o Tell learners your favourite English word, for example: *My favourite English word is (coconut).* Each learner writes their favourite word on the line in 7.

o Give each learner a small piece of paper. Ask them to write their favourite word on it. Then they stick their words on one of the classroom walls (or on a big sheet of paper). Tell them to read each other's words. (You will also need to look at the favourite words to prepare for the next activity.)

o Ask questions about the words:

Which word is really long?

Which letter is at the start of lots of these words?

Do you know all the words? No? Which ones don't you know?

Which words do you like?

Note: Use the learners' first language if necessary.

Larger classes: Use different areas of the classroom or have several big sheets. Ask different groups to stick their words in different areas.

o Write on the board: *My favourite colour is yellow.*

Ask: *How many words are there in 'My favourite colour is yellow'?* (five)

In pairs, learners think of a sentence with five words in it. (One of the words could be their favourite word.) Learners write their sentence on the line in 8.

Ask different learners to tell you their sentences.

o Write on the board: *?*

Ask: *Where do we write this?* (at the end of a question)

Write on the board: *Wh* and say: *Questions start with question words. Lots of questions start with these two letters. Can you tell me some question words starting with 'Wh'?* Learners tell you words (*What, Where, Which, Who, Whose* are on the Starters wordlist).

o Practise saying the /w/ sound at the start of these question words. Show learners that to make this sound, you shape your lips like a small 'o' (nearly closed). You tighten your lips then relax them as you make the sound.

o Say and/or write on the board:

1 ....'s your name?

2 .... is this bag? Is it yours?

3 .... do you live?

4 .... juice is your favourite: apple or orange?

5 ....'s your favourite teacher?

Learners complete each question with the correct question word.

> **Check answers:**
>
> **1** What **2** Whose **3** Where **4** Which/What **5** Who

o In pairs, learners ask and answer the questions. Go round and check that they are saying the /w/ at the start of the questions correctly.

o Learners write a *wh-* question with four words in it in **B** next to 9. Then they move about and ask three people in the class their question.

On your back

o Draw the numbers *4* and *8* on the board. Ask: *What are these?* (numbers)

Ask different learners to come to the board and draw: a tick, a cross, a line, their favourite letter of the alphabet, a question mark or their favourite number.

o Ask one learner to stay at the front of the class. They stand with their back to the rest of the class.

- Draw a cross with your finger on the learner's back. Ask: *What's this?*
- If the learner knows, they say: (*It's a*) *cross.*
- If the learner doesn't know the word, or can't decide what you have drawn on their back, the other learners can help by answering.
- Learners continue this activity in groups of 4–5. They take it in turns to 'write' another sign, number or letter on another learner's back.

C Look and read. Write *yes* or *no*.

Reading & Writing **Part 2**

- Point to the picture in **C** and say: *What can you see in this picture? Tell me!* When learners say a word, they come to the board to write it too. Continue until learners have run out of words. Leave the words on the board.

  Suggestions:

  apple, ball, bee, book, boy, car, dog, door, flower, frog, girl, hair, kite, paint, tree, trousers, T-shirt, wall, window

- Say: *Let's do a test now!* Point to the sentences below the picture and say: *Read these sentences and look at the examples in C. What do you do?* (Read the sentences, look at the picture and write *yes* or *no*).

- Point to and read out the first example sentence: *One of the boys is sleeping.* Point to the boy who's sleeping in the picture and ask: *Is this boy sleeping?* (yes) Read out the second example: *The girl in the tree has black hair.* Ask: *What colour is this girl's hair?* (brown) *Is this sentence correct?* (no)

- In silence (it is a test!), learners read sentences 1–5 and write *yes* if they are correct and *no* if they are not correct.

> **Check answers:**
> **1** no **2** yes **3** no **4** yes **5** no

- Tell learners to put ticks next to their correct answers and a cross next to any wrong answers. Anyone who gets all five answers right can draw a star!

- Ask learners why they wrote *no* after sentences 1, 3 and 5. (There are **four** apples, not six. The children are in the **garden**, not the house. The frog **isn't** on a book.)

- Point to the words on the board (the words for things in the picture). Explain that to clean the board, you will rub off words they use to talk about the picture. To start, they can use the sentences below the picture in their books.

  Ask learners to use any words left on the board in sentences (help them as necessary). See if you can clean the board!

D ▶ Listen and draw lines.

Listening **Part 1**

- Read out the instructions: *Listen and draw lines.* Ask: *Do I write 'yes' or 'no'?* (no) *Do I put a tick or a cross?* (no) *Do I draw lines?* (yes)

  Point to the line between the name Mark and the boy sleeping in the picture and say: *This line goes between Mark and this boy.* Play the example on the audio.

  Ask: *Is this line correct? Is Mark sleeping? Is Mark the boy with the black hair?* (yes)

  Say: *Now listen and draw lines between five names and the people in the picture.* Play the rest of the audio twice.

> **Check answers:**
> lines between **1** Kim – girl in tree   **2** Eva – girl painting bee
> **3** Hugo – boy with ball   **4** Pat – girl with kite
> **5** Sam – girl reading book

- Ask: *Which name has no line?* (Ben)

Audioscript

Look at the picture. Listen and look. There is one example.

Boy:	Hi, Miss Street! Here's a photo of me and my friends in our garden. We're having lots of fun!
Woman:	Oh, yes! But one child is sleeping … Who's that?
Boy:	The boy with black hair? His name's Mark.
Woman:	Mark? That's a nice name.

Can you see the line? This is an example. Now you listen and draw lines.

1 Woman: There's a girl here, too. She's in the tree!
    Boy: Yes. She loves trees! Her name's Kim.
    Woman: What's Kim doing in that tree?
    Boy: She's getting some apples.

2 Boy: And can you see Eva?
    Woman: No. Where is she?
    Boy: Eva's painting a bee. It's fantastic.
    Woman: Good! But she's getting paint on her clothes.
    Boy: I know!

3 Woman: I like the dog!
    Boy: That's Hugo's pet dog.
    Woman: Is Hugo the boy with the ball?
    Boy: Yes, that's right.

4 Woman: One of the girls is waving. What's her name?
    Boy: The girl with the kite in her hands?
    Woman: Yes. What's her name?
    Boy: That's Pat. Pat's fun! I like her.

5 Woman: And what's that girl's name? The girl with the book.
    Boy: That's Sam. She's in my class.
    Woman: Is she? What's she reading about?
    Boy: Polar bears! They're her favourite animals.
    Woman: I like those too!

E Mime the sentence.

- Point to sentence 1 in **B** and ask: *How many words are there in sentence 1?* (three – 'Draw a line'.)

  Learners show their answer by showing three fingers (one for each word).

- Explain that you are going to mime a sentence. First show them how many words are in the sentence by holding up a finger for each word.

  For example: for 'Put a cross in the box.' show six fingers. Learners say: *Six words!*

- Mime the whole sentence. If learners guess any of the words (for example: 'cross' or 'box'), confirm that that word is in the sentence and point to your third or sixth finger to show where it comes in the sentence. (For example, if learners guess 'draw', point to your first finger and nod your head.) Continue like this until the learners have guessed the whole sentence.

- Play the game in two teams. Put the sentence cards you have made from page 106 face down on a desk at the front of the classroom. A learner from one team comes up and picks up and reads a sentence silently. They show how many words it has by using their fingers to show the number of words and by miming the sentence. The other people in the learner's team guess the sentence. If they guess correctly, they get a point. If they can't guess the sentence and the other team can, the other team gets a bonus point. Continue like this until teams have each mimed the same number of sentences.

- The winners are the team with the most points.

  Note: Large classes: play this with more teams. You will need to make more copies of the sentences. Use one or two stronger learners to help you monitor the activity.

6   Animals and aliens

Topic body and face, animals, food and drink

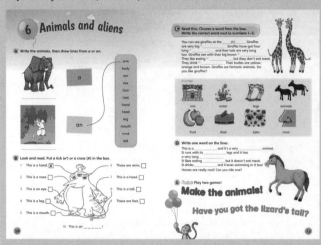

Equipment needed

O   One copy of page 107 for each group of 4 learners. See E.

Yes or no?

O   Teach/revise words for parts of the body. Point to your arm, body, ear, eye, face, foot, hand, head, leg, mouth and nose. Learners say the word or, if they don't know it, you say the word and they repeat it.

Do this several times, varying the order of the different face and body parts. Stop when learners can say the words quickly and confidently.

O   Show/remind learners how to write a tick and a cross. Do this on the board first. Next, draw a big tick and a big cross in the air.

Point to parts of your face and body again. As you point, say, for example: *This is my hand. These are my arms.*

Make some of these sentences true (*yes*) and some false (*no*).

If the sentence is true (*yes*), learners draw a tick in the air. If it is false (*no*), they draw a cross in the air.

Learners continue this in pairs. Learner A points to a part of their body and says its name. Learner B draws a tick or a cross in the air.

A Write the animals, then draw lines from *a* or *an*.

O   Write on the board: *a, e, i, o, u.* Say the vowels. Learners say them after you.

O   Teach/revise 'a/an'. Point to the picture of the elephant in **A** and say: *This is an (elephant).* Point to the mouse and say: *This is a (mouse).*

Write these two sentences on the board. Drill the pronunciation. Ask learners: *Why do we say **an** elephant, but **a** mouse?*

Underline the first letter of 'elephant' and 'mouse' on the board. Explain: *We use 'an' before words beginning with a, e, i, o or u. Before words that begin with other letters, we use 'a'.*

Tell learners to try and say 'a elephant' – it's very difficult!

Learners write 'an elephant' under the elephant picture and 'a mouse' under the mouse picture.

O   Learners look at the example in **A** (an arm). Check that learners understand that because the first letter of 'arm' is 'a', we say and write 'an arm'.

O   Learners look at the other words and draw purple lines between 'an' and the body words, or green lines between 'a' and the body words. Tell them to look carefully at the first letter of each word. They could also highlight or underline the first letters.

Check answers:

a + body, face, foot, hand, head, leg, mouth, nose, tail
an + ear, eye

O   Write on the board: *an alien, an egg, an ice cream, an orange, an ugly monster.*

Practise the pronunciation of each article + noun, making sure learners link the final /n/ of 'an' with the first vowel sound in each noun.

Learners draw pictures of the five things in their notebooks and write: *This is an alien. This is an egg.*, etc, under each drawing.

B Look and read. Put a tick or a cross in the box.

O   Learners look at the alien. Read out sentence 1: *This is a hand.* Point to the cross in the box. Say: *There is a cross here. This sentence is not correct. This line is going to its … ?* (head). Learners read sentences 2–9 and put a tick in the box for 'yes' sentences and a cross next to the 'no' sentences.

Check answers:

2 ✔   3 ✗   4 ✔   5 ✔   6 ✗   7 ✗   8 ✔   9 ✔

O   Ask: *Can you make the wrong sentences correct? What's the correct answer for 3?* (a hand) *And 6?* (eyes) *And 7?* (an arm)

O   Ask: *Can you see the five pink letters in the sentences? What letters are they?* (n, l, a, e, i) Write the letters on the board.

Point to the alien in **B** and ask: *What's this? Is it a boy?* (no) *Is it a robot?* (no) *Let's make a word from the five blue letters for it!* (alien) Learners write the letters for 'alien' on the lines in 10.

O   Say: *Colour the alien!* Learners use different colours for the different parts of its body.

O   Ask different learners questions about their pictures. For example: *What colour is the alien's ear?* (green)

In pairs, learners ask and answer each other about their alien pictures.

C Read and choose a word from the box. Write the correct word next to numbers 1–5.

o Say: *Look at the picture of the animal in C. What animal can you see?* (a giraffe)

o Write *giraffe* on the board.

o Learners read about giraffes and choose words from the box to complete the text. They write the words next to numbers 1–5.

o Check answers by reading out the completed text stopping at the gaps for different learners to say the next word.

> **Check answers:**
> **1** animals **2** legs **3** eyes **4** fruit **5** water

o Ask questions. Learners answer.
Are giraffes big or small? (big)
What colour are giraffes' eyes? (brown)
Do giraffes eat meat? (no)
Do they like apples? (yes)
What colour is a giraffe's body? (yellow, orange and brown)
Where do lots of giraffes live? In a house? (no) *In a garden?* (no)
In a park? (no) *In a zoo?* (yes)

D Write one word on the lines.

o Point to the horse in **D** and ask: *Which animal is this?* (a horse)

o Ask: *What do you know about horses?*
What colour are they? (brown / white / grey / black)
Are they big or small? (big)
How many legs have they got? (four)
Do they have a tail? (yes)
What do horses eat? (fruit)
What do horses drink? (water)
Ask the questions again. Learners write the answer to each question in the gaps in the text in **D**.

> **Check answers:**
> This is a **horse** and it's a very **big** animal.
> It runs with its **four** legs and it has a very long **tail/face/body**.
> It likes eating **fruit**, but it doesn't eat meat.
> It drinks **water** and it loves swimming in it too!
> Horses are really cool. Can you ride one?

E Play two games!

Make the animals.

o Give one set of the animal flashcards from page 107 to each group of four learners.
Tell them to make five different animals by putting together the different parts of the bodies. Ask: *Which five animals do you have?* (a frog, a fish, a bird, a crocodile, a lizard)

o Say: *Listen and make this animal: Take the frog's head, the bird's body and the lizard's tail.* In their groups, learners put the different parts together. Ask: *Do you like your new animal?*

o Different groups make new animals and tell the other groups which body parts to put together to make the same 'animal'.

Have you got the lizard's tail?

o In groups of four, learners sit together in a circle. Divide a shuffled set of cards between the four learners in each group so each learner has three cards. If one of the learners finds they already have three parts of the same animal, they place their three cards face up on the table, and say: *This is …* (a frog, etc).

o Learners must complete the animals in each set. One learner starts by asking another learner in their group for a part of an animal they need, for example: *Have you got* (the lizard's tail), *please?* If that learner has the lizard's tail, they give it to the learner who asked for it and the learner asks for another animal part.

o If they do not have the lizard's tail, they answer: *Sorry!* The turn then passes to the next learner who asks for the part of the animal they want.

o When a learner has made a complete animal, they put the three cards face up on the table and say: *This is a* (frog / crocodile / bird / lizard / fish). The winner is the learner who has made the most animals.

Note: You can also use these cards to play other games, for example: 'When the music stops!' (See Introduction for suggestions.)

7   Look, listen, smile, draw

Topic body and face, numbers, sports and leisure

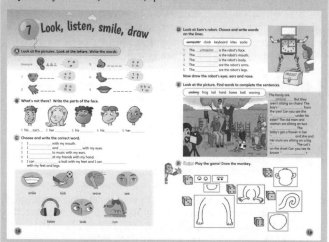

Not in YLE wordlists: *dice*

Equipment needed

- A camera or phone to take a class photo. See E. (optional)
- Pencils and a dice for every group of 4–5 learners. See F.

A Look at the pictures. Look at the letters. Write the words.

Reading & Writing Part 3

- Draw round both your hands on the board. Point to one of the hands and ask: *What's this?* (a hand)

  Point to both hands and ask: *What are these?* (hands)

  Write on the board: *1 hand 2 hands*

  Explain that we normally add 's' to the end of a word if we are talking about more than one thing. Point to two boys and/or two girls and say: *two boys / two girls*.

  Now point to your foot or draw a foot on the board. Ask: *What's this?*

  Write on the board: *1 foot*. Point to your feet or draw two feet on the board.

  Ask: *What are these? Are they 'foots'?* (No, they're feet.)

  Explain that some words like 'foot' are irregular and we don't add 's' to the end when we are talking about more than one of them. You could refer to irregular plurals in the learners' first language if helpful.

> **Starters tip**
>
> In Reading and Writing Part 3, candidates should cross off the letters as they use them to form each word. This will help them to spell the word correctly.

- Point to the example picture and ask: *What can you see?* (an ear).

  Point to the lines and the letters in the example and ask: *How many lines are there?* (three) *How many letters are there?* (three). *How do you spell 'ear'?*

  Point to the word 'ear' on the lines in the example.

- Learners put the letters from each speech bubble in the right order to make body words. For each word, they check that they are using all the letters by crossing them out when they write them on the lines.

> **Check answers:**
>
> **1** face **2** hand **3** nose **4** feet **5** mouth

Optional extension

Learners draw their own face in their notebook and label their picture with the words *ears*, *eyes*, *nose*, *mouth* and *hair*. They can just write the words or they can write short sentences, for example: *Here's my nose! This is my mouth.*

B What's not there? Write the parts of the face.

- Point to the first picture and ask: *Can you see the boy's eyes?* (yes) *Can you see his mouth?* (yes) *Can you see his ears?* (no) *His ears aren't there.* Point to the example answer: 'his ears.'

- Learners look at the other pictures and write the words for the parts of the face that aren't there. Check answers by asking different learners to come to the board to write the answer.

> **Check answers:**
>
> **2** eyes **3** mouth **4** nose **5** hair

- Tell learners to draw and colour the missing parts on the faces. Ask different learners: *What colour are the girl's eyes in your picture 2? What colour is the girl's hair in your picture 5?*

  Note: Check that learners understand why they can see 'his' or 'her' in front of the words they have written ('his' for a boy or man, 'her' for a girl or woman). Use their first language if helpful to explain this. Point out that we use 'his' and 'her' in front of both singular and plural words, for example: **2** her eyes **3** his nose.

- Learners choose two parts of the body or face from **A** in Unit 6 and draw them in their notebooks. Next to each drawing, learners draw a line for each letter of the word. Then they draw a circle or box and put the letters from the word inside it, jumbled up. Show learners how to do this before they start.

- Learners exchange notebooks and put the letters in the right order to make the words.

How many?

- Write on the board: *bodies, ears, feet, hands, heads, noses*.

  Learners work in pairs or small groups. Each pair or group counts the number of people in the classroom, then counts how many of these body parts on the board that there are in the classroom. Ask different groups for their answers. Answers should be all the same!

C Choose and write the correct word.

- Tell learners to look at sentence 1 in **C**: 'I … with my mouth.' Point to the picture of the smiling mouth and the word 'smile' in the box. Mime the word 'smile'. Ask: *What am I doing with my mouth?* (You're smiling.) Say: *That's right. I smile with my mouth.* Learners write *smile* on the line in 1.

- Learners complete sentences 2–5 with the other words.

> **Check answers:**
>
> **2** look, see (any order) **3** listen **4** wave **5** kick, run

- Ask learners: *What can you do with your mouth?* (Mime actions to teach or revise: drink, eat, talk.)

  Mime actions with your hands and ask: *What can you do with your hands?* (write, draw, paint, point, throw, catch, pick up, hold) Teach any new words.

I do it with my …

- Say an action word, for example: *listen*. Learners point to the part of the body that they use to do that action and say the word (*ears*).

- You can play this as an elimination game. If learners point to the wrong part of their body, don't know the word or hesitate for too long, they are out.

- Learners work in pairs. Learner A says a verb, for example, *Write!* Learner B does the action and says which part of their body they do it with: *I write with my hand!*

  Suggested actions: paint, walk, kick, look, point, eat, stand, see, write, colour, draw, wave, smile, throw, listen

D Look at Sam's robot. Choose and write words on the lines.

o Point to the boy in the picture in **D** and say: *This is Sam. He's making a robot.*

Point to the words in the box and ask: *Can you see the computer / clock / socks / kites?* (yes) *Where's the keyboard/clock? Where are the socks/kites?* Learners point to these things in the robot picture.

o Point to sentence 1 and to the words in the box. Say: *Look! The computer is the robot's face.* Point to the example answer: *computer.*

Say: *Look at Sam's robot. Write the words for the parts of the body in sentences 2–5.*

o Learners complete the sentences.

> **Check answers:**
> **2** keyboard   **3** clock   **4** socks   **5** kites

Now draw the robot's eyes, ears and nose.

o Draw a computer screen and keyboard on the board.

Say: *The robot hasn't got eyes or a … ?* (nose). Ask: *What can we put for the robot's eyes? What can we put for its ears? What can we put for its nose?*

Suggestions:

eyes: suns, eggs, oranges, grapes, balls

ears: bananas, ice creams, flowers, crosses, shells

nose: a phone, a pencil, a tick, a carrot

Draw two suns and a carrot on the screen on the board and say: *My robot's got sun eyes and a carrot nose.* Draw a shell on each side of the screen and say: *And look! My robot's got shell ears!*

o Say: *Now you choose!* Learners decide what to draw for the robot's eyes and nose and draw them on the robot in **D**.

o Write on the board: *My robot has got … eyes and a … nose.*

Learners copy and complete the sentence with words for the objects they chose. Ask different learners to read out their sentences and show their pictures.

 Find out about robots!

Learners find other examples of robots made from different objects. There are some great examples on the internet. You/ they use a search engine to find photos of these. They can print pictures and show the robots they find to the class and explain what they are made of and what the robots can do.

Alternatively, learners work in groups to design their own robot. They draw a picture and present it to the class, saying what their robot is made of and what it can and can't do.

E Look at the picture. Find words to complete the sentences.

o Point to the man at the front of the picture and ask: *What's the man doing?* (taking a photo) Point to the family and say: *This is the man's family. Where are they?* (in a garden) *How many people can you see?* (seven – the man, and six people in his family)

o Say: *Look at the words in the box. Can you find a frog, a tail, a hand, some boxes and a ball in the picture? Is one person smiling? Waving?* Read out the words in the word box again. Learners point to where they can see the word or action in the picture in **E**.

o Learners read the sentences and write words from the box on the lines.

> **Check answers:**
> **1** waving   **2** ball   **3** boxes   **4** hand   **5** frog   **6** tail

o Learners look at the picture again. Ask *What colour* and *How many* questions:

What colour is the boy's T-shirt? (yellow) *And what colour is the frog?* (green) *And the cat?* (brown) *How many eyes can you see?* (seventeen) *How many chairs are in this garden?* (three) *How many shoes can you see?* (ten)

o Say: *I want to take a photo of you! Sit down, please! Look at the camera! Smile! Don't close your eyes! Thanks!*

If you have a camera or phone, take the photo, but make sure you have parents' permission to take it and share it first.

F Play the game! Draw the monkey.

o Point to the eight parts of the body pictures and ask: *What can you see?* (two eyes, a nose, a mouth, a tail, two arms, two legs, a head with ears, a body).

Ask: *Which animal's eyes and ears can you see?* (a monkey)

o Ask: *What can you see next to the monkey's body?* (a dice) *What number can you see on the dice?* (6) Ask learners to tell you what numbers are on each of the other dice.

o Give each group of 4–5 learners a dice. They also need pencils and paper. Explain that they are going to draw a monkey. Show them how to play.

Throw the dice. They need to throw a 6 to start. Then they can draw a monkey's body on their piece of paper. If they throw 1, 2, 3, 4 or 5, they have to throw the dice again until they get a 6. When they have a body, they can draw a head (5), a leg (4), an arm (3) or a tail (1). To draw a mouth, nose or eyes (2), they need the head (5) first.

o Point out that they need two arms and legs and that they need to throw a '2' four times to be able to draw two eyes, a nose and a mouth.

o Learners play this game in groups of 4–5. The winner in each group is the first person to draw the whole monkey.

Note: You could make this game more exciting by only letting learners draw the different body parts if they can say or do these things:

To draw

a body   Say and spell three colours

arms   Say and spell three animals

legs   Say and spell three boys names

a tail   Say the alphabet

a face   Say and spell three girls names

a nose   Say and spell three numbers

eyes   Say and spell three toys

ears   Say four actions you do with your hands

8   In my clothes cupboard

Topic clothes, family and friends, the home

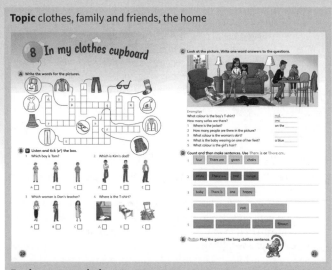

Equipment needed

- Starters audio 8B.
- Pictures of clothes. See A and B.
- Colouring pencils or pens.

Ⓐ Write the words for the pictures.

- Teach/revise words for clothes by pointing to learners' clothes and/ or to magazine or computer photos.
  Starters clothes words: bag, boot, (baseball) cap, dress, glasses, handbag, hat, jacket, jeans, shirt, shoe, shorts, skirt, sock, trousers, T-shirt, watch.
- Learners look at the pictures and write the words in the boxes in the crossword. They can check spelling in the list on page 103.

> **Check answers:**
> Down (left to right): dress, shirt, jeans, shoe, glasses, sock, hat
> Across (top to bottom): handbag, jacket, skirt, shorts, trousers

- Point to the pictures in **A** and ask: *Which picture am I talking about?*
  This is green and yellow. (the sock)
  These are blue. (the jeans)
  These are pink. (the skirt and the shirt)
  This has an apple on it. (the hat)
  This has three flowers on it. (the handbag)
  These are orange. (the shorts)
- Learners work in groups of six. Give each learner in the group a number 1–6. Explain that you are going to tell each learner in the group to colour one of the clothes in the circled pictures.
  Point to the jacket and say: *Number 1s! Please colour the jacket! You choose the colour for the jacket!*
  Now number 2s! What colour would you like to colour the trousers with? Choose a colour and colour the trousers, please!
  Number 6s. Find the hat. Colour it your favourite colour!
  Number 3s. You can colour the shoe! Which colour? I don't know! You choose!
  Number 5s. The handbag is yours. Colour it!
  Number 4s. Can you see the dress? Colour it, please!
- In their groups, Learner 1 tells the others what colour to make the jacket. He/she says: *Colour the jacket (blue), please.*
  Learners 2, 3, 4, 5, 6 do the same for the thing they coloured.

What am I drawing?

- Draw these clothes in the air with a pointed finger: a dress, a sock, a skirt, a hat.

Learners watch and say each word as you 'draw' it.

- In pairs, learners draw one of the clothes items from **A** in the air with their fingers. Their partner watches and says what they have drawn.
- Draw a cap in the air with a pointed finger (or draw a cap on the board). Ask: *What's this? What am I drawing?* (a cap) All the learners 'draw' a cap in the air. Ask: *Can you draw boots? Who can draw boots? (Angela/Boris), draw some boots on the board, please!* A learner draws some boots on the board.

Ⓑ ▶ Listen and tick the box.

> **Starters tip**
> In Listening Part 3, candidates need to look carefully at the three pictures and to notice the differences between them.

- Point to the pictures in 1 and ask: *What's the boy wearing?*
  A   yellow trousers, a green T-shirt, red shoes and a hat.
  B   blue trousers, a yellow T-shirt and red shoes.
  C   blue trousers, an orange T-shirt, glasses and blue shoes.
- Play the audio stopping after 1. (*Which boy is Tom?*) Learners put a tick in the correct box. (1A)
- Point to the pictures in 2. Ask: *What's the man wearing?*

> **Check answers:**
> **A** A white shirt and brown shoes.
> **B** A red and yellow T-shirt and white shoes.
> **C** A brown jacket, white T-shirt and brown shoes.

Play the audio for 2 (Which is Kim's dad?). Learners listen and tick the correct box: (2B)

- Play the rest of the audio. Learners tick the correct boxes for questions 3 and 4.

> **Check answers:**
> **3** C   **4** A

Audioscript

> *Look at the pictures. Listen and tick the box.*
>
> One   *Which boy is Tom?*
> Boy: Here's a photo of our class.
> Woman: Oh? Which boy is Tom? Does Tom wear glasses?
> Boy: No, he doesn't.
> Woman: Is Tom the boy with the hat?
> Boy: Yes. And red shoes!
>
> Two   *Which is Kim's dad?*
> Boy: Is that your dad, Kim? The man in the jacket and trousers?
> Girl: No. My dad isn't wearing a jacket today.
> Boy: What's he wearing?
> Girl: Jeans and a T-shirt.
>
> Three   *Which woman is Dan's teacher?*
> Woman: Is that your new music teacher, Dan?
> Boy: The woman in the skirt? No, that's not her.
> Woman: Is your teacher the woman in the trousers then?
> Boy: No. Our teacher's wearing a yellow dress today.
> Woman: Oh yes! I can see her. I like her green bag!
>
> Four   *Where's the T- shirt?*
> Girl: I can't find my white T-shirt, Dad!
> Man: Is it on your bed?
> Girl: No.
> Man: Is it on the chair in the garden?
> Girl: No. Oh, I know! It's in the car!

My favourite / new / clean / beautiful …

o Write on the board:
This is my favourite …
These are my favourite …

o Hold up a picture of a jacket and say: *This is my favourite jacket.* Give the picture to a learner. They hold up the picture and say the same sentence. (*This is my favourite jacket.*) This continues round the class, with each learner showing the picture and saying the sentence.

o Hold up a picture of a pair of jeans and ask: *What are these?* (jeans) Say: *This is my favourite jeans.* Or: *These are my favourite jeans. Which sentence is correct?* (These are my favourite jeans.) Pass the picture round the class. Learners show the picture and say the sentence. (*These are my favourite jeans.*)

Pass the different pictures around, starting with a different learner each time. The first learner says *This is my favourite …* or *These are my favourite … .* Then the others repeat the sentence and show the picture. Give out more pictures so that learners are showing and speaking about several pictures at the same time.

After a while, change the adjective in the sentences:
This is / These are my new … clean … beautiful …

Suggested clothes: trousers, dress, T-shirt, glasses, hat, handbag, shirt, shoes, skirt, socks

© Look at the picture. Write one-word answers to the questions.

o Learners write letters in their notebooks to make words.

Say: *Listen and write these letters: N-A-M. Can you make a word with these letters? You can see this in the picture in C. What's the word?* (man)

Words to spell:
s-r-t-i-h (shirt), t-a-c-s (cats), b-a-l-e-t (table), s-a-n-e-j (jeans), a-w-o-n-m (woman), d-a-n-h (hand), c-e-j-a-t-k (jacket), s-a-s-g-l-e-s (glasses)

o Check answers by asking different learners to point to the picture and to say the letters to spell the word.

Optional extension:
Learners work in pairs. Each learner chooses a thing in the picture and writes the word, then jumbles the letters. They say the letters to their partner, who writes them and then writes the correct spelling of the word and points to it in the picture.

o Read the two example questions and answers. Ask: *Can you see the boy's red T-shirt and the sofa?* Learners point to these things in the picture. Point to the answers in the two examples and ask: *How many words or numbers do you write in your answers?* (one)

o Learners read and answer questions 1–5.

o Ask different learners: *Can you spell your answer to question (1 / 3 / 4 / 5), please?* Write the words on the board.

Say: *Point to the (chair/orange skirt/blue sock on the baby's foot/ girl's black hair)!* Learners point to the correct part of the picture.

Check answers:				
1 chair	**2** 5/five	**3** orange	**4** sock	**5** black

o Ask more questions about the picture:
Where's the man's jacket? (on the chair)
What colour is his jacket? (grey)
What are the boy and his father doing? (playing a game)
Where's their game? (on the table)
What's the girl in the green dress listening to? (her mum / a story)
How many cats has this family got? (two)

Ⓓ Count and then make sentences. Use *There is* or *There are*.

o Point to 1. Explain that this is a sentence about the picture but it is in four parts and they are not in the correct order. Ask: *Can you make the sentence?* (There are four green chairs) Write it on the board. Learners copy the sentence onto the line in 1.

Point to the end of the sentence. Ask: *What's missing?* (the full stop). Make sure learners put the full stop at the end of the sentence in their books.

o Learners write the sentence for 2. (*There are two white lamps.*)

o Point to the baby and ask: *How many babies are there in the picture?* (one) Point to the words 'There is' on the second green part of 3. Say: *There is one … .* (baby) Point to the baby and ask: *Is the baby happy or sad?* (happy) *There is one happy baby. Is that right?* (yes) *Write that sentence on the line in 3!* Learners write the sentence.

o Point to the boxes for 4. Explain that some words are missing. Ask: *What colour are the cats in picture C?* (black) Say: *Write 'black' in the first box.* Say: *Count the cats. How many cats are there?* (two) *Write 'two' in the second box.*

Ask. *Which words go in box 4?* Tell learners they can find the missing words in sentences 1 and 2. (There are) Learners write *There are* in the last box. They then write the sentence under the boxes and put the full stop at the end. (*There are two black cats.*)

o Point to the word 'flowers' in the last orange box in 5. Say: *Count the flowers. How many flowers are there?* (three) Learners write *three* in one of the short orange boxes in 5. Ask: *What colour are the flowers?* (pink) Learners write 'pink' in the other short orange box. Ask: *Do we say 'There is three' or 'There are three'?* (There are) *Write 'There are' in the long orange box!*

Learners write the sentence on the line in 5: *There are three pink flowers.*

Ⓔ Play the game! The long clothes sentence.

o Say: *It's morning. I'm in my bedroom. I open my cupboard.* (Mime opening two big cupboard doors.)

Say: *In my cupboard, there are boots.* Make sure your voice (intonation) falls at the end of the sentence (boots).

Say the sentence again, but do not finish it (your voice/intonation rises): *In my cupboard, there are boots and … .*

One learner repeats the sentence and adds another word, for example, 'dresses'. Their intonation should fall at the end of the sentence (dresses). The next learner repeats that sentence and adds 'and' plus one more word (jackets). Their intonation rises when they say *shoes, dresses,* then falls when they say *jackets* at the end of the sentence.

Learner A: *In my cupboard, there are boots and dresses.*
Learner B: *In my cupboard, there are boots, dresses and jackets.*

o Play several times. Learners try to make the longest sentence.
Large classes: you could play this game in groups.
Stronger classes: learners add the colours of the clothes.
For example: *In my cupboard, there are brown boots, … .*

9 Funny monsters

Topic body and face, colours

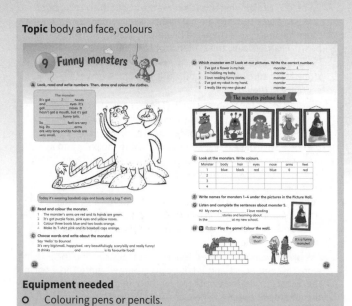

Equipment needed

○ Colouring pens or pencils.
○ Starters audio 9H.

Ⓐ Look, read and write numbers. Then, draw and colour the clothes.

○ Point to the monster and ask: *How many heads has the monster got?* (two) Point to the number 2 on the line. Ask: *How many eyes has this monster got? And noses? Feet? Arms? Can you count them? Count them and write the numbers on the lines.*

> **Check answers:**
> 6/six eyes, 3/three noses, 2/two funny tails, 5/five feet,
> 4/four arms

○ Read out the sentence about the monster's clothes: *Today, it's wearing baseball caps and boots and a big T-shirt.* Ask: *Can you see the monster's baseball caps and boots or T-shirt?* (no)

Say these sentences, pausing to give learners time to draw the clothes: *Take a pencil and draw two baseball caps. This monster needs two baseball caps. It's got two heads! Now, draw boots on the five feet! That's five boots! Oh, and a big T-shirt on the monster's body.*

Note: Learners do not colour the monster's body or clothes yet (they do this in **B**).

Ⓑ Read and colour the monster.

○ Learners read the sentences and colour the monster and its clothes.
○ Say: *Now, colour the monster's tails and legs. You choose the colours!*
In pairs, learners ask and answer questions about the tails and legs: *What colour are your monster's legs?*

Yes or no?

○ Read out the following sentences about the monster. Learners put their thumbs up if the sentence is right about the picture and down if it's wrong.
1 *It's got five feet.* (*Yes* – thumbs up.)
2 *It's got one nose.* (*No* – thumbs down.)
3 *It's got two funny tails.* (*Yes* – thumbs up.)
4 *The monster's eyes are pink.* (*Yes* – thumbs up.)
5 *It's got two green faces.* (*No* – thumbs down.)

Ⓒ Choose words and write about the monster!

○ Point to the monster in **A** again and say: *This monster's name is Bounce! You know, that's a good name for this monster! It bounces when it walks. It bounces when it runs!* Show learners how Bounce walks and runs! They could stand up and move like Bounce too!
Read the first part of the sentence: *It's very …*
Ask: *Is Bounce very big or very small?* (very big) Learners put a circle round 'big' in the first sentence.
Say: *Bounce doesn't have a mouth, so it isn't smiling, but is Bounce happy or sad? You choose! Is Bounce a very beautiful or a very ugly monster? Choose!* Learners circle 'happy' or 'sad', then 'beautiful' or 'ugly'.
Say: *Bounce is big. Is Bounce scary too, or is Bounce silly? Scary or silly? You choose.* Learners decide whether Bounce is scary or silly and circle the word to complete their sentence.

○ Ask: *What does Bounce drink? Milk? No!! What does it eat? Write words about Bounce's favourite drink and food!*

○ Say very slowly: *Bounce is very big.* (Show learners how we put our top and bottom lips together to say /b/ and put our top teeth against the inside of our bottom lip to say /v/). Say the sentence again. Learners say it too. Drill this several times. Do the same with: *Bounce is very beautiful.*

○ Learners read out and show each other their sentences in small groups. Walk around and listen, checking that learners are pronouncing /v/ and /b/ correctly. Tell the class what you think are the best answers for the monster's favourite drink and food.

○ Tell learners to draw a line down the middle of the page in their notebooks to make two columns. (They do not need to use the whole page – seven lines are enough) They write the letters 'b' at the top of the first column and 'v' at the top of the second column. Say: *Listen and write the words under 'b' or 'v'. For example: big. Can you hear 'b' or 'v' in that word?* (b) *Where do you write 'big'? Under 'b' or 'v'?* (b)
Say these words. Learners listen and write: *table, favourite, TV, bag, number, live, brown, love, robot, wave, body*

> **Check answers:**
> **b:** table, bag, number, brown, robot, body
> **v:** favourite, TV, live, love, wave

D Which monster am I? Look at our pictures. Write the correct number.

> **Starters tip**
>
> In Reading and Writing Part 2, candidates need to understand sentences that describe (or don't describe) a particular scene picture. They need practice in matching sentences to different pictures like they do here. They also need training in spotting words that make sentences incorrect, for example, prepositions of place, numbers, adjectives, etc.

o Learners look at the five monsters. Read out the first sentence: *I've got a flower in my hair.* Ask: *Can you see a flower? Where is it?* (Monster 4 has a flower in her hair) Point to the example answer: 4

o Learners read sentences 2–5 and write the numbers of the monsters on the lines.

> **Check answers:**
> **2** 3   **3** 5   **4** 2   **5** 1

E Look at the monsters. Write colours.

o Say: *Look at the monsters in D again.* Point to the first monster and to the words in line 1 in **E** and say: *This monster has got a blue body, black hair, red eyes and a blue nose. He has no arms and his feet are red.*

o Learners write the colours or 0 in the boxes for monsters 2, 3 and 4.

> **Check answers:**
> Monster 2: a green body, orange hair, blue eyes, a black nose, green arms, green feet.
> Monster 3: a grey body, red hair, green eyes, an orange nose, grey arms, grey feet.
> Monster 4: a pink body, yellow hair, green eyes, a purple nose, pink arms, white feet.

o Point to monster 1. Ask: *What's this monster doing?* (smiling)
Point to monsters 2, 3 and 4 in turn. Ask the same question: *What's this monster doing?* (2 waving 3 eating 4 dancing)

o Say: *Look at monster 5. How many feet has this monster got?* (two) *What colour are its feet?* (green) *What's this monster doing?* (reading)

o Write on the board: *How many ... has the monster got?*
Ask learners to suggest words to complete the question (*eyes, arms, noses, feet*). Write these words on the board.

o Write two more questions on the board: *What colour are they? What's this monster doing?*
Each learner chooses a monster. In pairs, learners take it in turns to ask and answer the three questions about monster 5.

F Write names for monsters 1–4.

o Point to the monster in picture 4 in the Picture Hall and say: *This monster's name is Candy. She really loves her name and she likes eating pink candy!!! Do you like pink candy too? Oh! And you spell her name C-A-N-D-Y! Can you write that name on the line under picture 4, please? C-A-N-D-Y! Thanks!*

o Learners think of a name for monsters 1–3 and write the names on the lines under the pictures in the monster picture hall.

o Ask different learners: *What's monster (1)'s name?* (Happy) Ask: *How do you spell Happy?* The learner spells the name. Ask the same questions to other learners about the other monsters.

G Listen and complete the sentences about monster 5.

o Point to monster 5 and say (in a funny voice): *Hi! My name's (Larry) and I love reading (scary) stories and learning about (aliens) in the (lessons) at my new school!* Say the sentences again.
Point to the sentences in **G**. Say: *Hi! My name's Larry. That's L-A-R-R-Y.* Learners write the letters on the first line.
Read out the second sentence, pausing for learners to say the words and write them on the lines: *I love reading ... (scary) stories and learning about ... (aliens) in the ... (lessons) at my new school.*
Walk around and check that learners are writing the words 'scary', 'alien' and 'lessons' correctly.

Draw then write about your monster.

o Learners draw a monster and colour it. They give it a name too. (With stronger classes, they could write what their monster likes drinking, eating and reading as well.)

o Write on the board:
big/small ... heads ... eye ... noses
... mouths ... legs ... feet ... arms ... hands
Learners copy this and write the numbers and colours for each part of their monster.

o Learners work in pairs. Learner A describes their monster. Learner B listens and draws the monster in their notebook. Then, they ask each other: *What's your monster's name? How do you spell it?* They write each other's monster names, and compare their monster pictures.

H ▶ Play the game! Colour the wall.

o Point to wall in the picture and ask: *What's this?* (a wall) *What's behind the wall?* (a monster)
Say: *Listen to the monster! Colour the wall.* Tell learners to colour each row of bricks in the wall. Use their first language if necessary/possible to explain this.
Note: If a box is white, learners don't need to colour it.

Audioscript

> 1 *red, green, yellow*
> 2 *black, grey, brown, orange*
> 3 *pink, purple, yellow, red, brown*
> 4 *white, red, blue, grey, brown, green*
> 5 *yellow, pink, white, purple, red, black, orange*
> *Thank you!*

o Play the audio several times to give learners time to colour all the boxes. Pause between each line as necessary.

10   Our families

Topics family, names, animals

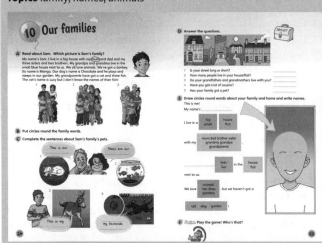

Movers words: *circle, grandparents, parents, round*

Equipment needed

- Colouring pencils or pens.
- Photos of learners' pets. See D.
- Paper for drawing families. See E, optional extension.
- Questions for C.

A Read about Sam. Which picture is Sam's family?

Starters tip
There are nearly always questions about families in Starters. Give learners practice in talking about their own family (their names, ages, number of brothers and sisters / cousins, etc).

- Point to the boy in the top picture in **A** and say: *There are three letters in this boy's name! Read sentence 1. What's his name?* (Sam) *Which letters are in the name Sam?* (S-A-M)

  Read the start of the next sentence: *I live in a big house with my mum … .* Point to the word 'mum'. Draw a circle in the air and say: *'Mum' is a family word and that's why there's a circle round it. Listen to me. When I say a family word, draw a circle!* Read out the rest of the text in **A**. Learners draw a circle in the air with their hand when they hear a family word.

- Point to the three pictures of the families and ask: *Which is Sam's family? Picture 1, 2 or 3?* (picture 2).

B Put circles round the family words.

- Learners read the text and, with a pen or pencil, draw circles round the other family words.

  Check answers:
  dad, sisters, brothers, grandpa, grandma, grandparents

  Note: Explain that 'grandfather/grandpa, grandmother/grandma, father/dad' and 'mother/mum' mean the same, but 'grandpa, grandma, dad' and 'mum' are more familiar. Use the learners' first language if necessary. Teach/revise 'parents' and 'grandparents'.

- Ask: *How many people live in Sam's house?* (eight) *Which pets has Sam got?* (a donkey and a dog)

  How many pets do his grandparents have? (four)

- Point to picture 2 and say: *Let's choose names for the people in Sam's family.* Learners can choose names from page 10 (Unit 3) Write the chosen names on the board.

  Suggestions: grandparents: *Mr and Mrs White.* Parents: *Mr and Mrs Love*, brothers: *Tom and Nick*, sisters: *Pat, Kim and Lucy.* Learners could also guess the ages of Sam's brothers and sisters. Ask: *How old is* (name)?

- Ask questions about the picture of Sam's family:
  1. *Who's wearing a red T-shirt?* (one of Sam's sisters)
  2. *What colour is Sam's T-shirt?* (green and red)
  3. *Which people are wearing glasses?* (two sisters, Sam's mother and grandmother)
  4. *Who's got white hair?* (Sam's grandfather)
  5. *Which people are wearing jackets?* (Sam's grandma/ grandmother and grandpa/grandfather)
  6. *Who's wearing white shoes?* (Sam)
  7. *Who's wearing red and white shoes?* (one of Sam's sisters)

Optional extension:
In pairs, learners could write questions about the people in pictures 1 and 3. Then, two pairs join together and ask and answer the questions.

C Complete the sentences about Sam's family's pets.

Starters tip
In Reading and Writing Part 1, the pictures will show one or more of each named item and, in the defining sentence, the named item will be singular or plural. See right and wrong answer examples below:
(a picture of a fish)   This is a fish. ☑
                 This is a foot. ☒
(a picture of two cakes)   These are cakes. ☑
                     These are cats. ☒

- Point to the picture of Sam's grandpa and grandma and ask: *Who are these people?* (Sam's grandparents) Point to the cat and ask: *What's this?* (a cat) *Who's got a cat – Sam or his grandparents?* (his grandparents) Point to the first bubble and read: *This is our … .* (cat). Learners write *cat* on the line.

- Learners write the words for the other animals on the lines in 2 and 3. (2 fish 3 donkey)

  Write on the board: *This is our cat.* and *These are our fish.* Ask: *How many cats have Sam's grandparents got?* (one) *There's one cat.* Point to the cat sentence on the board and say: *We say 'This is'. How many fish have they got?* (three) Point to the fish sentence and say: *We say 'These are' because there are three fish, not one.*

  Note: You can also explain that the words 'our' and 'my' do not change for singular or plural nouns.

  Point to the ball in 4. Ask: *What's this?* (a ball) *Which pet loves playing in the garden?* (Chocolate / the dog) *How many balls are there?* (one) *Do we say 'This is' or 'These are' for one ball?* (This is) Learners write *This is* and *ball* on the lines in 4.

- Point to the cat in C and ask: *What colour is this cat?* (white) *What's the cat doing?* (sleeping) *What are the fish doing?* (swimming) *What's the dog doing?* (running/playing)

- Say: *Look at the pictures in A and B. Can you find:*

  Two blue things (Suggestions: Chocolate's ball, Sam's trousers, one brother's sweater, one sister's shoes, one brother's shoes)
  Two brown things (Chocolate / the dog, Sam's hair, his sister's trousers)
  Two white things (the cat, grandpa's hair, Sam's shoes)

D Answer the questions.

○ Say: *Now, answer questions about your family!* Learners read the questions in **D** and write their answers. For 1, they write 'long' or 'short'. For 2 and 3, they write a number and for 4 and 5 they write *yes* or *no*.

○ Learners stand up. Go up to one learner (Learner A) and ask: *How many brothers and sisters have you got?* (two)
Say: *I've got one brother. Stand behind me.*
Learner A then asks a different learner the same question:
How many brothers and sisters have you got?
Learner B answers the question and stands **in front of** Learner A if they have fewer brothers and sisters and **behind** Learner A if they have more.

○ All learners ask each other the question:
How many brothers and sisters have you got?
They get into a line in the order of the number of brothers and sisters they have. Learners with no brothers or sisters stand at the front, those with the most stand at the back.

○ Learners now ask each other: *How many cousins have you got?*
They get into a line according to the number of cousins they have.

○ Learners then ask and move to stand in the order of the number of animals they have at home.

 My pet!

Learners draw a picture of their pet or bring in a photo and present their pet to the class.
If they haven't got a pet, learners can draw a pet that they would like to have, choose a name for it and talk about it to the class.

Complete the words.

○ Write on the board: *fa* and ask: *Can you tell me the four letters I need to add here to make a word for 'dad'?* (t-h-e-r) *What's the word for 'dad'?* (father) Point to *fa* again and say: *Now tell me four letters to make a word for your mum, dad, brothers and sisters.* (m-i-l-y, family)

Write on the board: pa
ma
mother
father

Ask: *Which five letters can I put in front of these words to make four family words?* (g-r-a-n-d, grand) Write the letters on the board in front of the four second parts. Point to and say each word. The whole class says the words after you, then different learners say them, then the whole class again.
Say: *Grandpa is great! My grandma's name is Grace.* Learners say these sentences too.

Note: For a lot of learners, saying two consonants like 'gr' together is difficult because this combination of letters does not exist in their first language, or they pronounce them differently.

Always encourage correct pronunciation, but make sure learners don't lose confidence. Explain that it is normal to make mistakes. If we don't try to say new words (and make mistakes – which is fine) we don't improve our language skills.

E Draw circles round words about your family and home and write names.

○ Point to the face in **E** and say: *This is you! Complete the picture!* (see Sam's face in **A** for help if necessary). Learners draw their hair, nose, and eyes. They can then colour their mouth, face, hair and eyes and T-shirt.

○ Point to the line after 'My name's' at the top of **E** and say: *Write your name on this line.* Ask different learners: *Do you live in a house or a flat?* Learners answer. Tell learners who live in a house to draw a circle round the word 'house' in the box. Learners who live in a flat draw a circle round the word 'flat'.
Ask different learners: *Is your flat big or small?* Learners who live in a big house or flat draw a circle round 'big' and learners who live in a small house or flat draw a circle round 'small'.
Ask: *Who lives with you? Draw a circle round the people who live in your house or flat.* Learners draw circles.
Point to the second line in front of 'lives/live in the house/flat next to us' and ask: *Who lives next to you?* Learners write the name of the person/people who live next to them on that line.
Point to the last line and ask: *Do you like animals? Do you like gardens? Draw a circle round 'animals', 'cats', 'dogs' or 'gardens'.* Learners end the text by drawing a circle round 'cat', 'dog' or 'garden'.
(Sam's text can be used as a model to help with this activity.)

○ Go round and help and check answers.

○ Ask 3–4 learners to stand up and read out their texts beginning with 'This is me!' (pointing to their drawing and showing it to the class).

Optional extension:
Learners make posters about their homes, their family members and pets. They use their own drawings or photos and write captions and/or a short continuous text. Their posters can then be displayed around the classroom.

F Play the game! Who's that?

○ Each learner writes a list of the names of the people in their family (including themselves) on a piece of paper. You could join in by writing your family's names on the board.
For example: *James, Margaret, David, John, Cristina, Victoria*

○ With a green pen, they number the names in alphabetical order. Ask different learners to read out the names.

○ With a red pen, they number the names from the youngest person to the oldest person. Different learners read out the names.

○ With a blue pen, they number the names from the longest (the most letters) to the shortest. Different learners read out the names.
Note: Use learners' first language to explain the meaning of 'youngest', 'oldest', 'longest' and 'shortest' if necessary.

○ In pairs, learners ask and answer each other about the names.
For example:
Learner A: *Who's James?*
Learner B: *He's my father.*

11 Whose is it?

Topics names, sports and leisure

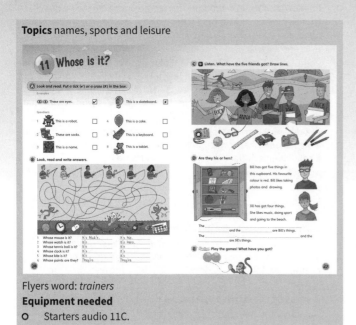

Flyers word: *trainers*

Equipment needed
- Starters audio 11C.

A Look and read. Put a tick or a cross in the box.

Reading & Writing Part **1**

> **Starters tip**
> Some of the words in Reading and Writing Part 1 look (and often sound) very similar, for example 'game' and 'name' in **A**. Point this out to your class and practise finding these small differences.

- Say: *Look at the pictures in A.* Point to the picture of the eyes and ask: *What are these?* (eyes) Read out the example sentence: *These are eyes.* Ask: *Is this sentence correct for this picture?* (yes) *Can you see the tick in the box? This sentence is correct. We tick the box!*
  Point to the ear in the second example and say: *Can you see the cross? This sentence is wrong. It isn't a skateboard. It's an … ?* (ear).
- Learners put ticks or crosses in boxes for sentences 1–5.

> **Check answers:**
> 1 ✔ 2 ✔ 3 ✘ 4 ✘ 5 ✔ 6 ✘

- Point to the picture in 3 and say: *This isn't a name, it's a game! This is a board game!* The whole class says these sentences and points to picture 3. Draw a big tick in the air and say: *You're right! Well done!* Do the same with picture 4: *This isn't a cake. This is a balloon!* Point to 6 and say: *This isn't a tablet. It's a …* (teddy).
  Learners work in A and B pairs. Learner A points at one of the things in A or B and says: *This isn't a ……., (saying a word that is NOT correct for the picture) it's a ……..* (saying the correct word). Learner B listens, draws a tick and says: *You're right! Well done!* Then Learner B says a different sentence about another picture and A draws a tick and says: *Well done!*

B Look, read and write answers.

- Point to the six children in the pictures and ask: *What are their names?* (Nick, Lucy, Tom, Jill, Bill, Anna) *Where are their names?* (on their T-shirts) *What's the first letter of Jill's name?* (J) *And of Anna's name?* (A) *Can you say 'J' and 'A'? How many letters are in their names?* (four) *What are they doing?* (fishing)
- Point to the six pictures of the objects and ask: *Are they catching fish?* (no) Point to the objects and ask: *What can you see here?* (a tennis ball, a clock, a [computer] mouse, a kite, a watch, paints/ a paintbox)

- Ask: *Have you got a watch?* Learners who have a watch put up their hands. Count hands. Ask: *How many children have got a watch?* (three)
  Repeat this with: *paints, kite, tennis ball, mouse* and *clock*.
  Note: in some languages, the word for 'clock' and 'watch' is the same. If this is true for your learners, tell them that in English, there are two words – a clock is something we put on a wall or table or is on our phones. A watch is something we wear on our arm.
- Point to the mouse and ask: *Whose is the mouse?* Learners follow the line from the mouse to Nick. (*It's Nick's*) Ask the same question about the kite, tennis ball and watch and clock: *Whose is the kite / tennis ball / watch / clock?* Learners follow the lines and answer: (The kite's Jill's. The tennis ball's Bill's. The clock's Anna's. The watch is Lucy's.) Ask: *Whose are the paints?* (Tom's)
  Note: Some learners confuse the words 'clock' and 'watch' because the word for both of these things is the same in their first language and because we use *o'clock* to talk about the time we see on both clocks and watches. Show the difference by pointing to the watch and to the clock in **B**.
- Point to and read out the first question and answer. *Whose mouse is it? It's Nick's.*
- Ask learners why there is 's on the end of *Nick.* (*It's his mouse – we put 's on the end of his name to show that the mouse is his.*)
- Learners complete the other answers in the first column.

> **Check answers:**
> 2 Lucy's 3 Bill's 4 Anna's 5 Jill's 6 Tom's

- Read out the second answer in 1: *It's his.* Remind learners that we use 'his' for boys' and men's things. Read out the second answer in 2: *It's hers.* We use 'hers' for girls' and women's things.
- Learners complete the second column with *his* or *hers*.

> **Check answers:**
> 3 his 4 hers 5 hers 6 his

- Point out that we use 'they' to talk about the paints because there is more than one paint here.

C ▶ Listen. What have the five friends got? Draw lines.

- Point to the five children in the picture and say: *The children aren't fishing now. Where are they?* (in the park) Point to the small pictures and say: *These are the children's things. Listen and draw lines between the children and these pictures.*
- Play the example on the audio. Ask: *Whose nose do you put the glasses on?* (Bill's) Make sure that they can see the line between the glasses and Bill's nose.
- Learners listen and draw lines from the things to the children. Play the rest of the audio twice.
- In pairs, learners check each other's answers.

> **Check answers:**
> Lines should be drawn between: **1** radio and in Lucy's bag
> **2** pencils and in Anna's hand **3** ruler and on Tom's book
> **4** camera and in Nick's box **5** car and on Bill's head

Audioscript

D Are they his or hers?

○ Say: *Bill has a sister. Her name's Jill.* Point to the girl in the green T-shirt and say: *This is Jill. Write Bill's and Jill's names on their T-shirts, please!* Learners write the names on the T-shirts.

○ Point to the shell in Bill and Jill's cupboard and ask:

    Teacher: *What's this?*

    Learner: *It's a shell.*

    Teacher: *Can you spell shell?*

    Learner: *Yes, I can. S-H-E-L-L.*

    Teacher: *Thanks!*

○ In pairs, learners write all the things they can see in the cupboard in their notebooks (phone, radio, robot (picture/drawing), shell, photo, camera, ball, pencils, guitar).

    Point to each thing in the cupboard and ask different learners: *What's this?* (It's a …) or *What are these?* (They're … .) *Can you spell … ?* All learners check their spelling.

○ Ask: *Whose is the guitar – Bill's or Jill's?* Learners say whose they think the guitar is. Ask the same question about the 'radio' and the 'camera'.

○ Learners read the sentences about Bill and Jill and write the words for Bill's things on the lines in the first sentence and for Jill's things on the lines in the second sentence.

> **Check answers:**
> Bill's things: camera, drawing/picture, pencils/crayons, phone, photo. Jill's things: (beach) ball, radio, shell, guitar.

○ Ask: *Whose camera is this? Is it his or hers?* (point to Bill and Jill) Learners put up their hands to answer: *It's his!*

○ Ask: *Whose beach ball is this?* (It's hers!)

○ Learners ask and answer questions about the other things in pairs. Go round and check they are using 'his' and 'hers' correctly.

    Possible extension: *Whose … ? It's his/hers!* Give more practice with this by asking questions about a boy and girl and their things. Ask a boy and a girl to stand up. Point to things that they're wearing or holding and ask: *Whose dress/pen/shoe is this?* Learners respond by calling out together: *It's his! / It's hers!*

E Play the games! What have you got?

○ Divide the class into two groups: A and B. All learners in group A look at page 96 of their book. All learners in group B look at page 98 of their book.

○ Learners look at the pictures in the first column and write the name of each object in the second column.

    Learner A: a camera, a watch, a bag/handbag, a ruler, a computer, shoes/trainers, a doll, toys, a kite, pens

    Learner B: a piano, a radio, sweets, a phone, an eraser / a rubber, a mirror, a cat, a skateboard, a tennis racket, a shell

○ Learners put a tick next to the things they have and a cross next to the things they don't have in the 'Me' column.

○ Learners work in A and B pairs. They write their partner's name at the top of the last column and ask each other *Have you got … ?* questions about the objects on their page. They put a tick or a cross in the last column.

○ Say: *Can you find the letter 'k' in some of the words on page 96? Put a circle round all the k's!*

    Different learners write the words with 'k' in their spelling on the board: *sock, cake, keyboard, Nick, clock, kite*

    Practise saying these words. Point out that we say the 'c' at the start of 'cake' and 'clock' with the same /k/ sound. 'C' in front of the letters 'a, l, o' and 'u' sounds like 'k'! Write: *cupboard* on the board. Say: *Listen: keyboard … cupboard, /k/ /k/!* Learners practise saying the words on the board.

    Say: *Listen and say! Kim's keyboard's in the kitchen!* Learners say this sentence, then they write it in their notebooks.

More games to play.

1

Choose eight things from pages 96 or 98 and make a list. Say: *I've got eight things. They are in the pictures on page 96 or 98.* Learners put up their hands to ask: *Have you got (a camera)?*

Each learner gets a point for each question that you answer 'yes' to.

Learners play this game in groups of four. (They should not be in the same group as the partner they had earlier.) Each learner looks at all of the things on both page 96 and on page 98. They write a list of the things they have. One learner tells the others how many of the things they have and the others ask *Have you got … ?* questions to guess which things. Then change and another learner answers questions about the things they have.

2

In pairs, learners look at pages 96 and 98. Say: *Close your books! What is in those pictures? Write words!* Different learners write words for the pictures on the board, spelling then saying the word as they do this. Pairs get points for every word on their list if their spelling is correct.

Next clean the board. Different learners say a sentence about one of the things. For example: *The ball's red. There are five photos.* Learners erase the words from the board as they say them in their sentence.

Pictures: bag, camera, cat, computer, doll, eraser/rubber, kite, mirror, pens, phone, photos, piano, radio, robot, ruler, sweets, television/TV, toys, watch

12   Who's got the red balloon?

Topics family and friends, the home, colours

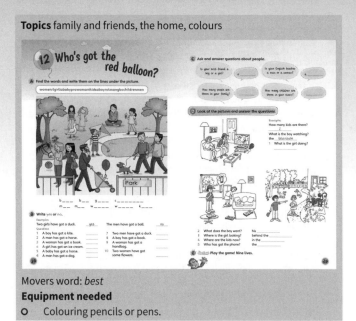

Movers word: *best*

Equipment needed

○ Colouring pencils or pens.

A   Find the words and write them on the lines under the picture.

> **Starters tip**
>
> In most parts of the Starters Tests, words for people ('baby', 'boy', 'girl', etc) appear. Make sure learners understand these words and are able to spell them correctly.

○ Write on the board: *one man – two men   one woman – two …*

○ Point to the gap and ask: *One man, two men, one woman, two … ?* Learners answer (*women*). Make sure learners pronounce 'women' correctly /ˈwɪmɪn/ .

    Show learners that we use 'men' in the plurals of both these words: '**men**' and 'wo**men**'.

○ Write on the board: *one man + one woman = two …*
    Point to the gap and ask: *Which word can I write here?* (people)

○ Write on the board: *one man + one woman + one boy + one girl = four …*
    Point to the gap and ask: *Which word can I write here?* (people)

○ Write on the board: *two boys + two girls = four …*
    Point to the gap and ask: *Which words can I write here?* (children/kids)
    Note: If you have both boys and girls in your class, demonstrate the difference between two boys and two children/kids. Ask two boys to come to the front. Say: *two boys*. Ask another boy and one girl to come to the front. Say: *two children. Two kids.*
    Explain that children and kids mean the same, but 'kids' is more informal. Use the learners' first language to explain this if necessary.

○ Learners find the words (they can circle them if they want) in the wordbox and complete the 'people words' on the lines under the pictures.

> **Check answers:**
>
> baby   boy   girl   children   man   men   woman
> women   kids

○ Ask 2–3 different learners: *How do you spell women/children/baby?* Learners say the letters to spell the words.

○ Say: *Look at the people in the picture. Find the boy with the kite, the baby, the girl with the ice cream, a man with a phone and a woman with a book.* Tell learners to also find the two children, two men and two women who are standing next to each other.

    Ask: *Where's the boy with the kite in the picture?* Learners point to the boy. Say: *Draw a line from that boy to the word 'boy'.*

    Learners then draw lines from the other people in the picture to their completed words. Walk around and check they are doing this correctly.

B   Write *yes* or *no*.

○ Learners look at the two example sentences.

    Ask: *Where are the two girls in this picture?* Learners point to the two girls. *Have they got a duck?* (yes) *What colour is the duck?* (white) Point to 'yes' on the line next to the first example.

○ Ask: *Where are the two men?* Learners point to the two men (with the dog). *Have they got a ball?* (no) Point to 'no' on the line next to the second example.

    Ask: *What have the men got?* (a dog) *What colour is their dog?* (brown)

○ In pairs, learners read sentences 1–10 and write *yes* or *no*.

> **Check answers:**
>
> **1** yes   **2** no   **3** yes   **4** yes   **5** no   **6** yes   **7** no   **8** no   **9** yes
> **10** no

○ Check pronunciation of 'ball' and 'balloon'.
    Write on the board: *Bill's got a blue ball and Ben's got a red balloon!*
    Explain that 'ball' and 'balloon' may look the same but they sound very different. 'Ball' sounds more like 'borl' /bɔːl/ and when we say 'balloon', we don't hear the 'a' /bəluːn/ (You could cross the 'a' out in the spelling.)

○ Drill the sentence with the whole class.

How much can you remember?

Note: This activity is for stronger classes.

○ Divide learners into teams A and B. Say to both teams: *Look at the picture of the people in the park again.* Give learners 30 seconds to try to remember the picture.

○ Say: *Close your books!* Write on the board:
Where?
How many?
What colour?
Who's got?

    Teams think of ten questions to ask the other team about the picture. They write these on a piece of paper. Walk around and help if necessary. When teams are ready, ask one learner from each team to come and sit at the front of the class. These two learners sit with their books open to check all the answers.

Note: If writing questions like these is too difficult for your learners, ask different learners the questions on the next page.

Suggestions and answers:

Where are these people? (in a park)
Where's the balloon? (in the baby's hand)
Where are the flowers? (under the tree)
How many trees are there in this park? (three)
How many animals are in the picture? (three)
How many people are in the picture? (eleven)
How many people are sitting down? (two)
How many people are standing up? (nine)
How many men are there? (three)
How many women are there? (three)
What colour is the balloon? (red)
What colour is the kite? (yellow and blue)
What colour is the ball? (blue)
What colour is the horse? (brown)
What colour is the woman's handbag? (brown)
Who's got the phone? (the man)
Who's got an ice cream? (the girl)
Who's got the duck? (the two girls)
Who's got the kite? (the boy)
Who's got the dog? (the two men)
Who's got the horse? (the two women)
Who's got the book? (the woman)
Who's got the red balloon? (the baby)

Teams A and B ask and answer their ten questions with their books closed. The two judges check the answers and keep the score (one point for each correct answer). The team with the most points at the end of the quiz are the winners.

C Ask and answer questions about people.

o   Learners look at the four questions in the yellow speech bubbles and write their answers on the dotted lines in the small green speech bubbles.

o   In pairs, learners ask and answer the four questions.

Optional extension:
Ask two learners to role play a conversation, adding a greeting and a conversation close. For example:

Learner A: *Hello!*
Learner B: *Hello! Is your best friend a boy or a girl?*
Learner A: *A boy. His name's Kerem.*
Learner B: *OK. Thank you!*

o   In pairs, learners repeat the role play. Go round and help with the greeting and conversation close if necessary.
Suggested greetings: *Hello! Hi! Good morning! Good afternoon!*
Suggested conversation closes: *Good! Great! Oh! OK! Thank you! Thanks! Wow!*

D Look at the pictures and answer the questions.

o   Learners look at the first picture and choose names for the girl and the boy. Write suggestions on the board. Learners vote for the best names. For example: *Peter* and *Natalie*.

o   Ask: *What colour is (Peter's) hat?* (green) *and Peter's T-shirt?* (orange/brown) *What colour is the balloon?* (red)

o   Write on the board: *the sofa, the lamp, the kite, the two dogs, the car, the lorry, (Natalie)'s T-shirt, the trees.*
Point to the words on the board and ask: *What colour are these? You choose!*
In pairs, learners choose colours for each of these things and colour them wherever they appear in the pictures. Ask 2–3 pairs: *What colour is the kite/sofa/lamp/car/lorry in your picture? What colour are the dogs/trees in your picture?*

o   Learners look at the first picture again and at the two examples. Point to question one and ask: *What's (Natalie) doing?* (She's reading a book.) Remind learners that they can only write a number or a one-word answer in this task. Ask again: *What's Natalie doing?* (reading). Learners write *reading* on the answer line.

o   Learners read questions 2–5 and write the answers on the lines.

Check answers:
2 phone   **3** sofa   **4** garden   **5** monkey

o   Say: *At the end of this story, the monkey has got the phone and the … ?* (red balloon!)

o   Write on the board: *Where … ?*

o   Ask learners to write two questions about anything in the pictures in their notebooks with this question starter. For example:
Where's the red balloon?
Where are the dogs?

o   Write on the board: *How many … ?*

o   Ask learners to write two questions about anything in the pictures in their notebooks with this question starter. For example:
How many trees are there?
How many books are there?

o   Write on the board: *Who's got … ?*

o   Ask learners to write two questions about anything in the pictures in their notebooks with this question starter now. Suggestions:
Who's got brown hair?
Who's got an orange T-shirt?

o   Each learner should now have six questions in their notebook.

o   Learners ask and answer their questions in pairs. Alternatively, one learner asks the class a question and other learners put up their hand to answer it.

o   (optional) Give learners time to finish colouring the pictures.

E Play the game! Nine lives.

o   Play 'Nine lives' with words from this unit (see page 104 of the Student's Book). See page 7 for how to play.

13 Who can do this?

Topics sports and leisure, names

Movers words: *well* (adv), *be good at*

Equipment needed

- Starters audio 13B.
- Magazine pictures of action/hobby verbs (someone swimming, jumping, reading, painting, running, etc). See C, Project.

Mime the verb.

- Teach/revise the verbs in the table by miming flying, swimming, reading, jumping, running and singing.
  Ask: *What am I doing?* (flying)
- Change the order of the verbs and say: *Swim! Jump! Fly! Sing! Run! Read!* Learners mime the actions.
- Revise 'be good at'. Say: *I'm good at swimming but I'm not good at jumping.* Ask: *What are you good at? Are you good at reading? Swimming?*
  In pairs, learners tell each other what they are good at and not good at.

Ⓐ Five funny monsters! Look at the ticks and crosses.

- Say: *Look at these five funny monsters!* Point to each monster in turn and ask: *What's his name? / What's her name?* Learners tell you the names of the monsters. (Alphabet, Bean, Carrot, Doll, Egg)
  Ask: *Are you good at spelling? How do you spell these names?* Ask different learners to spell the monsters' names.
  Ask 'Which?' questions:
  Which monster has got a book? (Carrot)
  Which monster is singing? (Bean)
  Which monster is flying? (Alphabet)
  Which monster has got very long feet? (Egg)
  Which monster has got long hair? (Doll)

Which monster? Write the names.

- Learners look at the ticks and crosses in the table. Say: *A tick shows this monster can do this. A cross shows this monster can't do this.* Learners read the three sentences and write the names of the monsters they describe.

  Check answers:
  1 Bean   **2** Carrot   **3** Egg

- Point to the boxes next to Doll. Say: *There are no ticks or crosses here. Listen and put ticks and crosses for Doll. Doll can't fly or run. She can swim and read and sing. She can't jump.* Learners put ticks and crosses for Doll: ✗ ✔ ✔ ✗ ✗ ✔.

Write the words for Alphabet and Doll.

- In pairs, learners write *can/can't* sentences in their notebooks about Alphabet and Doll.
  Suggestions (verbs can be in any order):
  Alphabet can fly, jump and run. He can't swim, read or sing.
  Doll can swim, read and sing. She can't fly, jump or run.
- Say to one learner: *You are one of the monsters now. You choose, but don't tell us. OK?*
  Ask questions to find out which monster the learner is. For example: *Can you jump?* (yes) *Can you read?* (no) *Is your name Alphabet?* (yes)
- Each learner chooses a monster and then, working in pairs, learners ask and answer *Can you … ?* questions to guess the monster's name.

Optional extension:

In pairs or small groups, learners make their own monster poster showing three or four different monsters doing different activities. Learners could choose and write the monsters' names and label them with 'can do' sentences. Pairs/groups take turns to show their posters to others in the class.

Ⓑ ▶ Listen and tick the box.   Listening **Part 3**

> **Starters tip:**
>
> In Listening Part 3, two of the pictures are wrong so candidates are likely to hear negative replies, for example: *Let's play tennis! No!, Not today!, Sorry, you can't … , I don't like … ,* etc. If they hear a negative reply, they will know that (in this example) the tennis picture must be wrong.

- Learners read the example question and look at its pictures A, B and C.
  Ask: *What's Egg doing in picture A?* (singing) *What's he doing in picture B?* (playing the guitar) *And what's he doing in picture C?* (playing the piano)
- Say: *Listen to a woman and a boy. They're talking about Egg. What's Egg doing now? Put a tick under the correct picture.* Play the example on the audio. Learners listen and tick the picture they think is correct.

  Check answer:
  C (Egg is playing the piano)

  Ask: *What does the boy say? Is Egg playing the guitar?* (Not now.) *And is Egg singing?* (No, he can't sing.)
- Play the rest of the audio. Learners tick the correct picture (A, B or C).

  Check answers:
  1 B   **2** A   **3** C   **4** A   **5** A

Audioscript

> *Look at the pictures. Listen and tick the box. There is one example.*
> *What is Egg doing now?*
> Woman: Is Egg playing his guitar in your story?
> Boy: Not now, Mum. He's playing the piano.
> Woman: Is Egg singing too?
> Boy: No, he can't sing!
> *Can you see the tick? Now you listen and tick the box.*
> **1**   *Where is Doll?*
> Man: Where's Doll? Is she at the park?
> Girl: No, she isn't there.
> Man: Is she in the street, then?
> Girl: No, Dad. She's in the sea. She's swimming!

2 *Where is Bean singing?*
Boy: Listen! Bean's singing! Where's he singing?
Girl: In his bed!
Boy: Does he sing in the bath, too?
Girl: No, and he can't sing on the TV. He isn't good at singing!

3 *What is Carrot reading about?*
Woman: Is Carrot reading again?
Boy: Yes, but she isn't reading about spiders now.
Woman: Is she reading about balloons?
Boy: No. She's reading about two funny cars.

4 *What can Egg's baby brother do?*
Girl: Can Egg's baby brother ride a bike?
Boy: No, but he can swim.
Girl: Can Egg's baby brother read?
Boy: No, he can't.

5 *What can Alphabet draw?*
Woman: Is Alphabet good at drawing?
Boy: He's OK. He can't draw horses.
Woman: Can he draw cats?
Boy: Yes, but he can't draw dogs!

o Say: *Alphabet can draw cats but he can't draw horses and he can't draw … ?* (dogs) Write on the board: .... *draw dogs.*
Ask learners to make the sentence. (Alphabet / He can't draw dogs.)
Say: *I can draw dogs, but I can't draw goats.*
Which animals can you draw? Which animals can't you draw?
In pairs, learners tell each other which animals they can/can't draw.
Ask 2–3 pairs about their partners: *Which animals can (Isabelle/ Daniel) draw?*

o Continuing in pairs, learners ask each other questions about another classmate:
Learner A: *Can Maria swim / drive a car / fly a kite / sing very well?*
Learner B: *Yes, he/she can. / No, he/she can't.*

C Read about me and my classmates. Write our names.

o Teach/revise 'classmates'. Point to one learner and to a circle of learners around him/her. Say: *These children are your friends. These children are in your <u>class</u>, too. These children are your <u>class</u>mates.* (You could also tell learners that some people call their 'friends', their 'mates'.)
Say: *Look at the picture.* Ask: *How many people can you see?* (ten) *How many children are there?* (nine) *Where are they?* (in their classroom)

o Say: *Look at the name in the example. It's next to number 1. What is it?* (Alice) Point to this girl in the picture and read out her sentence (second from last): *Alice has got a new tennis racket. She plays tennis with her sister.* Ask: *Can you see the tennis ball and tennis racket in Alice's hand?* (yes) Say: *Look! Alice has got a tennis ball in her hand. Can you see her tennis racket too?* (yes)
Read out the first description: *Kim has got a really big garden. He can play badminton with his dad there.* Ask: *Where's Kim?* Learners point to Kim in the picture. (classmate 4) Learners write *Kim* next to number 4 on the line.

o In pairs, learners read the other sentences and write the names under the picture.

> **Check answers:**
> **2** Anna **3** Grace **4** Kim **5** Dan **6** Nick **7** Lucy **8** May
> **9** Mr Page **10** Bill

o Ask nine children to stand together in a group. They should take their books with them so they can see the picture. The group should try to copy the children in the picture so three should sit down and the others stand. Put an empty chair to show where the teacher is sitting in the picture.
Learners should each stand or sit in the same way as the person they are copying in the picture and, for example, pretend to be playing a guitar, taking a photo or painting a picture.

o When the nine children are ready ask others in the class: *What can you say about your classmates?* Learners answer, for example: *Marina's painting. Tomas is taking a photo. Jess can ride a horse.*

o Write on the board: *Can you … ? Yes, but I can't.............*
Point to the question and answer on the board. Learners take turns to ask different classmates in the picture group questions, for example:
Marina, can you paint?
(Marina) *Yes! But I can't swim!*

o Ask questions about the group, for example: *Who's got a bike? A guitar? A camera? Which classmates are sitting? Standing?* Learners answer.

o The nine learners at the front of the class return to their seats.

> 📁 **Things we do!**
>
> o Ask learners to find and cut out magazine pictures, cartoons or photos of people doing different things. You could give learners a list of activities/hobbies to look for (see below) and bring to the lesson. Bring in some of your own pictures to add to the collection. You may also be able to download and print some cartoon pictures from online image searches.
>
> o Divide learners into groups of 5–6 and give each group a large sheet of coloured paper. Learners make a collage of their action/ hobby pictures and label them with the *-ing* form of the verb (*playing games, writing, jumping,* etc). Learners show their finished collage to other groups, point to pictures and say the verb. This will help prepare learners for the *What's … doing?* questions in Speaking Part 3 and Reading and Writing Part 5. Display the collages on the classroom walls if possible.
> Suggested verbs: bouncing, cleaning, colouring, drawing, drinking, driving, eating, flying, jumping, kicking, painting, reading, riding, running, singing, swimming, taking photos, talking, throwing, walking, waving, writing.

D Play the game! Stand up. Sit down again.

Note: Ideally, you need a lot of space to play this game, but if you don't have enough space for learners to sit in a circle, they can sit at their desks and move to another chair if their answer is 'yes' (see below).

o Play this game outside if possible. If this is not possible, use a large room in which everyone can move around easily, for example the school hall or gym.

o Learners sit in a circle.

o You say sentences which start with the words: *Stand up if you … .* Any learner whose answer is 'yes' has to stand up and change places with another learner whose answer is 'yes' and sit down again. (Either do this in the learners' first language, or demonstrate the activity and get learners to move.)
Suggestions:
Stand up if you:
can play hockey.
can fly a kite.
can spell really long words.
can jump.
can play baseball.
can draw monsters.
can drive a car.
can run.
can play the piano.
can play table tennis.

14 Big, small, happy or sad?

Topics the world around us

Equipment needed

- A book, a ruler, a pencil. See A.
- Colouring pencils and pens and a sheet of paper per two learners. See C.

A Look and answer the questions.

- Draw three circles on the board. In the first circle write the jumbled letters which spell 'book' in a random order, for example: *kobo*
  Do the same in the second circle for 'ruler' (*rleur*) and in the third circle for 'pencil' (*ipncle*).

- Hold up a book and ask: *What's this?* (a book). Point to the letters in the circle and ask: *How do you spell book?* (b-o-o-k). Ask the same questions for 'ruler' and 'pencil'.

- In their notebooks, learners could draw a book, a ruler and a pencil and then label them (a book, a ruler, a pencil).

- Learners look at the pictures in **A**. Point to the picture of the computer and ask: *What's this?* (a computer)
  Learners look at the jumbled letters on the right and the number of lines in the answer. They then put the letters in order and write *computer* on the lines. Write *computer* on the board so learners can check their spellings.

- Learners complete questions 2 and 3 by writing *computer* in the gaps.

- Ask four or five learners: *Have you got a computer?* (yes/no) Ask 3–4 learners who answered 'yes': *What colour is your computer?* Learners answer. To learners who answered 'no', point to the picture of the computer in **A** and ask: *What colour is this computer?* (blue)

- Learners write their answers to questions 2 and 3 (yes/no, big/small – accept either answer).

- Point to the socks and ask: *What are these?* (socks) Learners use the jumbled letters to write *socks* in the answer.
  In pairs, learners then complete questions 2 and 3 with the word 'socks' and answer the questions.
  Working on their own, learners then complete and then write answers for the questions about the phone and trousers. Walk around and help if necessary.

- Check answers for the socks, the phone and the trousers. Ask different learners to read the questions and different learners to answer them. For the first question about each item (*What are these? What's this? What are these?*), ask learners to spell the words 'socks', 'phone' and 'trousers'. Write these words on the board. Learners check they have spelled these words correctly.

Check answers:
(socks) **2** yes/no   **3** long   *(phone)* **2** red   **3** old
(trousers) **2** yes/no **3** dirty

- Ask different learners:
  What colour is your phone / are your socks/trousers?
  Where is your phone / your computer?
  Do you like wearing socks/trousers?
  Who do you talk to on your phone? Your friends? Your parents?
  What do you like doing on your computer? Playing games? Reading stories?

B Write the word under the picture.

- Point to the car in 1 and ask: *What's this?* (a car) Point to the word box and ask: *This car is … ?* (clean) *What can you see in 2?* (a car) *This car is … ?* (dirty) Learners copy *dirty* onto the line below car 2. They then cross out the word 'dirty' in the box.

- In pairs, learners do the same for the other pictures. They use all the words in the box above the pictures. If they don't know the meanings of some of the words, they could check them in a dictionary.

- Check answers by getting learners to say the whole phrase. For example:
  1 *This is a clean car.* Model and drill the pronunciation in each case.

Check answers:
2 a dirty car   **3** an old shoe   **4** a new shoe   **5** a young woman
6 an old woman   **7** a beautiful spider   **8** an ugly spider
9 a short skirt   **10** a long skirt

- Ask learners: Why do we say ***an** old shoe*, ***an** old man* and ***an** ugly spider?* (Because 'old' and 'ugly' start with a vowel sound.)

- Say different numbers. Learners say what they can see in that picture.
  For example: *Five.* (a young woman)

- Tell learners to listen very carefully. Read out the following text slowly and clearly. Make the text sound funny so that learners enjoy hearing about the old woman and her pet spider. If you can point to the pictures in **B** as you say the words, this will help learners remember the text.
  An old woman and her ugly pet spider are in the woman's new, clean car! The spider's got very long legs! The old woman has got short hair and she's wearing a long, pink skirt. The spider is black. It's wearing eight beautiful shoes on its feet!

- Read out the text again but don't point to any of the pictures in **B** this time. Leave some gaps in the text (shown here in brackets). Pause before each gap for the whole class to call out the missing word. If learners can't remember the words, mime the word or start the word with its first letter sound.
  An old woman and her (ugly) pet (spider) are in the woman's new, clean (car)! The spider's got very (long) legs! The old (woman) has got short (hair) and she's wearing a long, (pink) skirt. The spider is (black). It's wearing (eight beautiful shoes) on its feet!

- Divide the class into 3–4 large groups. Repeat the text leaving out more words. The groups take it in turns to say the missing words.

Stronger learners:
In pairs and from memory, learners try to write the complete text in their notebooks.

C Choose words and draw pictures.

o Point to the picture of the mouse and snake. Say: *What are these animals?* (a mouse, a snake) *Is the mouse happy or sad?* (happy) Say: *Make a happy face!* Learners smile. *Make a sad face!* Learners look sad.

Ask: *What colour is the mouse/snake?* (grey/yellow) *What's the mouse doing?* (riding the snake)

o Say: *Now find the right sentence!* Learners look at the options in the word columns and put up their hands when they know the answer. Ask the class: *What's the right sentence?* Learners answer in chorus: *A happy mouse is riding a yellow snake.*

o Teach/revise the other verbs if necessary (draw, paint, hold, play, watch). Ask learners to mime drawing and then painting a picture, holding a pencil, playing a guitar and watching TV.

o Learners work in pairs. They choose a sentence, write it on their piece of paper then turn their piece of paper over and draw their picture. For example: *A big elephant is holding a blue computer.*

o Pairs then get up and show their drawings to other pairs who must guess the sentence. Pairs show their sentence to confirm correct answers.

o **Smaller classes:** learners show their picture to the pair on their left (or nominate another pair) who try to guess their sentence.

D Look and read. Write *yes* or *no*.

Reading & Writing **Part 2**

> **Starters tip**
> In Reading and Writing Part 2, candidates should make sure that all parts of the sentence are right. For example: 'The old man is throwing a red ball'. For a 'yes' answer, there must be an old man in the picture, he must be throwing a ball and the ball must be red.

o Learners look at the picture. Ask questions, for example:
Where are the children? (in a/the park)
How many dogs are there? (two)
What colour are the trees? (green)

o Learners look at the picture. Ask: *Where's the small dog?* Learners find the small dog and point to it. Learners read the first example: *The small dog is happy.* Ask: *Is this sentence correct?* (yes)
Point to the word 'yes' next to the first example sentence.

o Learners look at the picture and find the big ball. They read the second example sentence: *The big ball is in the dog's mouth.* Ask: *Is that correct?* (no)
Point to the word 'no' next to the second example sentence.

o Learners read sentences 1–5 and write *yes* or *no*.

> **Check answers:**
> **1** no **2** no **3** yes **4** yes **5** no

Note: You could ask stronger learners to correct sentences 2 and 5.
Suggested answers:
One boy is wearing blue/brown shoes.
These children are in a park.

E Read, write and draw lines.

o Say: *Look at the four names. Point to the names above the big picture in* **D**. *What are the names?* (Anna, Eva, Hugo, Pat)
Ask: *Where's the name Pat?* Learners point to the name 'Pat' above the picture. Read out sentence 1 in **E**: *Pat's wearing jeans and a blue and white T-shirt.*

o Ask: *Where's Pat in the picture? Point to Pat!* Learners find the boy in the jeans and blue and white T-shirt. Say: *Now draw a line from Pat's name to Pat in the picture.* Learners draw a line between the name 'Pat' and the blond boy in the picture.

o Say: *Read the sentence about Anna.* Ask: *Anna's got long brown … ?* (hair). Learners write *hair* on the line and draw a line between the name *Anna* and the girl in the blue dress in the picture.

o Point to the name 'Eva' above the picture.
Ask: *Is Eva a girl's name or a boy's name?* (a girl's name)
Ask: *Which person in the picture is Eva?* (Learners point to the girl with the chocolate ice cream.) Say: *Draw a line from Eva's name to Eva in the picture.*
Point to the name 'Hugo' above the picture.
Ask: *Is Hugo a girl's name or a boy's name?* (a boy's name)
Ask: *Which person is Hugo?* (Learners point to the boy who is playing with Pat.) Say: *Draw a line from Hugo's name to Hugo in the picture.*

o Point to the sentences about Eva and Hugo. Ask: *What are Eva and Hugo wearing?* In pairs, learners complete the sentences about Eva and Hugo's clothes.

> **Check answers:**
> Eva's wearing a pink and red dress/T-shirt.
> Hugo's wearing a yellow and blue/purple T-shirt, brown shorts, white socks and blue shoes.

F Play the game! Opposites bingo.

o Say an adjective. Learners listen and tell you the opposite.
Suggestions:
beautiful/ugly, big/small, clean/dirty, happy/sad, long/short, old/new, old/young

o Practise this until learners are quick at producing the opposites.

o Tell learners to make a bingo board on some paper or in their notebooks. See page 7 for how to do this.

o Learners write one of the adjectives from this unit in each square (they should write nine different adjectives). If necessary, write the words on the board and they choose nine of them.

o Play bingo. You say an adjective. (Make a note of each adjective you call out as you will need this for checking later.) If they have written **the opposite** of it in one of their bingo squares, they cross the word out. (For example, if you call out *big*, learners cross out 'small'; if you call out *old*, they can cross out 'new' and/or 'young'.)

o The winner (who shouts *Bingo!*) is the first person to cross out all their adjectives. You could also ask learners to shout *Line!* each time they cross out a line of adjectives.

o To check that the winner has crossed out the correct adjectives, they have to read out the words they crossed out. You check them against the list of words you have called.

Note: You could play 'Nine lives' with the words from this unit. See page 7 for how to do this.

Note: In advance preparation for the next lesson (Unit 15), ask learners to bring in photos/drawings of their pets, if they have them.

15 One, two, three animals

Topics animals

Not in YLE wordlists: *match* (v)

Equipment needed

- O Pictures of learners' pets brought to class in advance.
- O Big pictures or flashcards of animals (optional). See 'Tell me about your pets.'
- O Photocopied animal cards cut out and hidden around the classroom (page 108) Red colouring pencil or pen. See C.
- O Scissors, photocopies of page 109 (one for each learner and one for yourself) and an envelope for each learner. See D.

Tell me about your pets.

- O If learners have brought pictures of their pets to class, give them time to show these to their partner. Walk around and ask questions, for example: *What's its name? How old is it? What does it like eating?*
- O Teach/revise: snake, fish, frog, mouse, spider, lizard. Write these words on the board.
- O Write on the board: *What's this? Have you got a pet … ?*
- O Draw a snake on the board (or show learners a picture of a snake). Ask learners the questions about the snake: *What's this?* (It's a) snake.
  Have you got a pet snake? Yes (I have). / No (I haven't).
- O Draw a fish in a goldfish bowl (or show learners a big picture/flashcard of a fish or a photo of a learner's pet fish if anyone brought one to this class). Ask the same questions about the fish.
- O In pairs, learners draw and then ask and answer questions about the other four animals. (Leave these six animal words on the board.)

A Match animal numbers and animal words.

- O Ask learners to find the snake, donkey, frog, spider and lizard pictures in **A**.
- O Teach/revise: cow, sheep, tiger, chicken, crocodile, goat, hippo, jellyfish, polar bear, zebra.
- O In a random order, say numbers (for example: *Number 3, 10, 2, 14*) that are next to the animal pictures. Ask: *What's this?* Learners answer. Check pronunciation.
- O Point to the number 5 in the yellow circle and the number 5 next to the picture of a chicken. Say: *Now you find the animal numbers. Write them in the correct yellow circles.* (Learners don't write any words on the lines yet.)

In pairs, learners find numbers 1–15 and write them in the other yellow circles.

> **Check answers:**
> (top to bottom) 4, 1, 10, 14, 7, 6, 15, 3, 11, 8, 2, 12, 13, 9

- O Point to the animals and ask: *Which is your favourite animal?* Learners secretly draw a star or heart next to the picture of their favourite animal.
- O Ask 2–3 learners just one or two questions about their favourite animal, for example: *Is your favourite animal big? Small? Ugly? Beautiful? How many legs has it got? What colour is it? Can it swim?*
- O Learners work in groups of 3–4. They take it in turns to ask questions to guess each learner's favourite animal. When groups have guessed all the animals, ask three different learners: *What is (Maria's/Lee's/Paula's) favourite animal?*
- O Ask: *Who likes monkeys? Stand up! Who likes elephants? You stand up now, too! Who likes tigers? Stand up, too! Who likes cats? Now you stand up!* Continue asking questions until everyone is standing then say, pausing for learners to add the animals: *So in this class, we like monkeys and … ?* (elephants) *and … ?* (tigers) *and … ?* (cats), etc.

B Write words next to the animals.

- O Learners look at the first animal on the list in **A** (chicken) and at the words in the three boxes (adjectives, colours and verbs).
  Ask: *Is a chicken big?* (no)
  What colour is a chicken? (red / brown / yellow)
  What can a chicken do? (walk, run, jump)
  Note: It doesn't matter if the words used to describe the animals are not completely accurate!
- O In pairs, learners choose five (or more) animals in **A** and write three (or more) words from **B** to help describe them.
  Ask different pairs to tell the class about one of their chosen animals. For example: *It is ugly. It is green. It can swim.* Other learners listen and guess the animal. (a crocodile)

C Where are Tom's pets? Draw lines.

- O Say: *Tom's got some funny pets.* Learners look at the picture. Ask: *How many pets has Tom got?* (six) Point to the lizard. Ask: *What's this?* (a lizard) *Where's the lizard?* (in the box)
- O Say: *Now you draw lines.* In pairs, learners draw lines with a red pencil to show where each animal is.

> **Check answers:**
> **2** spider (on the ball) **3** mouse (in the shoe)
> **4** snake (under the kite) **5** frog (on the cap)
> **6** fish (in the water)

- O Ask questions and learners answer. For example:
  Teacher: *Where's Tom's spider?*
  Learner: *It's on the ball!*

Optional extension:

Put the 15 animal cards from page 108 in different places in the classroom before the lesson. Don't make the cards too difficult to find, for example put them on a window/door/board/phone, under a chair/book/desk; next to a pair of glasses / apple; in a box/cup/cupboard.

Divide learners into groups of three. Ask one group to stand up, walk around the classroom and find three animals. When a learner finds an animal, on their own or as a group, they can win a maximum of three points by answering three questions correctly: *What is your animal? Where is it in the classroom? What colour is this animal?*

Note: The cards are in black and white so learners should say what colour the animal usually is in real life. Accept any appropriate colour answers.

Give learners two chances to get the right answer. Add up the points and put them on the board. Other teams do the same, each finding and talking about three different animals.

Groups of three working with one set of animal cards might not be appropriate for your class size. If necessary, change group sizes and/or use two sets of animal cards.

D Talk about the picture.   Speaking Parts **1,2,3**

> **Starters tip**
>
> In the Speaking test, candidates have to answer simple questions about everyday objects. To help them gain confidence, frequently use real objects, magazine photos or picture cards and ask questions, for example: *What's this? What colour is this? What's it doing? Do you like … ? Have you got a … ?*

o Ask different learners: *What's your favourite animal?* Write each answer on the board, writing animals more than once if necessary.

o Look at the list of animals on the board and ask: *How many children like (tigers, etc.)?*

o Check plurals. Teach/revise the irregular plurals: fish, mice, sheep.

o Give out a photocopy of page 109 and an envelope to each learner. Learners cut up the cards.
Say: *Find pictures of the kite, ball, watch, phone, guitar, chocolate, piano and board games. Put these eight pictures on your desk next to your book.* Learners put the other pictures in their envelope.
Note: For the following activities, check learners are pointing to the correct part of the picture. Then check they are placing the correct object card in the right place. Walk round the classroom as you give the following instructions.

o Point to the zoo picture in **D** and say: *Look! Dan is at the zoo! He likes taking photos of the animals there.*

1

o Point to Dan's camera and say: *Here's Dan's camera.*
Ask learners: *Where's the giraffe?* Learners point to the giraffe or say: *Here! / The giraffe is here. / It's next to the wall.)*
Ask: *Where are the trees?* Learners can just point to the trees or say: *Here! / The trees are here! / They're behind the animals.*

2

o Show learners the eight object pictures, one by one. Ask: *Which is the kite?* Learners point to the kite when they see it. Say: *I'm putting the kite on the elephant's head. You do that too!*
Learners put their kite on the elephant's head in their picture of the zoo. Say: *Now put the kite in the water.* Learners put the kite in the water in their zoo picture. (Learners leave the kite card and the two following object cards on the picture.)

o Show learners the other seven object pictures, one by one. Ask: *Which is the watch?* Learners point to the watch when you show the watch card. Say: *Pick up your watch card now. Put the watch between the flowers.* Learners put the watch card between the flowers.

o Show the remaining six object pictures (the ball, phone, guitar, chocolate, piano and board games.). Ask: *Which is the piano?* Learners point to the piano. Say: *Pick up your piano. Put the piano on the monkey's tail.* Learners put the piano card on the monkey's tail.

3

o Point to the yellow fish in the zoo picture. Ask: *What's this?* (a fish) *What colour is it?* (yellow) *How many fish are there?* (three)

o Point to the bird in the picture. Ask: *What's the bird doing?* (flying)

4

o Hold up the small picture card of the phone. Ask: *What's this?* (a phone)
Have you got a phone? (yes/no) *What colour is your/this phone?* (grey)

o Hold up the small picture card of the chocolate. Ask: *What's this?* (chocolate) *Do you like eating chocolate?* (yes/no) *What's your favourite food?* (ice cream, chips, bananas, etc.)

o Hold up the picture of the ball. Ask: *What's this?* (a ball) *Do you play ball games?* (yes/no) *Where do you play sports?* (at school, in the park, at home, etc.)

o Learners put all the object pictures back in the envelope with the others. You could collect the envelopes and keep them in a box for other activities. (See Introduction for ideas.)

Optional extensions:

1   Yes or no?

o Say sentences about the picture about place, presence, number or colour. Learners say *yes* or *no*. For example:

[place]	*The tiger is next to the giraffe!*	(yes)
[presence]	*You can see a frog!*	(yes)
[number]	*There are four fish!*	(no)
[colour]	*The snake is blue!*	(no)

o In pairs, learners write two true and two false sentences about the picture. Pairs ask and answer their questions with other pairs.

2   Write the animals on the zoo sign.

o Learners look at the signpost on page 97. Say: *You are at the zoo now. Lots of animals are in this zoo.* Point to the example and the small yellow sign and say: *Crocodiles are in the yellow part of the zoo. Crocodiles start with the letter … ?* (C).

o Ask learners if they can think of other animals that start with B or C. Learners write those animals on the yellow sign.

o In pairs, learners write animal names (or copy from the animals in **A**) on the colour-coded signpost. Alternatively, learners draw a larger signpost in their notebooks and add their animal words to that.

Suggested answers:

yellow sign: bees, birds, crocodiles, cats, chickens, cows.
green sign: dogs, donkeys, ducks, elephants, fish, frogs.
pink sign: giraffes, goats, hippos, horses.
blue sign: lizards, mice, monkeys.
orange sign: sheep, snakes, spiders, tigers.
Note: Allow any correct additional animals.

E Play the game! At the zoo.

o Divide learners into groups of 3–4 (or the whole class into three or four groups).

o Tell learners that they are at the zoo. Each group stands up and walks around the classroom. Tell them that different animals are in different corners!

o After a few seconds, tell the groups to stop. Ask each group: *Which animal are you looking at now?* (Groups whisper to each other and choose an animal, using their imagination!) Ask each group what colour the animal is, how many legs it has got and what noise it is making! Other groups guess what the animal is.

o After asking the questions, ask the groups to start walking again and to visit another animal. Repeat the same questions.

16   What's your favourite fruit?

Topics food and drink, colours, family and friends

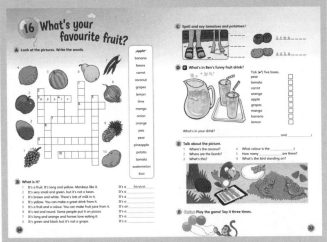

Movers words: *round, vegetable*; Flyers words: *pizza, toes*

Equipment needed
- Two fruits that learners are less familiar with (if possible). See A.
- Starters audio 16D.
- Pictures or flashcards of fruits (optional). See F.

A   Look at the pictures. Write the words.

> **Starters tip**
> There might be food items on the wordlist, for example, 'mango' or 'lime', that learners are unfamiliar with. It is important to tell learners about unfamiliar foods on the wordlist, for example, where they grow, what they look like, etc., so learners can recognise them in pictures. Use flashcards or find pictures of the food items in internet image searches.

- If possible, show the two fruits you have brought to the class. Ask: *What colour are these? Are they small? Big?* Tell learners where these fruits grow and what they taste like if possible. You might like to cut the fruit up so learners can taste them for themselves. Ask 4–5 learners: *What fruit does your family like eating? What's your favourite fruit?*

- Teach/revise 'vegetable'. To help with pronunciation, write *vegetable* on the board then cross out the second 'e' and first 'a' (v e g e̶ t a̶ b l e). Explain to learners that we don't hear these 'e' and 'a' letter sounds. The 'e' disappears and the 'a' becomes the /ə/ sound.

- Learners look at the fruit and vegetable pictures. Point to the example 'apple' and to its picture (3). Ask: *What colour is this apple?* (red and green)
  Write on the board and say: *I like eating apples.* Ask: *Do you like eating apples?* (yes/no) Point to the 's' at the end of *apples*. Say *apples* again stressing the final /z/ in this plural form. Change the sentence on the board to: *We like eating apples.* Learners say: *We like / don't like eating apples* in chorus.

- Point to the crossword again. Make sure that learners understand that each number shows where the fruit or vegetable word goes. The words for all the pictures are in the box.

- In pairs, learners help each other to write the words in the crossword. Tell learners to cross words out in the box as they use them.

> **Check answers:**
> Across: **3** apple   **6** pear   **7** beans   **9** pineapple   **10** potato
> Down: **1** grapes   **2** mango   **4** lime   **5** watermelon   **8** onion

- Learners look at the pictures again. Ask: *How many vegetables can you see?* (three) *What are they?* (beans, onions and potatoes)
- Check the pronunciation of 'beans', 'onions' and 'potatoes' (final /z/ in all three plural forms).
  Note: final 's' in 'grapes' is pronounced /s/.

B   What am I?

- Teach/revise 'round'. Point to one or two round objects in the classroom or draw a round window, a round ball and a round orange on the board and say: *Look! This is / These are round.*
- Learners look at the sentences in **B**.
  Read out 1: *It's a fruit. It's long and yellow. Monkeys like it.*
  Ask: *Which fruit is long and yellow?*
  Which fruit does a monkey like? (banana).
- Learners look at the remaining fruit and vegetable words in the box in **A**. They read the sentences 2–7 and write the words on the lines.
  Note: Help learners with any new words. Translate into their first language, if necessary.

> **Check answers:**
> **2** pea/grape   **3** coconut   **4** lemon   **5** orange   **6** tomato
> **7** carrot   **8** kiwi

- Write on the board: *It's (big/small/long/round) and It's (colour).* Point to this model sentence and say: *It's round and it's brown and white. What fruit is it?* Learners guess *coconut*. Say: *It's long and it's orange. What vegetable is it?* Learners guess *carrot*.
- In pairs, learners choose a fruit or vegetable and prepare their sentence. Ask 4–5 pairs to say their sentence. Other learners guess the fruit or vegetable.

C   Spell and say *tomatoes* and *potatoes*!

- Learners look at the picture of the feet.
  Ask: *Where are these people?* (on the beach/sand)
  What are they doing? (walking/standing)
  Are these two men? Two women? Two children? (one man, one child)
- Revise the word 'foot'. A useful word association is the word 'football'. Teach/revise the irregular plural 'feet' and teach learners the word 'toes'.
- Learners write *foot*, *feet* and *toes* next to the three arrows.
  Note: Don't focus on the singular form of 'toe'. This will not help learners with the following activity.
- Check the pronunciation of 'toes' (final /z/ in its plural form).
- Ask two different learners:
  How many feet have you got? (two) *How many toes have you got?* (ten)
- Learners look at the pictures of tomatoes and potatoes. Point to the tomato and ask: *Is this a potato?* (no) Point to the potato and ask: *Is this a tomato?* (no)
- Learners add four letters (-toes) to complete the words and draw an arrow from each word to the right picture. Ask: *Have tomatoes and potatoes got toes?* (no) Say: *That's right, but they <u>have</u> got 'toes' in their spellings!*
- Write on the board: *one potato – five potatoes, one tomato – ten tomatoes.* Explain that the 'e' in the plural does not appear in the singular form.
- In open class, learners help you to create a list of fruit and vegetables. For example:
  We've got ten bananas, nine lemons, eight potatoes, seven mangoes, six tomatoes, five beans, four onions, three apples, two pears and one potato!
  Note that in all these plural forms the final 's' is pronounced /z/.
- Point to one learner and say: *Now you choose. I've got ten … ?*
  The learner chooses a plural fruit or vegetable and says for example: *I've got ten onions.* Point to another learner and say: *Now you choose. I've got ten onions and nine … ?* The learner repeats the

sentence, adding another fruit or vegetable, for example: *I've got ten onions and nine bananas.*

Continue until all the numbers from ten to one have been used, or until learners can't remember the previous fruits and vegetables!

Optional extension:

Ask different learners to say a simple sentence, for example: *I've got eight pears.*

D ▶ What's in Ben's funny fruit drink?

o   Learners look at the picture of the drink. Ask: *What fruit is in this drink? Guess!* Learners guess *lemons, limes,* etc. Say: *Ben likes making funny fruit drinks.*

o   Say: *Ben is talking to his grandfather about his funny fruit drink. Listen. Which fruit and vegetables are in this drink? Tick the correct boxes.* Play the audio. Learners listen and tick boxes.

> **Check answers:**
> lemon, banana, pear, orange, carrot

o   Learners make up their own funny fruit or vegetable drinks. They can choose five different fruits or vegetables to put in their imaginary drink.

o   Learners write their five different fruits or vegetables on the lines.

o   Learners draw a picture of their imagined funny drink and label it with their choice of five different fruits or vegetables. Give each learner a number to put at the top of their funny drink picture. Display the funny drink pictures on a classroom wall if possible.

o   Call out five or six different numbers. Learners look at each funny drink picture in turn and vote whether the drink is great, good, OK or 'ugh!' Explain that some people say 'ugh!' and 'yuck!' when something tastes bad. Ask: *When you don't like food, what do you say?* Learners answer.

Audioscript

What's in Ben's funny drink? Listen and tick five boxes.

Grandpa:	What are you doing, Ben?
Ben:	I'm making a nice drink, Grandpa. It's called 'Funny Lemonade'.
Grandpa:	And what's in your drink?
Ben:	It's got a lemon in it, but, I'm putting a banana in it too.
Grandpa:	Right.
Ben:	And I'm putting a pear in it now.
Grandpa:	A pear?
Ben:	Yes, and I'm adding some juice from an orange to it.
Grandpa:	From an orange? OK.
Ben:	And now something long and orange.
Grandpa:	A carrot?
Ben:	That's right! I'm putting a carrot in this drink too!
Grandpa:	Yuck!

E Talk about the picture.

o   Point to the picture and ask: *Where's the sand? Where's the bird?* (Learners point.) *What's the bird wearing?* (glasses) *What's the bird doing?* (reading/standing/looking) *Where are the shells?* (Learners point.) *How many shells are there?* (three) *What colour are the shells?* (pink)

Point to the grapes and ask: *What are these?* (grapes) Say: *Write 'grape' in question four and 'grapes' in question five.*

o   Learners work in pairs or groups of three. They take turns to ask and answer questions 1–3, choosing what to point to in the picture for the 'What's this?' question.

o   Walk around and help learners if necessary.

o   Ask different learners questions 4, 5 and 6 (**4** green, **5** six, **6** *a/the tablet*).

Optional extension:

o   Make sure learners have their colouring pencils or pens.
Say: *Look at this picture again and listen.*

Draw an apple. Draw the apple next to the grapes … next to the grapes.

Draw a kiwi. Draw the kiwi behind the bird! Put it behind the bird.

Now draw an orange. Draw it between the lizards. The orange is between the lizards.

And now a potato. Draw a potato next to the shells … That's right! Next to the shells.

o   Give learners time to finish their drawings and to colour them. Learners show each other their drawings. To check understanding, ask four different learners where their apple, banana, orange and potato are.

F Play the game! Say it three times.

o   Write on the board: 1 *banana*   2 *coconut*   3 *pineapple*   4 *watermelon*   5 *mango*   6 *lime*   7 *grapes*   8 *orange*   9 *kiwi*

o   Point to the words on the board (or use pictures) to prompt these words. Check pronunciation and then drill the words.

o   Divide the class into two groups A and B. Say: *Listen to my numbers and look at the fruits on the board. Say the right fruit.*

To group A say (for example): *5!*

Group A calls out together: *mango!*

Repeat with group B saying a different number.

To Group B say: *4, 8, 1!*

Group B calls out together: *watermelon, orange, banana!*

Repeat with group A saying different numbers.

Continue calling out numbers to each group until learners tire of the game.

Optional extension:

Revise the vocabulary covered in this unit by playing various games with the learners. Set a time limit of one and a half to two minutes for each activity (see page 104 of the Student's Book for a list of words). See page 7 for different game ideas.

Suggested activities:

Longest to shortest.

Smallest to biggest.

Group according to colour.

Alphabetical order.

17   What's on the menu?

Topics food and drink, colours, the home

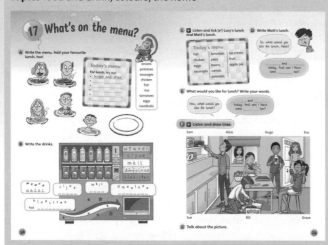

Movers words: *café, hot*; Not in YLE wordlists: *menu*

Equipment needed

o   Starters audio 17C, 17F.

o   Blue and red pencils. See C.

Ⓐ Write the menu. Add your favourite lunch, too!

o   Say: *Close your eyes! You're in a food shop. What food can you see?* Learners suggest different foods. Say: *You can choose four things. What food do you want?* In pairs, learners choose four things they would like from the shop. Ask 4–5 pairs: *What food do you want in this food shop?* Write the most popular foods on the board.

o   Teach/revise 'café' and 'menu'. Ask: *Do you like going to a café? Who do you go with? What do you like eating there? Is there a menu?*

o   Learners look at the food on the people's plates in **A**. Point to the woman's plate. Say: *These people are in a café now.* Ask: *What's the woman got for lunch?* (chips and a burger)

   Ask: *How many of you like chips?* (Learners put up their hands.) If *chips/fries* aren't already on the board, add them.

   Tell learners that 'chips' and 'fries' mean the same thing. 'Fries' is used more in American English and 'chips' is used more in British English.

   Learners look at the woman's lunch again. Check they can see the words 'burger and chips' on the menu under 'Today's menu'.

o   Learners complete the menu with the other food items on the plates. They use the words in the box.

o   Check answers by asking questions:

   What's the man got for lunch? (sausages and onions)

   What's the girl got for lunch? (fish and potatoes)

   What's the big boy got for lunch? (eggs and tomatoes)

   What's the small boy got for lunch? (chicken and rice)

   Point to the word 'meatballs' in the box under the monkey and ask: *Can you see any meatballs in the pictures?* (no) *Take your brown crayon! Draw three meatballs on the small plate!*

o   Say: *You're in this café too now. What would you like for lunch? You choose!* In pairs learners decide what they want to eat. Say: *Draw your lunch on the plate and write your lunch on the menu.*

   Learners add their meal to the menu board. Walk round and help with vocabulary adding useful food words to the board for everyone to copy into their notebooks.

Ⓑ Write the drinks.

o   Point to the drinks machine and say: *In this café, you can get your drinks from this. How many different drinks can you get?* (five) Learners put the jumbled letters in order and write the drinks in the boxes under the machine.

> **Check answers:**
> water, juice, milk, lemonade, (hot) chocolate

What would *you* like for lunch?

o   Say: *What would you like for lunch in this café?*

   Write on the board: *Would you like … ?* Drill questions using the foods in **A** and the drinks in **B**. For example: *Would you like fish and potatoes? Would you like hot chocolate?*

   Note: At Starters level, learners read or hear 'Would you like' plus noun or verb choices, for example 'Would you like an apple or an orange?' 'Would you like to go to the park?' The open-ended question 'What would you like?' is above Starters level but a useful question to practise.

o   Tell learners that you would like something to eat from **A** and a drink from **B**. Ask: *What's my lunch? Guess!*

   For example:

   Learner A: *Would you like chicken and rice?*

   Teacher: *No, thank you.*

   Learner B: *Would you like eggs and tomatoes?*

   Teacher: *Yes, please.*

   Learner C: *Would you like some lemonade?*

   Teacher: *Yes, please.*

o   Each learner chooses one thing from the menu in **A** and one drink from the drinks machine.

o   In groups of 3–4, learners take it in turns to guess which food and drinks their partners have chosen. Go round and check they are making questions with *Would you like … ?*

Ⓒ ▶ Listen and tick Lucy's lunch and Matt's lunch.

o   Learners look at the menu in **C**. Ask: *Can you see the words rice?* (no) *Potatoes?* (yes) *Burgers?* (no) *Chicken?* (yes) *Sausages?* (yes) *Fries?* (no)

o   Say: *Close your books now.* Learners close their books. Read out the words on the menu in **C** telling learners to listen carefully and to try to remember them. After reading out the words a second time, in pairs, learners write down as many words as they can remember in their notebooks. Learners then open their books again to check their answers.

o   Say: *Find your red crayon and listen to Lucy. What would she like for lunch? Tick Lucy's food.* Play the first part of the audio. Learners listen to Lucy and put a red tick next to the food she wants.

> **Check answers:**
> chicken, carrots, beans

o   Say: *Find your blue crayon and listen to Matt. What food does he want? Tick Matt's food now.* Play the second part of the audio. Learners listen to Matt and put a blue tick next to the food he wants.

> **Check answers:**
> fish, peas, apple pie

Audioscript

> *Listen and tick Lucy's food with your red crayon.*
> Man: Lucy. What would you like for lunch?
> Girl: I don't know … Yes! Some chicken, please.
> Man: What would you like with the chicken?

Girl: Carrots and beans for me.
Listen and tick Matt's food with your blue crayon.
Woman: What would you like for lunch, Matt?
Boy: Fish and peas today. And can I have some apple pie too?
Woman: OK.

D Write Matt's lunch.

o Learner look at the speech bubbles in **D**. Ask: *What would Matt like for lunch? What's he saying?* Learners look at the blue ticks in **C** and answer. (fish, peas and apple pie)

Say: *Write Matt's food on the lines now.* Learners complete Matt's speech bubble by adding *fish* (and) *peas* (And can I have some) *apple pie* (too?)

Ask 2–3 pairs to read out the question and Matt's answer.

E What would you like for lunch?

o Point to 'Today's menu' in **C**. Ask: *Where can you see the word 'fish'?* (in column 1) *Where can you see the word 'beans'?* (in column 2) *Where can you see the word 'ice cream'?* (in column 3)

o Ask: *What would you like for lunch? Now you choose!* Tell each learner to choose one thing from column 1 and write it on the first line. They then choose one thing from column 2 and write it on the second line. They choose 'ice cream', 'fruit' or 'apple pie' from column 3 and write it on the third line.

o Ask different learners: *What would you like for lunch?* Learners read out their choice of menu.

o In pairs, learners role play a conversation in a restaurant. One learner is the waiter and the other is the customer.

F ▶ Listen and draw lines.   Listening **1**
Part

o Point to the picture and ask: *Where are these kids? Are they in a classroom?* (No. They're in a kitchen.) *What fruit can you see in the box?* (kiwis) *And on the table?* (oranges, limes, lemons) *Can you see some cake, too?* (yes) *Is it banana cake?* (No. It's chocolate cake.) *How many kids can you see?* (6) Point to the names above and below the picture and ask: *How many names can you see?* (7)

> **Starters tip**
> In Listening Part 1, candidates might hear two different pieces of information about the person they need to name. For example, in this task, they hear that Eva is coming in the door and that she's wearing a yellow dress. Alternatively, learners might only hear one piece of information about the person they need to name, but this will be repeated.

Choose the best way for your class to complete this task.
Option 1: Learners complete this task as a Listening Part 1 test practice.

o Learners look at the picture and at the seven names. Play the audio. Learners listen to the example then to the rest of the audio. They draw lines from five of the names to the correct people in the picture. Play the audio a second time. Learners check and complete their answers.

Option 2: Learners practise a Listening Part 1 task.

o Say: *Listen to the man and the girl. They're talking about the people in this picture. You can see a line from Sue to the girl on the chair. This is an example. Listen!* Play the audio. Stop after the example. Ask: *What's Sue doing?* (listening to music)

o Point to the other children and say: *Now listen and draw lines from the names to these children.* Play the rest of the audio. Learners listen and draw lines.

o Check answers by asking different learners: *Who's eating chocolate cake?* (Sam) *Who's looking at the kiwis?* (Grace) *Who's drinking milk?* (Hugo) *Who's coming in the door?* (Eva) *What's Eva wearing?* (a yellow dress) *Who's really tall?* (Bill) *What's he opening?* (the/a cupboard)

> **Check answers:**
> **1** Sam – chocolate cake   **2** Grace – looking at kiwis in box
> **3** Hugo – drinking milk   **4** Eva – coming in door, yellow dress
> **5** Bill – tall, opening cupboard

Audioscript

Look at the picture.
Listen and look. There is one example.

    Girl: Hi! Here's a picture of our kitchen, Mr Chips.
    Man: Oh! Are these your brothers and sisters?
    Girl: No, they're my friends. There's Sue. Sue's listening to music.
    Man: I like listening to music, too.

Can you see the line? This is an example. Now you listen and draw lines.

1 Man: There are lots of kids! Who's that?
    Girl: The boy in the green T-shirt? That's Sam.
    Man: He likes chocolate cake, then!
    Girl: Yes! Sam loves it!
2 Man: And what's that girl's name?
    Girl: That's Grace.
    Man: What's Grace doing?
    Girl: She's looking in that box. There are some kiwis in that box!
3 Girl: And there's Hugo.
    Man: The boy with the milk?
    Girl: That's right. Hugo loves drinking milk.
    Man: Oh!
4 Girl: My friend, Eva, is in this picture too.
    Man: Which girl is she?
    Girl: Eva's coming in the door. Look!
    Man: Oh, yes. She's wearing a yellow dress.
    Girl: Mmm.
5 Man: And what's that boy's name? He's opening the cupboard.
    Girl: That's Bill. Bill's a really tall kid!
    Man: What does he want in the cupboard?
    Girl: Well, he wants some cake, too!
    Man: Cool!

G Talk about the picture.

o Point to the picture again. Say: *Look at this. This is a kitchen.* Point to the boy drinking milk and say: *This boy is drinking milk.*

o Point to the table and say: *Here's the table.*
Say: *Now listen and point.*
Walk around and check learners are correctly identifying different objects in the picture. Ask: *Where's the wall? Where's the window / the floor / the door / the cake / the milk? Where are the cupboards / the chairs / the kiwis?*
Learners point to these things in the picture. Stronger learners could label the picture showing where these things are.

o Point to the yellow crayon in the picture.
Ask three questions about the crayons:
Ask: *What's this?* (a crayon) *What colour is it?* (yellow)
How many crayons are there? (two)

> **Starters tip**
> In Speaking Part 2, learners are asked a *Tell me about* question. Learners can either say what they see or use their imagination to give two or three short answers. For example:
> *Q: Tell me about this boy.*
> *A: He's got brown hair. He's funny. He likes eating.*
> If learners can't think what to say, the examiner will ask two yes/no questions about the boy, for example: *Has he got brown hair? Is he eating cake?*

o Point to the girl who's sitting down and say: *Tell me about this girl.* Different learners tell you about the girl.
   Suggestions: *She's sitting down. She's listening to music. She's wearing shorts. She's 7. She's nice.*
   You could continue this with the other boys and girls in the picture.

18 A colourful house

Topics the home

Movers words: *dream, think*; Flyers words: *full*; Not in YLE wordlists: *colourful*

Equipment needed

o   Starters audio 18B.

A Look at the house. What colour are these rooms?

A colourful house.

Teach the meaning (but not the spelling) of 'full'. Show learners a bag or a cupboard that's full. You may like to show them (or draw) a glass that's full of water.

Write on the board: *colourful*. Explain that some words in English end in 'ful'. Point to the picture in **A** and say: *This house is colourful. Colourful means full of colour.* Ask: *Can you see lots of different colours in this house?* (yes) *Is your home colourful too?* Learners answer.

(You might like to point out that 'beautiful' ends in -ful too. That word means `full of beauty'!)

o   Before learners open their books, write on the board:

   bed_ _ _ _   bath_ _ _ _   living_ _ _ _   dining_ _ _ _

   Point to the four lines after all four words. Ask: *Which word can I put here?* (room) Four different learners come to the board and write *room* on the lines, point to the word and say it. The class repeats the word.

   Point to the words 'bedroom' and 'bathroom' and say: *'Bedroom' and 'bathroom' are one word.* Point to 'living room' and 'dining room' and say: *'Living room' and 'dining room' are two words.*

o   Ask learners: *Which room are we in now?* (a/the classroom)

   Is 'classroom' one or two words? (one) Ask learners to spell 'classroom'. One learner writes it on the board.

o   Learners open their books. Ask: *Where's the bedroom?* (Learners point to the bedroom in the picture.) *What colour is it?* (black and grey) Do this with the other rooms in the box in **A**.

Check answers:

bathroom / red and white

hall / yellow and brown

dining room / blue

living room / purple, grey and white

kitchen / green and white

Where am I?

o   Say: *I'm in that house in one of the rooms. Which room am I in?* Learners ask questions to guess where you are. For example:

Learners: *Are you in the living room?*

Teacher: *No, I'm not.*

Learners: *Are you in the kitchen?*

Teacher: *Yes, I am.*

Learners play the game in pairs or groups of three.

B Listen and draw lines.

Starters tip

In Speaking Part 3, learners might be asked questions about their home or routines, for example: *What's this?* (a television) *Do you like watching TV? Where's your television? Who watches television with you?* Make sure learners understand the difference between *What ... ?* and *Who ... ?* questions.

o   Point to the picture of the clock (1) and ask: *What's this?* ([a] clock) Point to the word on the line: 'clock'. Point to pictures 2–7 and ask learners: *What's this?* for each picture. Teach any new words. Practise pronunciation.

Check answers:

Learners say each word again and spell them too. Write each word on the board. Learners write the words under the pictures.

2 computer   **3** photo   **4** lamp   **5** radio   **6** mat   **7** mirror

o   In their notebooks, learners write the names of the objects and the room where they think each of them is (including the garden). For example: *computer – living room*

o   Play the example on the audio. Ask: *Where's the lamp?* (in the living room) *Can you see the line from the lamp to the small cupboard in the dining room?* (yes) *Good!* Point to the line between the lamp and the dining room.

o   Play the rest of the audio. Learners listen and draw straight, clear lines between the objects and the places in the picture.

Check answers:

radio – tree, mirror – sofa, photo – hall, clock – bed, mat – bathroom.

o   Learners check their notebooks to see who put the most objects in the correct room before they listened. Ask them how many objects they put in the correct room. Say: *Well done!* to the learner with the most correct guesses.

o   Ask: *Which picture has no line?* (the computer)

Audioscript

Look at the picture. Listen and draw lines.

   Man: Put the lamp in the dining room, please.

   Girl: Sorry, where?

   Man: Put the lamp in the dining room.

   Girl: OK.

This is an example. Now you listen and draw lines.

1   Man: Can you put the radio in the tree for me?

   Girl: Put the radio where?

   Man: Put it in the tree, please.

   Girl: Right.

2   Man: Now the mirror. Put it on the sofa, please.

   Girl: On the sofa? In the living room?

   Man: Yes. Put the mirror there, please.

   Girl: OK. I'm doing that now.

3 Man: Can you see the photo?
 Girl: Yes. Can I put the photo in the hall?
 Man: In the hall? Yes!
 Girl: Great!

4 Man: Now the clock. Can you see it?
 Girl: Sorry? What?
 Man: The clock. Put it on the bed.
 Girl: On the bed in the bedroom. Oh! OK.

5 Man: Now, put the mat in the bathroom.
 Girl: The mat? In the bathroom?
 Man: Yes, please.
 Girl: OK. It's there now!
 Man: Thank you!

C **Look, read and write one-word answers about the house.**

○ Learners look at the questions. Point to the example answer: 'hall'. Make sure learners understand they only have to write one word (one of the rooms in the house).

> **Check answers:**
> **2** bathroom   **3** bedroom   **4** dining room   **5** living room

○ Ask learners: *Where's the radio?* (in the tree/garden)

D **Read and write! Which home words can you see in the mirrors?**

○ Point to the example mirror and say: *Can you read the word in this mirror?* (wall) Explain that we can see the word 'wall' <u>backwards.</u> Point to the word 'wall' on the line under this mirror.
 Say: *Can you read the words in mirrors 1 to 5? Write the words on the lines under the mirrors.*

> **Check answers:**
> **1** window   **2** door   **3** table   **4** television   **5** bookcase

○ Ask about the windows and tables in the house in **B**:
 How many windows are there? (four) *Where are the windows?* (in the kitchen, dining room, living room and bedroom)
 How many tables are there? (three) *Where are the tables?* (in the dining room, hall and bedroom)

○ In pairs, learners ask and answer 'How many' and 'Where' questions about the chairs and bookcase in the house in **B**. (There are five chairs. Four chairs are in the dining room next to the table. There's a chair next to the desk in the bedroom. There's one bookcase. It's in the living room, behind the sofa.)

 Optional extension:
 Learners choose two more things from the picture in **B** and 'write' them in a mirror (backwards or upside down). They show these to their partner, who says what the word is and where that thing is in the picture in **B**.

E **Read this. Choose a word from the box. Write the correct word next to numbers 1–5.**   Reading & Writing **Part 4**

○ Point to the picture of the desk. Ask: *What's this?* (a desk) Ask: *Have you got a desk?* (yes) *What do you put in or on your desk?* (books, pens, pencils, paper, a tablet, etc.)

○ Read out: *A desk has four legs but it isn't an animal ...* Point to the four legs on the desk in the picture.
 Ask: *What are these?* (legs) Point to the picture and word 'legs' in the box under the text and to the word: 'legs' on the line in the first sentence.
 Note: In some languages, a different word is used to talk about a person's legs and the legs on a table, sofa, etc. Explain this to your learners if necessary.

○ Learners write the other words to complete the text.

> **Check answers:**
> **1** horse   **2** bedroom   **3** chair   **4** stories   **5** computer

○ Ask different learners: *What colour is your desk? Where's your desk? What do you do on your desk? Do you read books? Write stories? Play board games?*

F **Write about your home.**

○ Ask learners these questions. You could write them on the board too. Learners write their answers on the lines in **F**.
 1 *Where's your home?*
 2 *How many rooms has it got?*
 3 *Which rooms are there in your home?*
 4 *Which is your favourite room?*
 5 *What's in your favourite room?*

○ In pairs, learners ask and answer the questions.

G **Play the game! The long home sentence.**

○ Say a sentence about your home, for example:
 In my home, there are five rooms.
 The next learner has to repeat your sentence and add another thing to it.
 For example:
 Learner A: *In my home, there are five rooms and two sofas.*
 The next learner has to repeat Learner A's sentence and add another thing.

○ See how long your class can make the sentence!

> 🧳 **My dream room!**
>
> ○ Learners draw a picture of their ideal room. They can choose any room of the house. (For example: *My dream living room, My dream games room, My dream bedroom*) They do this in their notebooks or on pieces of paper, which can then be displayed on the classroom walls or made into a book.
>
> ○ Learners copy and complete sentences under their pictures.
> For example:
> *In my room, there's a ....*
> *From my window, I can see ....*
> *The walls are ....*
> *I sleep in ....*
> *I sit on ....*
> *I play with ....*

19   What's in your bedroom?

Topics colours, the home

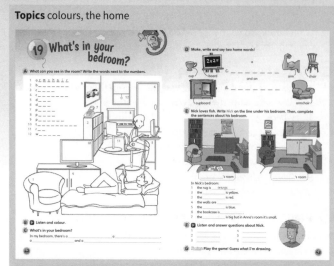

Movers words: *best, cup, first*

Equipment needed

- Starters Audio 19B, 19F.
- Colouring pencils or pens.

Ⓐ What can you see in the room? Write the words next to the numbers.

- Say: *Look at the picture. Listen to my questions. For 'yes' answers, put up your hand.* (Demonstrate putting up your hand if necessary.)

  Ask: *Is the boy watching television?* (no – hands down)

  Is the door open? (no – hands down)

  Is the boy wearing socks? (yes – hands up!)

  Is the robot sitting down? (yes – hands up!)

  Is the boy playing the piano? (no – hands down)

- Point to the boy and say: *Choose a name for this boy and write it on his door.*

- Point to the word *armchair* next to number 1. Ask: *What's the first letter in 'armchair'?* (a) *How many letters are there in armchair?* (8)

  Point to 2 and ask: *What's the first letter in this word?* (b) *Find number 2 in the picture. What is it?* (a bookcase) *How do you spell bookcase?* (b-o-o-k-c-a-s-e) *Write the letters in 2.*

  Say: *Write ten words for other things in the picture.* Remind them to look at the first letter and to count the lines to see how many letters they have to write.

- Ask questions about the picture: *What's in the bookcase?* (books) *What's on the bookcase?* (the phone) *Who's on the bed?* (the boy) *Who's looking at the computer?* (the robot)

> **Check answers:**
> **3** chair   **4** cupboard   **5** desk   **6** door   **7** phone   **8** piano
> **9** picture   **10** television   **11** rug   **12** window

Ⓑ ▶ Listen and colour.

> **Starters tip**
> Colours are tested in many parts of Starters, especially in Listening Part 4 and Speaking Parts 1, 2 and 3. Make sure learners understand and can write and say all the colours in the wordlist.

- Say: *Have you got your crayons? Now listen and colour the picture.* Play the audio twice. Learners listen and colour.

> **Check answers:**
> a green computer, a pink phone, a purple TV, a blue bookcase, a yellow armchair

Audioscript

Look at the picture. Listen and colour.

1   Woman: Look. Here's a picture of a bedroom. Do you want to colour it?
    Boy: Yes please!
    Woman: Can you see the computer?
    Boy: Yes.
    Woman: Colour it green, please.
    Boy: OK! There!

2   Woman: Now, can you see the phone?
    Boy: Yes, I can.
    Woman: Can you colour that for me too?
    Boy: What colour?
    Woman: Colour the phone pink.

3   Woman: There's a television in this bedroom too.
    Boy: Yes, I know.
    Woman: Can you colour it purple, please?
    Boy: What a funny colour for a TV! OK!

4   Woman: Now find the bookcase.
    Boy: Oh yes! I can see it. It's a big bookcase!
    Woman: Yes, it is.
    Boy: Can I colour it blue?
    Woman: Yes, you can. Thank you.

5   Woman: Now, find the armchair.
    Boy: Oh yes, I can see it.
    Woman: Good. Let's colour that yellow.
    Boy: Oh, great! That's my favourite colour!
    Woman: I like that colour too! Well done!

Ⓒ What's in your bedroom?

- Write on the board: *a big brown mirror, a small green table.* Point to the words 'big' and 'small'. Tell learners that these words tell us about the size of the mirror and table. Point to the words 'brown' and 'green' and ask: *What do these words tell us about the mirror and table?* (the colour – brown or green).

  Write on the board: *computer phone TV bookcase armchair*

  Point to the picture in **A**. Pairs say sentences about the colour and size of these things. For example: *The computer is green. It's a small computer.*

  Note: You could explain that if we say words like 'big' or 'small' <u>and</u> words for colour like 'brown' or 'green' in front of the thing (*mirror/table*), we say 'big' or 'small', then the colour.

- Ask: *Is there a bed in your bedroom?* (yes!) *Is there a cupboard?* (yes) Ask them to tell you other things that are in their bedrooms. They can use words from **A**.

  Learners write four things that are in their bedroom on the lines in **C**. They write *big* or *small* and the colour too. For example: *In my bedroom, there's a big blue bed, a big white cupboard, a small black computer and a small red chair.*

  Ask different learners: *In your bedroom, is there a rug on the floor?* (yes/no)

  Note: Explain to learners that we put both mats and rugs on floors. Mats are usually smaller than rugs. Some people put mats on their bathroom floor or just inside the entrance to their house or flat. Rugs are more decorative and people might put them on the floor in their living room or bedroom.

  Use the learners' first language to explain this if necessary.

o   In pairs, learners read their lists to each other, starting with: *In my bedroom, there's a …*
    Learners ask and answer questions in pairs about the other things that are in the picture in **A**, for example, *Is there a piano in your room?* (If necessary, revise *Is/Are there ..?* and the short answer forms: *Yes, there is/are. No, there isn't/aren't.*)

Ⓓ Make, write and say two home words!

o   Point to the picture of the cup and ask: *What's this?* (a cup) Point to the board and ask: *What's this?* (a board) Point to the picture of the cupboard and ask: *What's this?* (a cupboard) *And what's in this cupboard?* (a cup!) Write *cupboard* on the board to show learners that the word 'cupboard' has the words 'cup' and 'board' in it.

o   Point to the picture of the arm and ask: *What's this?* (an arm) Point to the chair and ask: *What's this?* (a chair) Point to the picture of the armchair. Ask: *What's this?* (an armchair) *And how many arms has this armchair got?* (two!) *How many arms have you got?* (two!)

o   Learners write letters to complete the words 'cupboard' and 'armchair'. They draw a line and an arrow from each word to the correct picture.

    Note: Although 'armchair' sounds exactly like 'arm' + 'chair', 'cupboard' does not sound like its two parts. Check/practise the pronunciation of 'cupboard': /kʌbəd/.

    Optional extension:
    Learners copy the two picture clues into their notebooks and draw and colour their own cupboard and armchair. This will help them to remember the spellings.

Ⓔ Nick loves fish. Write *Nick* on the line under his bedroom. Then, complete the sentences about his bedroom.

o   Say: *Look at these two bedrooms. One bedroom is Nick's and one bedroom is Anna's. How do you spell Nick and Anna?* Ask a learner to write *Nick* and *Anna* on the board. The rest of the class say the letters to spell the names.
    Say: *Nick likes fish.* Ask: *Which bedroom is Nick's?* (the room on the right) *How do you know?* (Nick's bedroom has the fish picture and the fish in the bowl.) Ask: *What does Anna like doing?* (drawing) *How do you know?* (Anna's bedroom has a drawing and pencils on the bed and next to the computer.)

o   Learners write the names *Anna* and *Nick* on the lines under the pictures.

o   Point to the desk in the two rooms and say: *In Anna's bedroom the desk is blue, but in Nick's bedroom the desk is …* (green)
    Learners look at the first sentence and the example answer: *In Nick's bedroom, the rug is orange.* Ask: *Can you see the orange rug? Where is it?* (on the floor) Say: *In Anna's bedroom, the rug is …* (brown).

o   In pairs, learners write words on the lines about the things in Nick's bedroom.

    Check answers:
    2 cupboard   **3** armchair   **4** white   **5** bed   **6** small   **7** window

o   Read sentence 7: *In Nick's bedroom, the window's big but in Anna's bedroom it's small.*
    Learners work in A and B pairs. Tell A learners to read out sentences 2, 4 and 6 about Nick's bedroom. They should begin each sentence with 'In Nick's bedroom'. B learners reply adding 'but' and then talk about the differences. For example:
    Learner A   *In Nick's bedroom, the cupboard is yellow, …*
    Learner B   *… but in Anna's bedroom, it's purple.*
    Learners then reverse roles. B learners read out sentences 1, 3 and 5 about Nick's bedroom and A learners talk about the differences.

Ⓕ ▶ Listen and answer questions about Nick.

o   Point to the picture of the boy in **F** and say: *This is Nick.* Ask: *What colour is his hair?* (brown) *What's he wearing?* (a blue T-shirt)

o   Write on the board or read the questions for learners to write in their notebooks:
    1 *How old is Nick?*
    2 *What's Nick's family name?*
    3 *How many brothers has Nick got?*
    4 *How many sisters has Nick got?*
    5 *Who is Nick's best friend?*
    6 *What's the name of Nick's pet fish?*
    Ask learners to guess the answers to these questions.

o   Say: *Listen to Bill. He's talking about Nick.* Play the first part of the audio. Ask: *How old is Nick?* (ten) Write *ten* after this question on the board.
    Say: *Listen and write the answers to questions 2–6.* Play the audio twice.

    Check answers:
    2 Bird   **3** 7/seven   **4** 1/one   **5** Tony   **6** Small

o   Erase the name *Nick* from the questions on the board. Say: *Choose one of the children from the picture on page 27. Write the answers for that girl or boy.* In pairs, learners write the answers for that child. Two pairs join to form groups of four. They ask and answer questions about the children they chose.

Audioscript

Listen and write a name or a number.

1 Woman: Who's this boy in your photo, Bill?
   Boy: That's my school friend. His name's Nick.
   Woman: Oh! How old is he?
   Boy: He's ten.
   Woman: Ten?
   Boy: Yes.

2 Woman: What's Nick's family name?
   Boy: His family name is Bird.
   Woman: Bird?
   Boy: Yes. You spell that B-I-R-D.
   Woman: Thanks.

3 Boy: Nick's got lots of brothers!
   Woman: How many?
   Boy: He's got seven brothers. Seven!
   Woman: Wow! What a big family.

4 Woman: So, has Nick got a sister too?
   Boy: Yes, he's got one sister.
   Woman: Pardon?
   Boy: He's got one sister. I like her. She's nice.

5 Woman: And who is Nick's best friend?
   Boy: Tony is his best friend.
   Woman: How do you spell Tony?
   Boy: T-O-N-Y.
   Woman: Oh! OK.

6 Boy: Nick's got a pet fish. It's in the picture.
   Woman: Oh yes. What's the name of the fish?
   Boy: Small. Small is a good name for a fish, I think. You spell it S-M-A-L-L.
   Woman: What a funny name for a fish!

Ⓖ Play the game! Guess what I'm drawing.

o   See how to play this on page 8. Learners choose words from this unit or Unit 18 and draw them line by line.

20 Ben and Kim live here!

Topics the home, places, family and friends

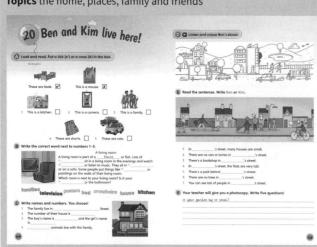

Movers words: *tall, home*

Equipment needed

- Starters audio 20D.
- Colouring pens or pencils. See D.
- Counters for the spelling game. See F.
- Photocopies of page 110. One for each pair. See F.

Ⓐ Look and read. Put a tick or a cross in the box.

Reading & Writing Part 1

- Draw a tick and a cross on the board. Point to the tick and say: *This is a tick. It means 'yes'.* Point to the cross and say: *This is a cross. It means … ?* (no)
- Say: *Listen and say 'Tick!' or 'Cross!'* Hold up a pencil and say: *This is a pencil!* Learners say *Tick!* Point to a window and say: *That is a door!* Learners say *Cross!* Learners could also draw ticks or crosses in the air.
- Learners look at the two examples in **A**. Point to the picture in the first example and ask: *What are these?* (beds) Point to the first example sentence and say: *These are beds. Is this sentence correct?* (yes) Point to the tick and say: *These are beds. That's right. We put a tick in the box!* Point to the picture in the second example and say: *Can you see the cross? This sentence is wrong. It isn't a mouse. It's a … ?* (house). Ask: *Is your house like this?* (yes/no)
- Learners put ticks or crosses in boxes for sentences 1–5.

> **Check answers:**
> 1 ✔ 2 ✘ 3 ✔ 4 ✔ 5 ✘

- Ask: *What can you see in 2?* (a photo [of a dog]) *But the word is … ?* (camera) *What can you see in 5?* (cars) *But the word is …?* (cats) Write *photo/camera* and *cat/car* on the board. Explain that these two were wrong for different reasons: *The words 'cat' and 'car' look almost the same. You take photos with a 'camera'!*

Ⓑ Read this. Write the correct word next to numbers 1–5.

> **Starters tip**
>
> In Reading and Writing Part 4, candidates complete a text about, for example, an animal, a place, an item of food or clothing. Make sure learners look at words around each gap and that they read the whole text at the end to check it makes sense. They should also cross out words after they have used them.

Note: in Starters Part 4, candidates will see both words and pictures. Here, they only have the words.

- Point to the words under the text and ask *How many words are there?* (seven)
  Read the first sentence in **B**: A living room is part of a <u>house</u> or flat. Say: *This is an example. Find the word 'house'.* Learners cross out 'house'.
- Learners read the text and choose and write the correct words for 1–5. They should cross out words as they use them.
- Check answers by reading the text and stopping at each gap. Ask different learners to say the missing word.

> **Check answers:**
> 1 families 2 television 3 armchairs 4 posters 5 kitchen

- Ask different learners questions about their own living room, for example:
  Are there photos on the wall in your living room?
  Is there a television in your living room?
  Is there a sofa in your living room? Are there armchairs?

Ⓒ Write names and numbers. You choose!

- Learners work in pairs. Say: *Look at the picture of the house. A family lives here. There are two children in the family – a boy and a girl.*
- Say: *Look at the four sentences in C. Which answers are names?* (1 and 3) *Which are numbers?* (2 and 4)
  Say: *Write your names and numbers on the lines.* Learners write their chosen answers. Walk round and help if necessary.
- Tell learners to imagine the family and this house. Ask the following questions, pausing between questions to let learners choose one of the answers or think of one of their own. They should not answer the questions out loud. *What's the name of this street? Is this house in Happy Street? Green Street? Or has this street got a different name? You choose!*
  What's the number of this house? Is this house number 14, 3 or a different number? You choose.
  What's the children's family name? Is it Wall? Rice? Or have they got a different family name? You choose.
  What's the boy's name? How old is he? What's the girl's name? How old is she? Have this family got a cat? A dog? A bird? A monkey? You choose.
- Learners exchange ideas for answers in pairs. Ask 3–4 pairs a name and a number question again, for example, *What's the name of this street? How old is the girl?* Pairs tell their chosen answers to the rest of the class. Ask pairs to spell any names.

Listen and write your names and numbers.

- Say: *Now listen to five questions and write answers about you and your home. Write a name or a number in your answers.*
  Ask the following questions. Learners write their answers in their notebooks.
  1 *What's your name?*
  2 *How old are you?*
  3 *What's the name of your street?*
  4 *What number is your house or flat/apartment?*
  5 *How many people are there in your family?*
- Repeat the questions and ask different learners for the answers.
- In pairs, learners ask and answer the same five questions.

Ⓓ ▶ Listen and colour Ben's street.

Listening Part 4

- Learners look at the picture. Ask: *Is your home in a street like this? Who lives in this street?* (Ben)
- Learners work in pairs. Ask: *What can you see in the picture of this street? Find six things.* Pairs note answers. Ask different pairs for their words and write them on the board.
  Suggestions: *houses, flats/apartments, a shop, trees, cars, a bus, a lorry/truck, windows, water, a clock, a bookshop, doors, a park, people, birds*

- Ask: *How many trees are there in this picture?* (seven)
  Say: *One tree in the picture has a colour. Point to that tree.* Learners point to the tree behind the number 10 flats. Ask: *What colour is that tree?* (red)
- Check learners have their colouring pencils or pens. Play the audio, stopping after the example.
- Say: *Now listen and colour five trees.* Tell learners they will hear the colour and the information about each tree twice.
- Play the rest of the audio. Learners listen and colour the five other trees.

> **Check answers:**
> colour tree on lorry – yellow, tree in front of bookshop – blue, tree in street – orange, tree next to clock – purple, tree behind the water – green

Audioscript

> *Look at the picture. Listen and look. There is one example.*
>
> Man: Look at the flats in this street! Can you see the tree behind the number 10 flats?
> Girl: Yes, I can.
> Man: Great. Colour the tree behind those flats red, please.
> Girl: OK.
>
> *Can you see the red tree behind the number 10 flats?*
> *This is an example. Now you listen and colour.*
>
> **1** Man: Colour the tree on the lorry now.
> Girl: Pardon?
> Man: Colour the tree on the lorry.
> Girl: OK! Can I colour it yellow?
> Man: Yes, you can! Thank you.
>
> **2** Man: There's a tree in front of the bookshop, too.
> Girl: Oh yes! I'd like to colour the tree in front of the bookshop blue!
> Man: OK!
> Girl: Thanks. There!
>
> **3** Girl: I can see a tree in the street! Can I colour that one now?
> Man: Yes. Make it orange, please.
> Girl: OK. I've got that colour.
> Man: Fantastic!
>
> **4** Man: And there's a tree next to the clock.
> Girl: Yes. That's a funny tree. I've got purple here. Can I colour it that colour?
> Man: OK!
> Girl: Right. I'm colouring the tree next to the clock now.
>
> **5** Man: Now, the tree in the park. It's behind the water. Can you see it?
> Girl: Yes, I can. What colour for that tree?
> Man: Green! Is that OK?
> Girl: Yes. I'm colouring it now. There!
> Man: Thanks a lot. This street is great now.

- Learners finish colouring the picture of the street. They choose their own colours and then show their pictures to their classmates.
- Teach/revise 'tall'. Point to a tall child in the class and the flats in the picture of Ben's street and ask: *Is (Rosa/Tomas) tall? Are these flats tall?* (yes)
- Ask learners what they can see from their windows at home. Point to the picture of Ben's street and ask: *Can you see a street like this? Can you see cars and lorries? A park? The sea? What can you see?* Ask two or three confident learners in the class then allow learners time to ask and answer in pairs.
- Ask more questions about Ben's street, for example: *Is the park in Ben's street open or closed?* (open) *Are the birds flying or eating in the park?* (flying)
- Ask: *What's the name of Ben's street?* Learners suggest names. Write a popular answer on the board, for example 'Park Street'. Ask: *Does Ben live at number 10 Park Street? You choose!* Add a number to the name of the street on the board. Say: *So, where does Ben live?* Learners read out Ben's address together.

- Point to the picture of Ben's street again and ask: *What can Ben see from his window?* Learners can imagine the view (The beach! His school! Lots of shops! His friends!) or say what they can see in the street (Cars! Buses! Lorries/Trucks! People!).

E **Read the sentences. Write *Ben* or *Kim*.**

- Point to the picture in **E** and say: *Kim lives here. Look at the first sentence.* Ask: *Are there any houses in Ben's street?* (no) *Are the houses small in Kim's street?* (yes). Learners write *Kim* in sentence 1.
- Learners read the other sentences and write *Ben* or *Kim*.

> **Check answers:**
> **2** Kim **3** Ben **4** Ben **5** Ben **6** Kim **7** Kim

- Ask questions about the street outside your own school to prompt 'no' as a determiner. Point to a street that's outside your classroom window and ask, for example: *Are there lots of cars / buses / tall flats / trees in this street?* Different learners answer: *There are no cars / buses / tall flats / shops / trees in this street.*

F **Write five questions.**

- Learners work in A and B pairs. Give out the top half of the photocopy of page 110 to A, and the bottom half to B. Point to the example questions in A and B: *Is your garden big or small? Is the window in your bathroom closed or open?* Show learners that the words to complete these questions are in the box.
- Learners find the second half of each of the questions and write it on the lines.

> **Check answers:**
> **2** or closed? **3** or dirty? **4** or sad? **5** or new?

> **Check answers:**
> **2** or old? **3** or long? **4** or clean? **5** or beautiful?

- Learners work in A and B pairs. A says the first part of their questions and B finishes them. Then B reads the first part of their questions and A finishes them. They do not answer the questions yet.
- Each learner answers their own questions. They underline the word which is their answer. For example, a learner who has a big garden underlines the word 'big' in the first question. Ask different learners to say their answers, for example: *The shops in my street are open. Our school is new. The children in this class are happy!*
- In pairs, learners show their answers to each other. They say sentences about each other's street, house, flat, school or classmates.

Optional extension: Play the game! Spelling challenge.

- Say the following words and ask learners in pairs to write them in their notebooks. After each word, ask different learners to spell them out loud. Remind them that for double letters, we usually say 'double':
  mirror, bookcase, street, dinner, wall, rubber, egg, bee, teddy
- Form teams (the number of teams will depend on the size of the class). Learners in each team choose seven words that they think are difficult to spell and write a list of those words. Go round the class and make sure they have spelled the words correctly.
- Each team has a counter which is stuck on the board. You could use pictures of different animals or transport (one for each team). The board is divided into five columns. Teams have to move their counters to the end of the board.
- Play the game. One team starts by asking the next team: *How do you spell … ?*
  The other team has to spell the word (a different learner each time). If they spell the word correctly, their counter moves forward one space. If they spell it incorrectly, they stay where they are.
- The winning team is the team whose counter reaches the end of the board first.

21 Play with us!

Topics transport, toys, names

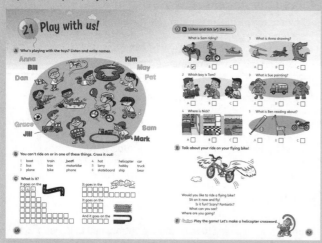

Movers words: *move, ride* (n), *up*; Flyers words: *high, sky*

Equipment needed

o (Optional) Your own favourite toy or photo of it.
o A piece of card or paper for each learner to draw on. See A.
o Photocopies of page 111, cut up into 14 phrases (one set per group of 4 learners). See C.
o Starters audio 21D.
o (Optional) Colouring pencils and pens. See E.

Ⓐ Who's playing with the toys? Listen and write names.

o If you have a favourite childhood toy, or a photo of it, show it to learners. Ask: *Do you like it, too?* Ask 4–5 learners: *What's your favourite toy?* Learners answer.

o Revise possessive -'s. Learners draw their favourite toy on a piece of card (or paper). Learners then put their drawings on a table or on the floor face-down so other learners cannot see the drawings. Learners take turns to pick up a card and guess whose toy is on the card by saying, for example: *It's Miguel's!* If they are correct, they can keep the card. The winner of the game is the learner with the most cards.

o Point to the names in **A**. Ask: *How many names can you see?* (10) Point to the picture. Ask: *How many children can you see?* (10) *How many toys have they got?* (13)

o Use the pictures to teach/revise the transport words: bike, boat, bus, car, helicopter, lorry/truck, motorbike, plane, ship, train.
   Explain that ships are always much bigger than boats. Lots of people can travel in a ship and ships are always big enough to cross the sea. We might only see one or two people in a boat.

o Ask *Where's the kite/balloon/ball/doll?*
   Learners point to the toys in the picture. Stronger learners could answer in sentences, for example: *It's behind the boy. It's in the girl's hand. It's behind the truck. It's next to the red car.*

o Say: *Look at the line to the girl with the toy bus.* Ask: *Who's playing with the toy bus?* (Jill)
   Point to the boy with the plane and ask: *What's this boy's name? Guess!*
   Point to the girl on the motorbike and ask: *And what's her name? Guess!* (Remind learners that Kim, Pat and Sam can be boys' or girls' names.)
   Learners choose one of the names for this boy and this girl.

o Ask: *Are your names right? Find a pencil and listen! Draw five lines from names to five children in the picture.*
   Note: Learners can use a ruler to help them draw straight lines if they prefer but this isn't obligatory in the test.

Say (pausing after each sentence to give learners time to draw their line):

Who's playing with the plane?	*Dan! Dan's playing with the toy plane!*
Who's sitting on the truck?	*It's Bill! Bill's sitting on the truck!*
Who's holding the helicopter?	*Anna is! Anna's got the helicopter!*
Who's playing with the red car?	*Pat! That's Pat's red car!*
Who's sitting on the toy motorbike?	*Sam! Sam's got the toy motorbike!*

o Ask: *Who's playing with the toy plane?* (Dan) *Who's got the toy motorbike?* (Sam) Ask learners if any of them guessed these names correctly before they heard the answers.

o Ask: *Which children haven't got names? The boy with the … ?* (boat) *and the boy with the … ?* (train) *The girl with the … ?* (yellow car) *and the girl on the … ?* (bike).
   Write on the board: ....*is playing with the* ....

o In pairs, learners write four sentences by choosing a name from the remaining four (Grace, Bill, May and Mark) and copying and completing four sentences in their notebooks, for example: *Grace is playing with the yellow car. (The words they need for the toys are in B.)*

o Ask different pairs to read out one or two of their sentences.

Ⓑ You can't ride on or in one of the things. Cross it out!

o Teach/revise 'move'. Mime 'moving' and then ask: *Can a pen move?* (no) *Can a bird move?* (yes)
   Learners look at sets 1–6. Say: *Look at the three words. You can ride on or in two of these things but you can't ride on or in one thing!* Learners cross out the word which isn't part of the set.

Check answers (crossed out):
2 box **3** phone **4** hat **5** hobby **6** bear

o Check that learners understand that 'lorry' and 'truck' can be used to talk about the same thing. 'Lorry' is used in British English and 'truck' in American English. In British English, 'truck' is often used to talk about a smaller vehicle that carries things in an open back, like the truck in **A**.

   Optional extension:
   Teach learners the tongue twister, *'Red lorry! Yellow lorry!'*
   Divide learners into two groups A and B. To begin with, direct group A to just say *Red lorry!* followed by group B saying *Yellow lorry!* Then direct the whole class to chant both halves of the tongue twister faster and faster until they find it too hard to continue!

Ⓒ What is it?

o Learners look at the four small pictures in **C**.
   Point to the street/road picture and ask: *What's this?* (a street/road)
   Point to the water/sea picture and ask: *What's this?* (water / the sea)
   For the two other pictures, teach 'sky' and 'railway line'. Pointing to the street picture and the example 'car', read out *I go on the street.* Make sure learners understand that the other boxes under this heading are for things that go on the street.

o Learners decide which words to write under each heading. They can find and copy all of the ten words they need from the lists in **B**.

Check answers:	
(street/road)	bus, bike, lorry, truck, motorbike, skateboard
(sky)	plane, helicopter
(water/sea)	boat, ship
(railway line)	train

Stronger classes:

o Learners work in groups of four.

Give each group a set of phrases to make up the poem from page 111. Groups divide up the phrases into four piles of 'look alike' cards.

Learners then try to order the phrases from each pile so they make one verse. The first phrase in each verse begins with a capital letter and the last phrase in each verse ends with a full stop.

Groups then choose how to order their verses and take turns to recite their version of the poem to the rest of the class.

Possible answer:

Buses, bikes and motorbikes, / trucks, lorries and cars / start, cross and stop / in School Street.

Helicopters and planes / fly happy people / here and there / in the blue sky.

Wave at the train, / it's there again / on the railway line.

And look … / at the boats and ships / big and small / on the blue, blue sea.

Groups could glue their poem onto a large piece of paper and illustrate it. Stronger learners could add extra lines. Display the finished poems on a classroom wall if possible.

D  Listen and tick the box.

Listening Part **3**

> **Starters tip**
>
> In Listening Part 3, train learners to read the question before they listen. If they do that, they will know what information to listen for. They hear the question before each conversation and the question is often heard again at the start of the conversation.

Option 1: Learners complete this task as a test on their own.

o Learners look at the pictures. Play the audio. Learners listen to the example then the five conversations. They tick the correct box (A, B or C). Play the audio a second time. Learners check and complete their answers.

Option 2: Learners complete this task as a class activity.

o Say: *Look at the example pictures. This girl's name is Sam. What's Sam riding in picture A? a … ?* (horse) *And in B? a … ?* (bike) *And what's she riding in in picture C?* (a boat)

o Play the example on the audio. Ask: *What's Sam riding? A bike?* (no) *Is she in a boat?* (no) *Is she riding a horse?* (yes) Point at the tick box in A.

o Play the rest of the audio. Learners tick the correct boxes. Play the audio a second time. Learners check their answers.

> **Check answers:**
> **1** B **2** C **3** A **4** B **5** C

Audioscript

> *Look at the pictures. Listen and look. There is one example.*
> *What's Sam riding?*
>
> Man: Is Sam riding her bike this morning?
> Girl: No, she's riding her friend's horse!
> Man: Wow!
> Girl: Her friend's family have got a boat, too! But Sam can't ride in that.
>
> *Can you see the tick? Now you listen and tick the box.*
>
> *One* What's Anna drawing?
> Woman: What are you drawing Anna? Are you drawing a crocodile?
> Girl: No, Mum! Look!
> Woman: Oh! It's a plane. It's very good.
> Girl: Thanks. But I can't draw helicopters …
>
> *Two* Which boy is Tom?
> Girl: There's my brother. His name's Tom.
> Boy: The boy with the toy car?
> Girl: That's right. Tom doesn't like playing with trains. Do you?
> Boy: No. I like playing with robots!

> *Three* What's Sue painting?
> Boy: Sue's painting one of her toys, Dad.
> Man: Which one? Her toy bus?
> Boy: No, one of her dolls. It's blue now.
> Man: Like her blue monster! She loves that!
>
> *Four* Where's Nick?
> Girl: I can't find Nick, Dad. Is he in the garden?
> Man: No, and he isn't in his bedroom.
> Girl: Oh listen! He's in the kitchen. He's singing that song about a red lorry!
> Man: Not again … !
>
> *Five:* What's Ben reading about?
> Woman: What's Ben reading?
> Girl: It's a story about a funny motorbike.
> Woman: And what are you reading about? That baseball game?
> Girl: No, Mum. I'm reading about giraffes.

E Talk about your ride on your flying bike!

o Point to the picture of the flying bike and ask: *Would you like to ride a bike like this?* (yes/no) Say: *Close your eyes! Listen to the questions and answer them in your head. Don't tell me the answers.*

o Read out the questions, pausing after each question so learners can imagine their answers. Give learners a few seconds to continue to imagine flying then quietly say: *Open your eyes, now.*

You can see your flying bike! What a beautiful bike! What colour is it?
Would you like to ride this flying bike?
You're sitting on your flying bike now. Are you happy?
Your flying bike is moving now. It's going up and up into the sky! Are you OK? Are you having fun? Is it scary? Fantastic?
What can you see?
Where are you going on your flying bike?
Enjoy your ride! Isn't it great!

o In pairs, learners ask and answer the questions in **E**. Ask different learners other questions. For example: *What colour is your flying bike? Where do you go on your flying bike? To the beach? The park? Your house? Has your friend got a flying bike too? Where does your friend go on their flying bike?*

F Let's make a helicopter crossword!

o Say: *Look at all the toys in A again. What are they?*
Learners answer. Write the words on the board: *kite, doll, ball, balloon, bus, car, bike, boat, plane, train, truck, lorry, motorbike, helicopter.*

o Cross out *helicopter* and write *helicopters* vertically on the board instead.

o Learners make a crossword in their notebooks by writing the toy words around the letters in *helicopters*. They should try to use words only once. Do this as a whole class activity or learners write the words in groups of 3–4.

Suggestion: s**h**ip, kit**e**, **l**orry, motorb**i**ke, **c**ar, b**o**at, **p**lane, **t**ruck, bik**e**, t**r**ain, bu**s**

22   In our bags and in our school

Topics school

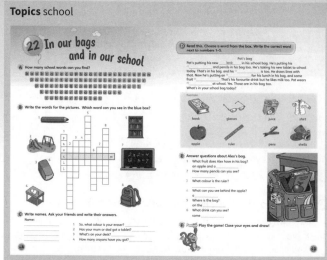

Movers word: *take*

Equipment needed

o   A big (non-transparent) bag with the following objects: a book, a blue pen, an apple, a ruler, some juice, a pair of glasses. See C.

o   Large sheets of paper. See F.

A   How many school words can you find?

o   Point to the keyboard drawing and say: *Look at this funny keyboard! There are lots of school words on it. Find the school words. Draw circles round them.*

o   When learners have finished, ask: *How many school words are there?* (20)

Check answers and teach/revise any words as necessary: book, bookcase, cupboard, board, desk, crayon, poster, teacher, ruler, eraser, paper, bag, computer, pen, pencil, keyboard, page, mouse, rubber, tablet.

o   Say: *You can see the word 'board' in two long words. Which words?* (cupboard, keyboard) *You can see 'book' in a long word too. Which word?* (bookcase)

Which word can you find 'pen' in? (pencil)

Which words are parts of a computer? (keyboard, mouse)

Which word is a computer too? (tablet)

o   Learners try and find all 20 things in their classroom. They say where each thing is. For example: *The board is on the wall, behind our teacher.*

B   Write the words for the pictures. Which word can you see in the blue box?

o   Point to the pictures in **B** and ask: *How many pictures are there?* (seven)

Point to the picture of the pencil and ask: *What's this?* (a pencil)

Point to the letters in the boxes under 1 and say: *Let's spell 'pencil'.* Learners call out the letters. (P-E-N-C-I-L).

Say: *Write the words for pictures 2, 4, 5, 7 and 8 now. Write them under the numbers. Don't write the words for 3 and 6!*

> **Check answers:**
> **2** playground   **4** desk   **5** bookcase   **7** board   **8** schoolbag

Point to the eraser/rubber and the numbers 3 and 6. Ask: *There are two different words for this. What are they?* (eraser and rubber) Write *eraser* and *rubber* on the board.

Explain that 'eraser' is used in American English and 'rubber' is used more in British English. Tell learners to write *eraser* in the boxes under 3 and *rubber* in the boxes under 6.

o   Point to the long word across the middle of the crossword and ask: *Which word can you see here now?* (classroom)

How many desks are there in this classroom? Is there a board? Can you see a bookcase, too?

C   Write names. Ask your friends and write their answers.

o   Tell learners to choose four people in the class. They write the names of these people on the lines in front of 1–4 (four different names.)

o   Learners stand up and move around to ask each of the four people the question after their name. They write each answer (one-word answers) on the lines next to the questions.

o   Write on the board:

1   … 's eraser is … .

2   … has/have got … a tablet.

3   … has … on his/her desk.

4   … has got … crayons.

o   Learners copy the four sentences in their notebooks and complete them with their classmates' answers.

o   Ask different learners to read out one of their sentences.

Ask: *What colours are your erasers? Has your mum or dad got a tablet? Have you got books, pens, crayons on your desk? Who has got a lot of crayons?*

What's in the bag?

o   Show learners the bag you have brought in. Tell them there are six school things inside it. In pairs, learners write down six things they think could be inside it.

o   Ask different learners to put their hand inside the bag and take out a different thing. They show it to the rest of the class and ask: *What's this?*

(It's an apple / a ruler / a pen / a book / juice. They're glasses, etc.) Learners tick the objects they guessed correctly.

o   Ask if anyone guessed all six things.

o   Write on the board: *In my bag, I've got … .*

Ask different learners to come to the board and write the words for the six things to complete the sentences:

Suggestion:

In my bag, I've got an apple, a ruler, a pen, a book, some juice and some glasses.

o   Tell learners to write a sentence in their notebook about the things in their own school bag.

o   In pairs, learners try and guess the words that their partner wrote about their bags. They ask questions, for example: *Have you got some pens / books / a ruler / a rubber in your bag?*

After 2–3 minutes, learners show their partner the sentence that they wrote.

D Read this. Choose a word from the box. Write the correct word next to numbers 1–5.

Reading & Writing **Part 4**

Starters tip
In Reading and Writing Part 4, the words 'a' or 'an' before the gap will help candidates choose their answers because they tell them that the word they need is singular, and 'an' tells them that the word starts with a vowel too. In this activity, for example, they have to choose 'an apple'.

o   Write these sentences on the board:

1   *I eat an …*
2   *I drink …*
3   *I draw lines with a …*
4   *I read a …*
5   *I wear a … or … and some …*
6   *I can find … on the beach.*
7   *I write with my …*

o   Point to the pictures in **D** and ask: *Can I eat shells?* (no) *Do we eat a ruler?* (no) *Can I eat an apple?* (yes) Point out that the word 'an' here tells us that the word that comes next begins with a, e, i, o or u.

o   Ask learners where to put the other words for the pictures in **D** in the sentences on the board. Write the words in the sentences:

Check answers:
2 juice   **3** ruler   **4** book   **5** shirt/glasses   **6** shells   **7** pens

Note: Point out that in the first gap in 5, we say *a shirt* but we can't say *a glasses* because 'glasses' is a plural word.

o   Explain to learners that they are going to read about Pat's bag. Say: *It's the morning and Pat is at home. It's a school day today.*

o   Read out the first two sentences of the text. Point to the example word 'book' on the line, and to the picture and word 'book' in the wordbox below.

o   Learners read the text, choose the words and write them next to the numbers.

Check answers: ask learners to say which words helped them choose their answers.
1 pens (and pencils)   **2** ruler (draws lines, that)
3 apple (an, lunch)   **4** juice (That, drink)
5 glasses (wears, Those)

o   Ask: *In this class, who wears glasses? Do you eat an apple at school? What's your favourite drink? Is an apple your favourite fruit? What's your favourite juice?*

E Answer questions about Alex's bag.

o   Say: *Alex is Pat's friend. He has a schoolbag too.* Point to the picture and say: *This is Alex's bag.*

o   Read out question 1 and the first part of the answer: *What fruit does Alex have in his bag? an apple and a …*

Point to the apple and then the banana. Ask: *What's this?* (a banana) Learners write *banana* on the line in 1.

o   Learners write the answers to the other questions.

Check answers:
2 2/two   **3** purple   **4** (green) book   **5** floor   **6** (apple) juice

F Play the game! Close your eyes and draw!

o   Learners take a big piece of paper and a pen or pencil.

o   Read out the description of the classroom scene below. The first time you read it out, learners don't draw anything. They just listen with their eyes closed so they can imagine the picture. Learners then open their eyes to pick up a pencil, then close their eyes again. Read out the description again. Learners listen and, this time, draw the picture of Alex's bag without opening their eyes. Pause between details if learners need more time to complete their drawings.

Drawing with eyes closed is really difficult so make sure learners understand that this is a fun thing to do, that everyone's picture will be different and most drawings will be very messy!

Say: *You can see a classroom.*
Your teacher's standing in front of the board.
He/She's drawing on the board with a pen.
He/She's drawing Alex's bag.
Can you draw Alex's bag now too?
Alex's bag is on a desk.
Can you draw the bag on the desk? Draw the bag, the apple and the banana. And the apple juice too!
Put the ruler and the book in the bag. Draw the two pencils too, please!

o   When learners have finished drawing, they open their eyes and look at their pictures so they can see how funny and how different they all look. You could display the pictures on the classroom walls.

23 At our school

Topics school, numbers, names

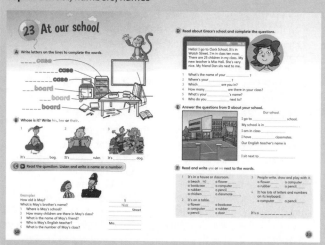

Not in YLE wordlists: *case*

Equipment needed

○ Starters audio 23C.

○ A pencil case, glasses and glasses case, two pencils, three pens, a rubber, a ruler, an English book, a story book, a desk, a chair, a schoolbag and a bookcase (optional). See A.

A Write letters on the lines to complete the words.

○ Point to a book. Ask: *What's this?* (a book) Point to the books on the floor in the picture in **A** and ask: *What are these?* (books) *Where are these books?* (on the floor) Point to the books in the bookcase and ask: *And where are these books?* (in the bookcase)

Follow the line with your finger from the bookcase to the blue word next to the picture. Point to the four lines in front of 'case'. Ask learners: *Which word goes here?* (book) Learners write *b-o-o-k* on the four lines.

○ Hold up a pencil and ask: *What's this?* (a pencil) Say: *We can put books in a bookcase. Where do we put pencils?* (in a pencil case!) Point to the pencil case on the desk in the picture, then follow the line to the purple word next to the picture. Ask: *Which word do I write here?* (pencil) Learners write *p-e-n-c-i-l* on the lines.

○ Point to a pair of glasses. Ask: *Where do we put glasses?* (in a glasses case) *Where's the glasses case in this picture?* (on the desk) Learners write *glasses* on the lines in the pink word.

○ Explain that we can put (and keep) things in a case. The first word ('book', 'pencil', 'glasses') tells us what we put in the case.

○ Point to the cupboard and ask: *What's this?* (a cupboard) Point to the three lines in front of the word 'board' in the green word and ask: *Which letters do we put here to write 'cupboard'.* (c-u-p) Learners write the letters on the lines.

Say: *There are two more words with the word 'board'. Do you know what they are?*

Point to the keyboard and ask: *What's this?* (a keyboard) *What's the first part of this word?* (key, k-e-y) You could explain that the letters and numbers on a keyboard are on keys. Learners write *k-e-y* on the lines in the yellow word.

Point to the whiteboard and ask: *What colour is this board?* (white) Say: *It's white, so we can say … ?* (whiteboard) Learners write the letters w-h-i-t-e on the lines.

Note: If you have a blackboard, not a whiteboard, in the classroom, you could explain that that's a blackboard because it's black!

Note: You could point out that we write some compounds as one word (bookcase) but others as two words (pencil case).

○ Explain that in compounds like these, which are made from two words, the first word is usually stressed. Write on the board:

bookcase 0 o   *pencil case* 0 o oo   *glasses case* 0 oo
cupboard 0 o   *keyboard* 0 o   *whiteboard* 0 o

Practise the pronunciation of these things. Point to each thing in the picture or in your classroom. Learners say the word.

○ Point to all the things on the floor of the classroom in the picture and say: *Listen and draw lines between these things and where I tell you to put them.* Tell learners to listen to you and to draw lines between the things on the floor and where you tell them to put them.

For example, say: *Put the open book in the bag.* Learners draw a line from the open book to the bag.

Put the <u>glasses</u> in the <u>glasses</u> case.

Put one <u>pen</u> behind the <u>pencil</u> case on the desk.

Put the <u>two</u> closed books in the <u>bookcase</u>, please.

Put the <u>ruler</u> in the <u>pencil</u> case.

Put one of the <u>pencils</u> in the <u>school bag</u>.

Put the <u>eraser</u> in the <u>pencil</u> case, please.

Put the <u>mouse</u> next to the <u>keyboard</u>, please.

Thank you!

○ If you have the objects in the picture, put them in the same position in your classroom as they are in the picture. Say the sentences again. Ask different learners to pick up the objects and to put them in the places you tell them. Learners check they have drawn the seven lines from the correct objects to the correct places in the picture.

B Whose is it? Write *his, her* or *their*.

○ Point to picture 1 and ask: *What can you see?* (a girl with a tennis bag) Say: *Look at the words under that picture.*

Ask one learner to read it out: *It's .... bag.*

Ask: *Which word goes here? Is it 'his', 'her' or 'their'?* ('her' because it refers to a girl).

○ Learners look at the other two pictures and sentences and write *his, her* or *their*.

> **Check answers:**
> **2** his (masculine, singular)   **3** their (plural)

○ Ask: *What colour is the girl's bag?* (red) *What's in her bag? A piano?* (no) *Her tennis things?* (yes)

The boy's got a ruler. What colour is his ruler? (brown) *Have you got a brown ruler?* (yes/no) *What's the dog doing?* (jumping/playing) *This dog lives with this family. Is their dog big or small?* (small)

Draw pictures and write about them.

○ Learners draw their English book on a piece of paper or in their notebook.

○ Say: *Let's write about your English book.* Write on the board: *This is my English book. It's .... and there are .... pages.*

Learners copy this under their picture of their English book. Ask: *What colour is your English book?* Learners write the colour of their book after 'It's' in the first gap. Ask: *How many pages are there in your English book?* Learners look at the number of pages and write the number in the second gap.

○ Learners draw a picture of something else they can see in the classroom. They then write two sentences about it. They could write about its colour and where it is. For example: *This is my (pencil case). It's (purple) and you can see it (on my desk).*

C ▶ Read the question. Listen and write a name or a number.
Listening Part **2**

> **Starters tip**
> In Listening Part 2, part of a name (for example, 'Street', 'Miss') might be on the answer paper. Candidates will hear these words on the audio (for example, 'Good Street', 'Miss Hall') but they are not spelt out. The part of the name that they have to write (for example, 'Good', 'Hall') <u>is</u> always spelt out on the audio.

o Point to the picture of the girl and say: *This is May. She's talking to this policeman about her family and her school.*

o Play the first part of the audio. Ask: *Whose birthday is it today?* (May's) *How do you spell Nick?* (N-i-c-k)

   Point to the two examples. Explain that the first answer (8) is a number. May is eight years old. The second answer is a name (Nick) Ask: *Who's Nick?* (May's brother)

   Point to the five questions and ask: *Which questions ask about a name and which questions ask about a number?*

   Answer: names – 1, 3, 4 numbers – 2, 5.

o Play the rest of the audio twice. Learners write names or numbers.

> **Check answers:**
> **1** Good   **2** 15/fifteen   **3** Kim   **4** Hall   **5** 8/eight

o In pairs, learners role play the conversation between May and the policeman.

Audioscript

Read the question. Listen and write a name or a number. There are two examples.

> Girl: Hello, Mr Line! It's my birthday today!
> Man: Happy birthday! How old are you now? Eight?
> Girl: Yes, that's right. I'm eight today.
> Man: Is that your brother behind you?
> Girl: Yes. That's Nick.
> Man: Does he spell his name N-I-C-K?
> Girl: Yes.

Can you see the answers? Now you listen and write a name or a number.

1 Man: Where do you go to school, May?
    Girl: I go to school in Good Street.
    Man: And how do you spell Good?
    Girl: G-O-O-D.
    Man: Oh yes. I know.

2 Man: How many children are there in your class?
    Girl: Umm … there are fifteen.
    Man: Fifteen! That's a small class.
    Girl: Yes. I like that.

3 Man: Now, May. Who are your friends in your class?
    Girl: Well … , I like Kim. Kim sits next to me.
    Man: Do you spell her name K-I-M?
    Girl: Yes, that's right.

4 Man: Do you learn English at school, May?
    Girl: Yes. I'm good at English.
    Man: Who's your English teacher?
    Girl: Her name's Miss Hall.
    Man: Oh, Miss Hall. Do you spell that H-A-L-L?
    Girl: Yes.

5 Man: And which class are you in now?
    Girl: I'm in class 8.
    Man: Class 8? OK. Thank you for answering my questions.

D Read about Grace's school and complete the questions.

o Point to the girl and say: *This is Grace.* Point to the tablet and say: *This is Grace's tablet. Read the text about Grace's school.*

   Give learners time to read the text, then say the name and numbers below. Learners tell you what the names or numbers are. For example: Say: *25.* (There are 25 children in Grace's class.)

   Clock: (Grace goes to Clock School.)

   Miss Hall: (She's Grace's new teacher.)

   Dan: (He's Grace's friend and he sits next to her.)

   Watch: (Grace's school is in Watch Street.)

o Point to the questions in **D** and say: *Grace answers these questions. You can read her answers in the text.*

   Look at the questions and at Grace's answers. Which words are missing in the questions?

   Learners write one word on each line to complete the questions.

o In pairs, one learner asks the questions and the other learner answers them, using the information in the text in **D**.

> **Check answers:**
> **1** school   **2** school   **3** class   **4** children/students   **5** teacher
> **6** sit

E Answer the questions from D about *your* school.

o Read out the first question in **D**: *What's the name of your school?* Ask one learner to answer (for example, (Dickens) school). Point to the first sentence in **E**: *I go to … school.* Learners write the name of their school on the line in the first sentence.

o Point to the next sentence in **E**: *My school is in …* . Ask one learner: *Where's your school?* Learners write the name of the town/city or the street where their school is on the second line in the text.

o Learners answer the other questions from **D** and complete the sentences in **E**.

o Check answers by asking different learners to read out sentences from the text in **E**.

o Learners can make the text into a poster by copying text from **E** onto a piece of paper and adding pictures or photos. They could also email another school with their information or put it on their school blog.

F Read and write *yes* or *no* next to the words.

o Say: *It's in a room.* Write on the board: *in a room.*

o Ask: *What can you find in a room?* Learners say things you can find in a room. Write their words on the board under *in a room.* Suggestions: *bed, chair, table, sofa,* etc.

o Say: *It's on the wall.* Write *on the wall* on the board next to *in a room.* Ask: *What can you find on the wall in a room?* Write learners' words on the board.

o Say: *People look at it.* Write *look at it* on the board next to *in a room, on the wall.* Ask: *What do people look at on the wall in a room?*

o Say: *Children at school paint me.* Ask: *What do children at school paint and look at on a wall in a room?*

   Write *paint* on the board next to *in a room, on the wall, look at it.*

   Ask: *Do you paint a photo?* (no) *Do you paint a clock?* (no) *Do you paint a poster, picture or a painting?* (yes)

o Read out the first sentence in **F**: *It's in a house or classroom.* Ask: *Is a beach in a classroom?* (No!)

   Ask the same question about *a flower, a bookcase, a computer, a rubber, a pencil* and *a chicken* and *a classmate.* Learners write *yes* or *no* after each word.

   Answers: no: a chicken   yes: a flower, a bookcase, a computer, a rubber, a pencil, a classmate

o In pairs, learners read sentences 2–4 and write *yes* or *no.*

> **Check answers:**
> **2 yes:** a flower, a rubber, a computer, a pencil
> **no:** a bookcase, a classmate
> **3 yes:** a computer, a pencil **no:** a flower, a rubber
> **4 yes:** a computer **no:** a pencil

o Learners write *computer* on the lines after *It's a …* .

o Learners write three 'It's …' sentences about the thing they drew and wrote about in the **Draw pictures** activity. For example: *It's in a classroom. It's on a desk. People put pencils and pens in it.*

   They show or read out their sentences. The other learners say after each sentence what the thing could be. (a pencil case)

24   What's the class doing?

Topics school, names

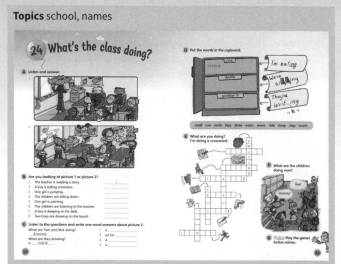

Not in YLE wordlists: *crossword*; Flyers word: *rocket*

Equipment needed

o   Photocopies of page 112 (large classes: one for every ten learners; small classes: one copy, made into flashcards). See G.

A   Listen and answer.

o   (Books closed) Ask questions: *Where are we?* (in a classroom) *How many children are there in this room? How many boys are there? How many girls are there?* Learners answer.

o   Say: *Now, open your books. Look at page 52. Look at pictures 1 and 2 in A.*

     Where are the children? (in the classroom)

     How many children are there? (seven)

     How many boys are there? (four)

     How many girls are there? (three)

     Where's the teacher? Is she in picture 1 or 2? (1)

     In which picture can you see the names? (2) *How many names can you see?* (seven)

o   Say: *Look at picture 2. Answer my questions.* Read out the questions below, pausing after each question to allow learners time to answer. Then, ask the questions two or three times more until learners answer promptly. Ask:

     1   *Who's eating?* (Sam)

     2   *Who's sleeping?* (Ben)

     3   *Who's jumping?* (Anna)

     4   *Who's painting* (Lucy)

     5   *Who's drawing?* (Tom and Nick)

     6   *Who's throwing a ball?* (Alex)

o   Mime different activities (reading/writing/sleeping/sitting/drawing/listening). After each mime, ask: *What am I doing?* each time. Learners answer. For example: *You're reading.*

     Write each answer on the board. Underline 'ing'.

o   Ask two or three questions about different learners in the class. For example: *What's Mario doing?* (He's listening.)

B   Are you looking at picture 1 or picture 2?

> **Starters tip**
>
> The pictures in Reading and Writing Part 5 often show the same people doing different things or in different places. These differences are often the focus of some of the questions for the second and third pictures. For example: 'What are the children doing now?' Training learners to notice what different people in the pictures are doing will also help them with Reading and Writing Part 2.

o   Read out the first sentence: *The teacher is reading a story.* Ask: *Where's the teacher? In picture 1 or 2?* (picture 1) Point to the number 1 on the line after sentence 1. Learners read the sentences. If the sentence is true for picture 1, they write *1* after the sentence. If it is true for picture 2, they write *2.*

> **Check answers:**
> 2 2   3 2   4 1   5 2   6 1   7 2   8 2

o   Ask questions about picture 1:

     1   *What's the teacher doing?* (looking at a book / reading [a story])

     2   *What are the children doing?* (looking at the teacher / sitting)

o   Write the verbs on the board and underline the endings: *look<u>ing</u>, read<u>ing</u>, sitt<u>ing</u>*

o   Ask questions about picture 2:

     1   *What's Sam doing?* (eating)

     2   *What's Ben doing?* (sleeping)

     3   *What's Tom doing?* (drawing)

     4   *What's Lucy doing?* (painting)

     5   *What's Alex doing?* (throwing a ball)

o   In pairs, learners ask and answer '*What's .... doing?*' questions about picture 2.

C   Listen to the questions and write one-word answers about picture 2.

o   Ask: *What are Nick and Tom doing?* (drawing) Point to the word 'drawing' on the line in **C.** Ask: *What are Nick and Tom drawing?* (a rocket) Point to the word 'rocket' on the line in **C.**

     Explain that when someone asks what a person is doing, we answer with an '–ing' verb (for example: drawing, eating). When we ask what a person is drawing or eating, we answer with a noun (for example: a picture, a sweet).

o   Ask these questions about picture 2. Learners listen and write one-word answers on the lines in **C.** Remind them that some words (a, on his) are already written. They only need to write one word.

     What's Sam eating?

     Where's Ben sleeping?

     What's Alex throwing?

     What's Lucy painting?

> **Check answers:**
> **1** banana   **2** desk   **3** ball   **4** sheep

Yes or *no?*

o   Say: *Now, listen to questions about you! If your answer is 'yes', stand up. If your answer is 'no', sit down!* Ask:

     1   *Are you listening to me?*

     2   *Are you wearing blue socks?*

     3   *Are you standing up?*

     4   *Are you writing with a black pen?*

     5   *Are you sitting on a chair?*

     6   *Are you drawing a funny face?*

     7   *Are you sleeping?*

o   Different learners ask: *Are you ..?* questions about their class. Learners stand up or sit down to answer.

D Put the words in the cupboard.

○ Write these questions on the board. Learners say and spell the missing word. Write the letters on the board on the lines.

Are you _ _ _ _ _ _ a banana? (eating)

Are you_ _ _ _ _ _ _ on a chair? (sitting)

Are you _ _ _ _ _ _ _ with a pen? (writing)

○ Explain to learners that there are three ways of adding '-ing' to a verb.

eat + ing = eating (most verbs – just add 'ing')

sit + t + ing = sitting (some verbs – double the last letter, then add 'ing')

write + ing = writing (some verbs – take away the 'e', then add 'ing')

Explain: Verbs where the final consonant doubles before adding '-ing' only have <u>one</u> syllable and <u>one</u> vowel + <u>one</u> consonant at the end (the 1–1–1 rule), ('w' and 'y' are not classed as consonants for this rule.)

○ Point to the cupboard in **D** and say: *This is the ''ing'' cupboard'.* Learners look at the three yellow sentences and at the three shelves in the cupboard.

The example: 'reading' is on the **+'ing'** shelf because we don't change the verb before we add '-ing'. Learners write 'eating' there too.

Now point to 'sitting'. Explain that 'sitting' goes on the **double** shelf because we need to add another 't' before we add '-ing'.

Point to 'writing'. Explain that 'writing' goes on the '**goodbye 'e''** shelf because it loses its final 'e' before we add '-ing'.

> **Check answers:**
> eating (**+'ing'**), sitting (**double**), writing (**goodbye 'e'**)

○ Learners look at the words in the box below the cupboard. They write the '-ing' forms for the words in the box on the shelf according to their '-ing' spelling group. Go round the class and help, if necessary.

> **Check answers:**
> **+'ing'** (drawing, sleeping, counting), **double** (running, stopping, swimming, clapping), **goodbye 'e'** (smiling, waving, riding)

Learners find three more '-ing' words in the sentences in **B** and add them to the cupboard.

> **Check answers:**
> jumping, painting, listening (all go on the **+'ing'** shelf)

Note: Starters verbs where the final consonant doubles before adding '-ing' are: *get, hit, put, run, sit, stop, swim.*

E What are you doing? I'm doing a crossword.

○ Point to the smiling face clue at the top of the crossword. Ask: *What's this person doing?* (smiling) *How do you spell smile?* (s-m-i-l-e) Point to the example answer 'smiling' in the crossword. Say: *'Smile' is a goodbye 'e' verb too!*

○ In pairs, learners look at the other picture clues and complete the crossword with '-ing' words. Tell learners that all of the answers are in the '-ing' cupboard.

> **Check answers:**
> **Across (top to bottom):** drawing, sitting, listening, eating, writing, running
> **Down (left to right):** waving, reading, sleeping

F What are the children doing now?

○ Point to the picture of the children outside the school and say: *It's the afternoon now. Are the children in the classroom now?* (no) *Are they going home?* (yes)

Learners work in pairs. Say: *Look at the children in the picture. What's Anna saying?* (Hooray!) *Is she happy?* (yes) *What's Ben saying?* (Bye!) *Who's he saying 'bye' to?* (Sam) *What are the kids doing? What are they holding?*

Ask different pairs to say what one of the children is doing or holding.

Suggestions: *Anna's jumping. Tom's pointing. Nick's looking. Ben and Sam are waving.*
Lucy's holding some paints / a box of paints. Alex is holding her ball. Nick's holding a book. Ben's holding a guitar.

○ Say: *It's the evening now. The children in the class are doing different things.*

Divide the class into two groups – A and B. Learners in group A look at page 97. Learners in group B look at page 99. Each group talks about what the boy or girl is doing in the different pictures.

Suggestions:

Group A: Tom is playing games with his grandmother. Nick is phoning / talking on the phone. Ben is doing a crossword. Anna is writing music. Sam is making a plane. Lucy is cleaning a/the car. Alex is fishing.

Group B: Lucy is phoning / talking on the phone. Ben is playing games with his grandmother. Anna is making a plane. Tom is writing music. Sam is doing a crossword. Nick is fishing. Alex is cleaning a car.

○ Make pairs of learners – one learner from group A works with a learner from group B.

Learner A says a sentence about their first picture. (*Tom's playing games with his grandmother.*) Learner B says what Tom's doing in their picture: (*Tom's writing music.*) Then, Learner B says a sentence about another boy or girl and Learner A says what that boy or girl is doing in the picture they have. Continue like this until learners have talked about all the pictures.

G Play the game! Action mimes.

○ **Large classes:**
Make copies of page 112 (one for every ten learners, cut up into word cards).

○ Run across the front of the classroom. Ask learners: *What am I doing?*

○ Learners put their hands up to answer. (*You're*) *running*.

○ The learner who answers correctly comes to the front of the class, takes a card and mimes the action on it. The other learners put their hands up to answer. The learner who answers correctly then mimes another action in front of the class and so on.

○ Learners continue this game in groups of 8–10, divided into two teams (A and B) of 4–5 learners, who compete to guess the most sentences.

○ **Small classes:**
Make one photocopy of page 112. Cut up the words and make flashcards. Give out one or two cards (depending on the size of the class) to each learner. Each learner then mimes the activity they have been given.

Note: For stronger groups, you could add an extra challenge: as well as saying the sentence (for example: *You're running.*), learners have to say if the verb is '**+'ing''**, '**double**' or '**goodbye 'e'**'.

25 Animal challenge

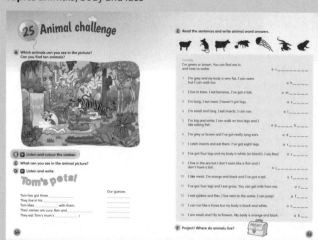

Movers words: *fly, grass, plants*; Flyers words: *insects, wild*

Equipment needed

o   Starters audio 25B, 25D.

o   Colouring pens or pencils.

o   Large pieces of paper. See F.

o   A map of the world (in an atlas or online). See G.

A   Which animals can you see in the picture?

o   Teach 'wild'. Say: *I like cats and dogs but I like watching wild animals on TV too!* Point to the picture in **A**. Say: *These animals don't live in our homes. These are wild animals!*

Ask: *What's your favourite wild animal? Which wild animals are funny/big/small/ugly?*

o   Learners work in pairs. Say: *Look at the picture. Can you find ten wild animals here?*

Note: Learners should not draw in the picture or write anything yet.

Give pairs time to find the animals and say what they are (bird, crocodile, fish, elephant, giraffe, hippo, monkey, spider, tiger, snakes).

Note: there are six snakes in the picture.

Point at two or three different animals in the picture and say: *Look! It's a … ?* Learners complete your sentences.

o   Ask different learners: *Do you like drawing animals? Which animals can you draw? Do you like reading about animals? Which ones? Do you like watching animals on TV? What's your favourite wild animal?* Make a list of each learner's favourite wild animals on the board. Ask learners to spell the animal words as you write them. Point to the list and ask which wild animal is most learners' favourite.

B ▶ Listen and colour the snakes.   Listening Part 4

> **Starters tip**
>
> In Listening Part 4, candidates only have 15 seconds to colour each object in the picture. Make sure they know that they don't have to finish colouring the object in order to get the mark and there are no extra marks for beautiful colouring!

o   Say: *There are six snakes in the picture. Can you find them all?* Ask different learners to point to a snake and say: *Here's a snake.*

Snakes are: next to the flower, on the elephant's ear, in the water, under the tiger, in the tree, between the monkey and the bird.

o   Check learners have colouring pens or pencils. Play the example then stop the audio and say: *Can you see the grey snake behind the big flower? This is an example. Now you listen and colour the five snakes.* Play the audio twice. Learners listen and colour.

o   In pairs, learners compare pictures.

Check answers:	
snake on elephant's ear	blue
snake in the water	red
snake under tiger	yellow
snake in tree	purple
snake between monkey and bird	brown

o   If they are happy with their answers, give learners time to complete their colouring.

o   Write on the board: *In my picture, there's a … snake in the water.* Learners repeat the sentence adding the colour (red) in the gap. Repeat for the snake that is in the tree (purple) and under the tiger (yellow).

o   Say: *Some people have pet snakes. Would you like a pet snake?*

Audioscript

Look at the picture. Listen and look. There is one example.

Girl: There are lots of snakes in this picture!

Man: Yes, there are. Can you see the snake behind the big flower?

Girl: The snake behind the big flower? Yes! Can I colour it grey?

Man: Yes. That's a very good colour for it.

1   Man: There's a snake on the elephant's ear. Colour that snake now.

Girl: OK. Which colour?

Man: Colour the snake on the elephant's ear blue, please.

Girl: OK! There!

2   Girl: There's a snake in the water, too!

Man: I know! Colour that snake now.

Girl: What colour?

Man: Colour the snake in the water red.

Girl: OK. I'm doing that now.

3   Man: And there's a snake under the tiger!

Girl: You're right!

Man: Colour that snake yellow. Can you do that?

Girl: Yes, I can. I'm making it that colour now.

Man: Good!

4   Man: One snake is in the tree. Let's colour that one now.

Girl: OK. Can I colour it purple?

Man: Yes, you can.

Girl: Great! The snake in the tree is my favourite colour now. Look!

5   Man: I can see a snake between the monkey and the bird.

Girl: Me too. Can I colour that one brown, please?

Man: Yes, you can.

Girl: The one between the monkey and the bird? Great! There!

Man: Well done!

C   What can you see in the animal picture? Put a tick or a cross in the box.

o   Learners look at the animal picture in **A** again.

Write on the board: *Can you see the bird's tail?*   ☐

Can you see the hippo's feet?   ☐

Read out the questions. When learners answer *yes* to the first question, put a tick in the box on the board so learners can clearly see what to do. When learners answer *no* to the second question, put a cross in the box on the board.

o   Learners work in A and B pairs. Say to A Learners: *Look at the animal picture again.* Say to B Learners: *Don't look at the animal picture. Look at page 99.* B learners turn to page 99. Say to B Learners: *Look at the two examples and sentences 1–10 now.*

○ B Learners ask A Learners the example *Can you see* questions to check they understand what they need to do. They then ask other *Can you see* questions. A Learners answer *yes* or *no*. B learners put a tick or a cross in each box.

○ Say to B Learners: *Look at the animal picture.* Say to A Learners: *Look at the sentences on page 99.* A Learners ask the *Can you see* questions and B Learners answer *yes* or *no*. A Learners put the ticks and crosses.

> **Check answers:**
> ✔ 1, 2, 5, 6, 7   ✘ 3, 4, 8, 9, 10

D ▶ Listen and write.

○ Ask 3–4 learners: *Have you got a cat or dog at home? What's its name? What colour is it?*

○ Learners work in pairs. Say: *Listen! Tom's got three animals at home.* Learners look at the sentences in **D**. Say: *Look at sentence 1. What animals has Tom got? Has Tom got three cats? Three lizards?* Pairs guess the missing animal word and write their guess (for example: *dogs*) on the first dotted line under 'Our guesses'.

○ Learners read the other four sentences and talk together in pairs to guess the missing information (for example: *kitchen, playing, Bill, apples*)

○ Say: *Now listen to Tom. He's talking about his pets. Write the answers.*

○ Play the audio twice. Learners listen and write. Before checking answers, ask: *How many of your guesses are right/wrong?*

> **Check answers:**
> sheep, garden, playing, Pat, flowers

Note: To give learners more support, write the answers plus some wrong answers in random order on the board (see below). Learners listen, choose and copy the right answers into the sentences.

Suggested list:

cows   park   playing   Sue   bananas   flowers   walking   Pat   garden   sheep

Audioscript

Hello! My name's Tom. I love animals. We've got three pets. They're sheep! They say Baaa Baaa! Our sheep live in our garden. You can come and see them in our garden! I really like playing with them. They have funny names. Their names are Lucy and Ben and Pat. You spell Pat, P-A-T. They're funny sheep. They eat Mum's flowers! Mum doesn't like that! She loves her flowers! The sheep love them too!

E Read the sentences and write animal word answers.

○ Teach/revise the following verbs by telling learners to do the actions: Jump! Run! Swim! Fly! Sing! Catch!

○ Learners look at the pictures of the animals at the top of the page. Ask: *Which animals can you see?* (a sheep, a mouse, a cow, a bee, a jellyfish, a lizard, a frog)

○ Learners read the example and say the important words in the 'crocodile' sentence (*green or brown, water*). Learners write the letters on the lines to complete the word 'crocodile'.

○ Learners read sentences 1–14 and write the letters to complete the names of the animals.

> **Check answers:**
> **1** a hippo   **2** a monkey   **3** a snake   **4** a lizard   **5** a polar bear
> **6** a donkey   **7** a spider   **8** a sheep   **9** a jellyfish   **10** a tiger
> **11** a cow   **12** a frog   **13** a zebra   **14** a bee

○ Write on the board: *I can fly. I can swim. I can jump. I give you milk.*

○ Ask: *Which animals can fly?* Write learners' answers under *I can fly*. Do the same with the other three headings: *Which animals can swim / jump / give you milk?* (Learners can answer using animal words in this unit and in Unit 14.)

Note: The complete animal list at Starters is:

bear, bee, bird, cat, chicken, cow, crocodile, dog, donkey, duck, elephant, fish, frog, giraffe, goat, hippo, horse, jellyfish, lizard, monkey, mouse/mice, polar bear, sheep, spider, tiger, zebra

○ Each learner chooses an animal and writes it on a big piece of paper. Read out the sentences below. If it is correct/true for their animal, learners stand up and hold out their animal paper.

Sentences: *I am very big. I don't have legs. I live in water. I live in hot places. I eat meat.*

Play the game! O and X.

○ Draw the following grid on the board.

old	young	beautiful
long	small	big
short	clean	dirty

○ Divide the class into O and X teams. Each team tries to 'win' squares in the grid.

○ Team O starts. They have to make a short sentence using any adjective in the grid and any animal word. The sentence has to be logical – the teacher is the judge! For example:
*My spider has **long** legs!*
This is acceptable, so write O in the 'long' square. Team X then tries to win another square in the grid.
*It's a **beautiful** word.*
This is not acceptable because there is no animal in the sentence. Team X cannot win that square so you don't write an X in the 'beautiful' square.

○ The team which gets three squares forming a row (horizontally, vertically or diagonally) wins that round and the game starts again. Each time an adjective is used, it must be about a different animal.

F 🧳 Where do animals live?

○ Show learners a map of the world in an atlas or online.
Ask them to find and point to: South America, USA, Asia, Africa, India and Australia.

○ Ask: *Where do wild hippos, crocodiles, tigers, elephants, zebras and giraffes live?* Learners can find out online or in books.

○ Learners could each draw a map of the world (or print one out).
They label the countries/continents above, then they draw arrows to show where wild hippos, crocodiles, tigers, elephants, zebras and giraffes live, adding those animal words to their map too. Learners can also add other animals to their maps.
Display learners' animal maps on the classroom wall if possible. Alternatively, learners add their animal maps to their project file.

General reference:
Wild hippos live in Africa, crocodiles live in South America, Asia, Africa, India and Australia, tigers live in Asia, elephants live in Africa, Asia and India, zebras and giraffes live in Africa.

Note: Not all areas where crocodiles live are mentioned.

26   How many pets?

Topics animals, the home, names, numbers

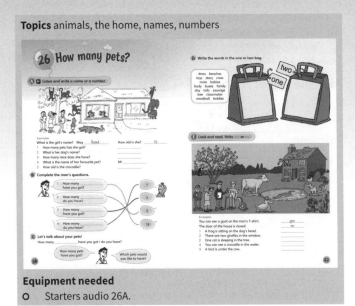

Equipment needed
○   Starters audio 26A.

Ⓐ ▶ Listen and write a name or a number.
Listening **Part 2**

○   Point to the picture and say: *Look at this house.* Point to the girl and say: *May lives here. May has got a lot of pets. How many animals can you see?* (nine) If necessary, explain that 'a pet' is an animal that lives with a person or family at home.

○   Say: *In pairs, write the animals you can see in the picture.* (Learners write: *monkeys, tigers, a crocodile, a giraffe, an elephant, a hippo.*)
Ask: *How many crocodiles/tigers/monkeys has May got?* (one crocodile / two tigers / three monkeys)
Ask: *Where are the tigers?* (in the house) *Where are the monkeys?* (two are in the tree and one is next to the house)
Which animal is next to the girl? (the crocodile)
Which three animals are next to the house? (the elephant, giraffe and hippo) *Who's talking?* (a man and May / the girl) *Who's holding a camera?* (a/the woman) *Who's writing?* (a man)

○   Point to the man who's talking to May and explain that this man is from the television studios. Point to the questions under the picture and say: *He's asking May some questions about her pets.*

○   Play the first two questions on the audio. Learners look at the example answers: *Read* and *10.* Say: '*Read*' is May's family name and May is '10' years old. Look at questions 1–5. Which answers are names and which are numbers? (2 and 4 are names. 1, 3, 5 are numbers)

○   Say: *Listen to the man and to May. Write names or numbers.*
Tell learners to listen carefully to the spellings when they write their answers. Play the conversation twice.

> **Check answers:**
> **1** 18/eighteen   **2** Sue   **3** 5/five   **4** Mr Big   **5** 14/fourteen

Write on the board: *How many … live in your house?*
What's the … of your house?   *What's the … of your street?*
Learners suggest words to fill the gaps (people/animals, colour/number, name).

○   Learners work in A and B pairs. Learner A is the man from the TV. Learner B is May. They ask and answer the questions on the board.

Audioscript

Look at the picture. Listen and write a name or a number. There are two examples.

Reporter:	Hello! What's your name?
May:	May Read. You spell Read, R-E-A-D.
Reporter:	Thank you. And how old are you, May?
May:	I'm ten.
Reporter:	You're ten?
May:	Yes, that's right.

Can you see the answers? Now you listen and write a name or a number.

1   Reporter: And are these your pets, May?
     May: Yes, they are.
     Reporter: How many pets have you got?
     May: I've got 18 pets.
     Reporter: 18?
     May: Yes!

2   May: I've got some birds, a cat and a dog too!
     Reporter: Wow! What's your dog's name?
     May: Her name is Sue.
     Reporter: Sue. That's a nice name. Do you spell that S-U-E?
     May: Yes.

3   May: I've got some pet mice too.
     Reporter: How many mice do you have?
     May: I've got five mice now.
     Reporter: Five?
     May: Yes. They've got very long tails!

4   Reporter: And which is your favourite pet?
     May: My favourite pet is my crocodile. His name's Mr Big! You spell that B-I-G. Say hello, Mr Big!
     Crocodile: *Croak!*

5   Reporter: And how old is your crocodile?
     May: Erm … He's 14.
     Reporter: Sorry?
     May: He's 14 now.
     Reporter: What does he eat?
     May: He loves sausages!

Ⓑ Complete the man's questions.

○   Ask: *How many pets has May got?* (18) Write on the board: *18.* (Leave space above this number to write nine more numbers)
Point to the picture in **A** and ask: *How many monkeys does May have?* (three) Write *3* at the top of the board above *18.*

○   Ask learners to tell you the questions you asked about May's pets and May's monkeys? (*How many pets has May got? How many monkeys does May have?*) Write both questions on the board, omitting the words *pets* and *monkeys.* Explain that *have you got?* and *do you have?* mean the same here.
Point to the questions on the board and ask: *Can you ask this question about May's crocodile?* (How many crocodiles does May have? / has May got?) (one) Write *1* on the board under *3.*
Explain to learners that they need to use the plural form in this question (even if the answer is 'One!').

○   Learners ask and answer *How many* questions about the giraffe, elephant, hippo and tigers. Write the answers (*1, 1, 1, 2*) on the board above *18.*

○   Ask different learners to come to the board and write the different animals after the numbers.
3 monkeys, 1 crocodile, 1 giraffe, 1 elephant, 1 hippo, 2 tigers, 18 pets
Play the audio for questions 2 and 3 again. Ask: *How many cats/dogs/mice does May have?* Learners say the answer, then different learners add the numbers and animals to the list on the board. (One cat, one dog, five mice.)

Add up the numbers on the board with learners (not including the number 18): *3+1+1+1+1+2+1+1+5 = 16*

Say: *May has 18 pets. Which pets are not on the board?* (her birds) *How many birds has May got?* (two) A learner writes *two birds* in the list on the board.

Teach the word 'plus'. Point to and say the first two numbers: *3 + 1 is* (four). Point to each number in the list on the board. Learners add the numbers together, saying: *Three plus one is four. Four plus one is five. Five plus one is six.*, etc., until they have the total number (18).

o Point to the man and May in **B**. Point to the first question bubble and ask: *What's the man asking about?* Learners follow the line from this question to 18, May's answer. (about her pets.) Learners write *pets* on the line in question 1.

Do the same with questions 2 and 3. Point to the yellow line from question 2 to the number 5. Say: *May has five … ?* (mice). Learners write 'mice' on the line in question 2.

Ask: *Which number is the answer to question 3?* (three) Say: *May has three … ?* (monkeys) Learners write 'monkeys' on the line in question 3. Point to question 4 and say: *May has one … .* (cat, dog, giraffe, elephant, hippo, crocodile.) Learners write one of these animals on the line in question 4. In pairs, learners ask and answer the questions in **B**.

C Let's talk about your pets!

o Learners work in A and B pairs (Greta and Jonas). Point to the questions in **C** and say: *(Greta), you ask these two questions about pets. (Jonas), you answer the questions.* Learner A asks and Learner B answers questions about the pets that they have or would like to have.

o Say: *How many pets does this class have?* Learners who have pets come to the board and say and write the pets they have. (For example, *I've got a dog.* The learner writes *one dog* on the board) Continue like this. At the end, add up the numbers and write, for example: *This class has (15) pets.*

D Write the words in the *one* or *two* bag.

> **Starters tip**
> Candidates write nouns in Reading and Writing Part 4 and also in some Reading and Writing Part 5 answers. Some of the nouns are singular and some plural. Make sure they know how to spell singular and plural versions of all Starters nouns.

o Point to the bag labelled 'one'. Ask: *How many crocodiles has May got?* (one)
Say: *Write the word 'crocodile' in this bag.* Learners write *crocodile.*
Point to the bag labelled 'two'. Ask: *How many tigers does May have?* (two) *Write the word 'tigers' in this bag, please. May has two birds. Write the word 'birds' in the bag too!*

o Point to the words in the box. Explain that if a word could follow the number 'one', they write it in the bag that says 'one'. If a word could follow the number 'two' (or higher), they write it in the bag that says 'two'.

> **Check answers:**
> **1:** dress, story, cross, body, family, day, sausage, bee, meatball.
> **2:** beaches, toys, mats, babies, buses, tails, classmates, teddies.

o Explain we add '-s' to most words in English when we talk about two or more things. For example: one tiger, two tigers; one bird, two birds; one bee, three bees.
Say: *tiger, tigers.* Learners repeat the words. Make sure they say the 's' at the end of 'tigers'. Do the same with *bird, birds* and *bee, bees.*

o Write on the board: *one toy, two … .*
Ask a learner to write *toys* on the board after *two.* Write on the board: *ay   ey   oy   uy*
Explain that when a word ends in a vowel (a, e, o, u) plus 'y', we add 's' to the end of it when we talk about two or more toys, etc.

o Write on the board: *one baby   two babies*
Explain that when a word ends in a consonant (for example, 'b', 'd' or 'l') plus 'y', we take the 'y' away and add '-ies'.

Write: *a family, three.* Ask a learner to write *families* on the board after 'three'.

Write: *one … , two teddies.* Point to the line after 'one' and ask: *What do I write here?* (teddy) Ask a learner to write 'teddy' on the board after 'one'.

o Write: *one box, two boxes.* Circle the letters 'es' at the end of 'boxes'. Explain that we add '-es' to words that end in '-s', '-x', '-ch' or '-sh'.
Say: *box, boxes* Learners repeat the words. Make sure they pronounce the '-es' ending in 'boxes' correctly: /ɪz/
Learners say the words. Check pronunciation. Say: *bus, buses   sausage, sausages   beach, beaches*

o Divide learners into two groups: A and B. Learners in group A make the words from the 'one' bag in **D** plural. Learners in group B make the words in the 'two' bag in **D** singular.
Different learners from group A come to the board and say and write the singular forms. Learners from group B come to the board and say and write the plural forms.

o Say: *Listen! Put the sausage in the box! Put the sausage in the box!* Ask: *How many sausages are there?* (one) *How many boxes are there?* (one)
Say: *Listen again! Put the sausages in the boxes! Put the sausages in the boxes! Is there one sausage or more?* (more)
Say: *Put the sausage in the box. Sorry! Put the sausages in the boxes!*

o Say the sentences again. Ask different learners to come to the board and write the next word in the sentence. (Learner 1: Put, Learner 2: the, Learner 3: sausage, Learner 4: in, etc.) Continue until both sentences are on the board.

o In pairs, Learner A says one of the sentences, Learner B listens and says *one sausage* or *more sausages.*

E Look and read. Write *yes* or *no*.
Reading & Writing Part 2

o Point to the picture and say: *This man lives in the house next to May. The TV people are talking to him now.*
His name's Mr Zoo. Can you spell his name? (m-r, z-o-o)
Mr Zoo has lots of animals too! Which animals can you see? (Real animals: three cats, two giraffes, a bird, a frog, a crocodile. Animal statues: a cow, duck, an elephant)

o Read out the first example: *You can see a goat on the man's T-shirt.* Ask: *Which animal is on the man's T-shirt?* (a goat) Say: *This sentence is correct.* Point to the word 'yes' on the line next to this sentence.
Read out the second example: *The door of the house is closed.* Point to the door and ask: *Is this door closed?* (no) Say: *This sentence is wrong.* Point to the word 'no' next to this sentence.

o Say: *Read sentences 1–5. Write 'yes' next to the correct sentences and 'no' next to the wrong sentences.* Learners read and write *yes* or *no.*

> **Check answers: 1** no **2** yes **3** no **4** yes **5** yes

o Say: *Sentence one is wrong. Which word in this sentence is wrong?* (dog – The frog is sitting on the **duck**'s head, not the dog's.)
Say: *Sentence three is not correct. Can you make this sentence correct?* (One cat is sleeping on the **house**, not in the tree.)

o Say: *Look at the pictures in A and E.* Ask learner to find things that are similar and things that are different.
Suggestions:
Similar: two animals in the tree, two animals at the window, four people, one elephant, crocodile
Different: girl/man, blue T-shirt / yellow T-shirt, no animal / goat on T-shirt, two tigers/giraffes at window, door closed/open, monkeys/cats in tree, a frog, a bird, a cow, cat on house, one giraffe / two giraffes, no flowers / flowers in tree, two windows / four windows

67

27 Food I really like!

Topics food and drink

Equipment needed

o An apple and an orange or other fruits that are used to make juice (and which learners are likely to drink).

o Starters audio 27D.

o Colouring pens or pencils.

o Photocopies of the food pictures on pages 113 and 114, made into flashcards. See F.

Ⓐ Bill's big breakfast.

o If you have brought an apple and an orange to class, show these to learners and ask: *Do you like apple juice? Orange juice? What do you like drinking with your breakfast?* Learners answer.

o Learners look at the picture. Say: *This is Bill.*

Point to the food and drink on the tray. Ask: *Where is Bill?* (in his kitchen) *What's on the wall behind him?* (a clock, a cupboard) *What's Bill looking at?* (the food)

Say: *Bill loves eating! Bill wants this food for his breakfast!*

o In pairs, learners draw lines from the blue words to each food item. To check answers, ask: *What's between the bread and the fruit?* (an egg) *What's between the beans and the bread?* (some sweets) *What's behind the juice and next to the beans?* (the peas) *What's between the juice and the egg?* (the fruit)

o Ask: *How many purple grapes are there?* (eight) *How many long sweets can you see?* (four) *How many peas are there?* (seven)

o Ask: *Which words have orange letters?* Write these on the board.

Write on the board the other six food words underlining the two vowels in each one: br<u>ea</u>kfast, fr<u>ui</u>t, p<u>ea</u>s, j<u>ui</u>ce, b<u>ea</u>ns, br<u>ea</u>d. Learners find two words in which the vowel pairs sounds like the /e/ in '<u>e</u>gg'. (br<u>ea</u>kfast, br<u>ea</u>d)

o In pairs, learners find a sound pair with the /uː/ sound in 'f<u>oo</u>d' (fr<u>ui</u>t, j<u>ui</u>ce) and another sound pair the /iː/ sound in 'sw<u>ee</u>ts' (p<u>ea</u>s, b<u>ea</u>ns)

o Say: *Bill eats sweets, peas, beans, fruit juice, bread and an egg for breakfast!*

o Forward chain drill this, for example:

Bill eats sweets.
Bill eats sweets, peas
Bill eats sweets, peas, beans
Bill eats sweets, peas, beans, fruit juice
Bill eats sweets, peas, beans, fruit juice, bread and an
Bill eats sweets, peas, beans, fruit juice, bread and an egg
Bill eats sweets, peas, beans, fruit juice, bread and an egg for breakfast!

o Make sure learners have yellow, red, brown, purple and blue colouring pencils. Say: *Listen and colour.* Read out the instructions, pausing between each one to give learners time to colour five things in the picture if necessary.

o Read out the instructions:

Can you see the clock in Bill's kitchen? Colour the clock yellow, please.
Now the long sweets. Colour the long sweets red. Good. They're red now.
And colour Bill's hair. Colour his hair brown. That's right. Colour it with your brown pencil.
And the peas. Colour the peas green. Can you find your green pencil? Good!
Now colour the cupboard. Can you see it? It's on the wall behind the table. Colour the cupboard blue. Blue is the right colour for that.

o Check answers by asking: *What colour is/are the clock / the sweets / Bill's hair / the grapes/ the cupboard?* Learners point to these things in the picture and say: *yellow/red/brown/purple/blue.*

Ⓑ Write six things that Lucy likes for lunch.

o Point to the picture of the girl. Say: *This is Lucy. Lucy likes food which has the letter 'c' in its word, for example 'ice cream'.*

o Write *ice cream* on the board. Say: *Write ice cream on Lucy's first line.* Tell learners to find five more foods for Lucy in pairs. Each food item should have the letter 'c' somewhere in its spelling. Learners write their food words on the lines. Pairs can look for words in this and previous unit for ideas. Alternatively they can look in their wordlists or dictionaries if they can't think of enough answers.

Suggested answers: cake, candy, carrots, chicken, chips, chocolate, coconut, ice cream, juice, rice.

o Write on the board: *Lucy likes … for lunch.*

Ask different learners to come to the board and write food words with the letter 'c' in, in the gap.

Point out that 'ce' in 'ice' and 'juice', sounds like /s/ and 'ca' in 'carrot', 'cake' and 'co' in 'coconut', the 'c' sounds like /k/.

Ⓒ Dan's funny dinner.

o Learners look at the picture. Point to the eggs and ask: *What are these?* (eggs) Point to the basket with the letters for 'eggs' and to the word 'eggs' on the lines.

o Learners look at the other food on the table, follow the lines from the food items to the baskets and unjumble the letters to write the words.

Check answers:				
2 bread	**3** apples	**4** burger	**5** potatoes	**6** pineapple

o Write on the board: *Dan's having … for dinner.* Leave a big gap in the middle of the sentence. Point to the gap and ask: *Which words can I write here?* (bread, eggs, apples, burger, potatoes, pineapple) Write the words in the gap in the sentence on the board:

Dan's having eggs, bread, apples, a burger, potatoes and pineapple for dinner.

o Underline the double letters in the words. (*Dan's having e<u>gg</u>s, bread, a<u>pp</u>les, a burger, potatoes and pineapple for di<u>nn</u>er.*) Point to the underlined words and say: *These words have double letters in them.* Ask different learners to spell the words, using the word 'double'. For example: *Dinner: d – i – double n – e – r.*

o Ask the whole class, then different learners, to say the sentence about Dan.

o Challenge learners to write, then say, all three sentences about Bill's breakfast, Lucy's lunch and Dan's dinner!

Bill eats sweets, peas, beans, fruit juice, bread and an egg for breakfast!

Lucy likes cakes, candies, carrots, chicken, chips and chocolate for lunch!

Dan's having eggs, bread, apples, a burger, potatoes and pineapple for dinner!

D 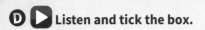 Listen and tick the box.   Listening Part 3

o Learners look at the questions and pictures in **D**. Ask: *What food can you see?* They put up their hands to answer. (chicken, rice, chips/fries, potatoes, meatballs, burgers, sausages, egg, bread, fish, peas, kiwi pie, apple pie, ice cream) *Which drinks can you see?* (orange juice, milk, lemonade, tomato juice, pineapple juice)

o Say: *Look at the pictures and listen to people talking. Tick the correct boxes.*

o Play the audio stopping after the example. Learners listen. Ask: *Why is C the correct answer?* Learners try to remember. Say: *Mum says, We've got chicken and … ?* (rice). *Kim says, Can we have some orange … ?* (juice) Ask: *Does Mum say yes or no?* (yes)

o Play the rest of the audio. Learners tick the correct boxes. In pairs, learners could look at each other's answers before they listen to the audio the second time to carefully check their answers.

Check answers:
1 B **2** A **3** B **4** C **5** A

Audioscript

Look at the pictures. Listen and look. There is one example.
What can Kim have for lunch?
Boy: What can we have for lunch, Mum? Have we got potatoes?
Woman: No, we've got chicken and rice!
Boy: Great! Can I have some orange juice, too?
Woman: Yes, Kim!
Can you see the tick? Now you listen and tick the box.

One   *What's May's favourite meat?*
Man: What's your favourite meat, May? Is it sausages?
Girl: No, I don't like them.
Man: Do you like eating meatballs?
Girl: No, I don't, but I really love burgers. Those are my favourite!

Two   *What does Alex want for breakfast today?*
Woman: Do you want some bread for breakfast, Alex?
Boy: Not today. I'd like an egg, please.
Woman: OK. And do you want some milk too?
Boy: No thank you, Mum.

Three   *What can Hugo have for dinner?*
Boy: Can I have fish for dinner, Dad?
Man: Yes, Hugo. You can have some peas too.
Boy: Great! And can I have some fries?
Man: Sorry! Not today.

Four   *Which drink does Anna like?*
Man: Which drink do you like, Anna? Do you like pineapple juice?
Girl: Yes, but I don't like lemonade.
Man: Oh. Do you like tomato juice, too?
Girl: No, but my dad likes that.

Five   *Which is Sue's favourite?*
Woman: What's that, Sue? Is that apple pie?
Girl: No. It's coconut ice cream. It's for my lunch.
Woman: Is that your favourite?
Girl: No. Kiwi pie is my favourite!

E Listen and write the food and drink.

o Learners look at the table. They listen to the food and drink words that you read out (see below). They write the words under 'like' or 'don't like' headings. If learners have never tasted a food, they can write that word under the 'I don't know' heading. Pause between each word and help with spellings if necessary.

Food and drink words:
sausages, watermelon, ice cream, fish, meat, bananas, carrots, orange juice, chicken, tomatoes, onions, peas, coconut, burgers, pears, mangoes, juice, beans, rice, limes, eggs, carrots, cakes, milk, water, kiwis, meatballs, apple pie.

o Tell learners that you have also completed this table. Learners take turns to guess one food or drink that you wrote in the 'like' or 'don't like' columns. Stop when learners have correctly guessed four likes/dislikes. For example: *You like carrots, ice cream, tomatoes and coconut. You don't like eggs, fish, milk and mangoes.*

o In pairs, learners continue this guessing game, trying to guess their partner's likes/dislikes.

F Play lots of games with food!

Put the pictures in order.
Learners work in pairs. Give each pair the photocopies of food pictures from pages 113 and 114. Learners then group foods and drinks:

1 in alphabetical order
     beans, bread, burger, cake, chicken, egg, fish, fruit, ice cream, lemonade, milk, orange juice, rice, sausages, water

2 in groups of the same number of letters in their words
     egg (3 letters); cake, fish, milk, rice (4 letters); beans, bread, fruit, water (5 letters); burger (6 letters); chicken (7 letters); ice cream, lemonade, sausages (8 letters); orange juice (11 letters)

3 in order from small to big (food only)

Suggestion: rice, bean, egg, cake, sausage, burger, ice cream, fish, bread, chicken

Which one is missing?
See page 8 for how to play this.

Run to the food and eat it.
o Choose 7–8 learners and give each of them a different picture card. For example: a banana, an apple, a drink of milk, juice, etc.

o Learners stand in different parts of the room. Say one of the food or drink items, for example: *banana*.

o Large classes: all the learners without pictures run to the learner who has the picture of the banana and mime eating a banana.
   Small classes: everyone runs to the learner with the picture of a banana and mimes eating a banana.

o Continue with the other food and drink items.

o After a while, change the pictures.

28   My favourite food day

Topics food and drink

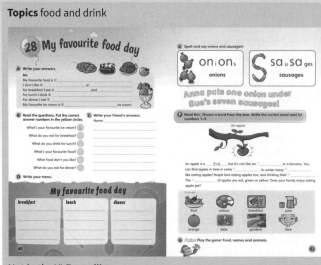

Not in the YLE wordlists: *menu*

Equipment needed

○ Colouring pencils or pens.

○ A larger sheet of paper or coloured card per group of four. See D.

A Write your answers.

○ Ask: *What food do you like? Do you like chocolate cake? Bananas*?

In pairs, learners ask and answer. Ask 2–3 pairs: *What food does (Tuncay/Adriana) like?* Write a few answers on the board. Teach popular food and drink words if learners don't already know them, for example: pizza, pasta, strawberry (ice cream), cola.

○ Learners draw pictures of their favourite food in their notebooks and write, for example, *I ♥ pizza.* under their drawing.

○ Learners look at **A**. On the board, write your own answers for the gaps, for example:

1 chicken   2 beans, sausages   3 eggs, bread   4 water   5 rice 6 lemon

○ Learners point to the sentences as you read your completed answers out. Pause before and after adding your own food word answers, for example:

My favourite food is … chicken …. I don't like … beans … or … sausages ….

○ In pairs, learners plan their answers, then each learner completes the text with their own answers.

B Put the correct answer numbers in the yellow circles.

○ Choose one A and B pair to help explain this task.

Ask Learner B to read out the first question in **B**: *What's your favourite ice cream?*

Ask Learner A to find and read out the answer to this question (in **A**): *My favourite ice cream is (chocolate) ice cream!*

Say: *Ask and answer the question again.* Learners B and A ask and answer the question.

○ Point to the last answer in **A** and ask: *Can you see a number in that circle? What is it?* (6). Point to the number 6 in the yellow circle at the end of the question in **B**. Make sure learners have understood that they need to match the questions with the answers this way.

○ In pairs, learners look at the other questions in **B** and find their matching answers in **A**. At the end of each question, they write the numbers 1–5 in the yellow circles to show the matching pair.

Check answers:
(top to bottom) ③ ④ ① ⑤ ②

C Write your friend's answers.

○ Learners work in pairs. They write their partner's name on the top line.

○ Learners read the questions in **B** in the order that they appear and write their partner's answer on the same line but under his/her name. Say: *Write one or two words in each answer* (for example: *What do you eat for breakfast?*) *bread, milk.*

Stronger classes:

Continuing in pairs, learners choose two more food questions and answers using 'our' or 'we' and write these on a piece of paper. Write suggestions on the board for pairs to complete:

What are our favourite …………? Our favourite ………… are …………

What are we making? We're making …………

What do we eat for …………? We eat …………

What do we drink for …………? We drink …………

Pairs take it in turns to ask the rest of the class one of their questions. 3–4 learners try to guess the pair's own answer, for example:

Learners A and B: *What are our favourite fruits?*

Learner C: *Bananas and pineapples?*

Learners A and B: *No!*

Learner D: *Bananas and oranges?*

Learners A and B: *Oranges are one of our favourite fruits.*

Learner E: *Oranges and grapes?*

Learners A and B: *Yes! Our favourite fruits are oranges and grapes.*

D Write your menu.

For your class level and size, choose from options 1 or 2.

1

○ Learners write a menu of their favourite food and drink. Help with vocabulary if necessary. Learners work in groups of four taking turns to read out their menu. The group votes for the best menu and reads that out to the rest of the class.

2

○ Learners work in groups of four. They produce a menu on a larger sheet of paper using all their favourite food and drink options. They can decorate the menu and add prices if they like. If necessary, learners can find food ideas in unit 25 and from menus in unit 17.

Options:

○ If learners haven't created their own menu, copy the menu idea from unit 17 and give that to each group to use here.

Learners continue to work in groups of four. Groups choose one learner to be a waiter and the three others to be customers who are coming into a café. Help groups take turns to role play their café scenes at the front of the class.

1 The customers mime opening a door and say: *Hello!, Hi!* or *Good morning/afternoon!*

2 The waiter says: *Hello!, Hi!* or *Good morning/afternoon!* and then shows the customers to the table.

3 The customers sit down. The waiter gives them their menu and the customers say *Thank you!*

4 The waiter says to each customer: *What would you like to eat/drink?*

5 The customers reply with their choices.

6 The waiter mimes writing down the order, says: *Thank you* and leaves the scene.

E Spell and say *onions* and *sausages!*

o   Teach/revise 'onions' and 'sausages'.

o   Ask: *Who likes onions? Put up your hands!* Learners count the 'yes' answers. Ask: *How many children like onions?* Learners answer.

o   Learners look at the letter pattern for 'onions'. Build the word with the learners by writing in big letters on the board: on_ on_. Then write in the "*i* and the '*s*' in smaller letters.

o   Ask: *Who likes sausages? Put up your hands!* Learners count the 'yes' answers. Ask: *How many children like sausages?* Learners answer.

o   Learners look at the letter pattern for *sausages*. Build the word with the learners by writing in big letters on the board: sa_ sa___. Then write in the *u* and the *ges* in smaller letters.

o   Learners draw onions and sausages and copy each of the letter patterns in their notebooks. This will help them to remember the spellings.

o   Check the pronunciation of both words. Show learners that the two 'on's in 'onions' and the two 'sa's in 'sausages' do NOT sound the same.
    Say: **on***ions,* stressing the first syllable   /ˈʌnjənz/
    Say: **sau***sages,* stressing the first syllable   /ˈsɒsədʒɪz/

o   Read out the tongue twister. Learners repeat it in a chain:
    Anna puts one onion under Sue's seven sausages!
    If you would like to practise other numbers, colours or names and can bring other food items into class, hold these up (or use flashcards) to prompt different tongue twisters, for example:
    Pat puts one onion under Tom's twenty tomatoes!
    Peter puts a potato under Sue's seven sausages!
    Sam puts six sausages under Ben's black beans!
    Grace puts green grapes under Fred's fourteen fries!
    Lucy puts eleven lemons under Bill's baby's bread!
    Anna puts an apple under Fred's four fish!
    Jack puts some juice under Charlie's children's chips!
    Stronger learners could create their own tongue twisters using names, numbers and food words and illustrate them. If possible, display the tongue twisters on a classroom wall.

F Read this. Choose a word from the box. Write the correct word next to numbers 1–5.

Reading & Writing Part **4**

> **Starters tip**
> In Reading and Writing Part 4, there are five gaps but eight options. Make sure candidates understand that of these three extra words, one is the example and two are wrong words for this text.

o   Say: *Close your eyes! You are not boys and girls now. You are apples! Where are you? What colour are you? Who eats you?* Different learners answer.

o   Learners look at the text. Point to the gaps. Say: *The words are in the box. You can see pictures of the words there too! Look!*

o   Ask: *How many words must you choose?* (five) Learners count the number of words in the box. Ask: *Are there five?* (no) *six?* (no) *seven?* (no) *eight?* (yes). Say: *So three of these words aren't answers for questions 1–5.*
    Ask: *Which word is correct for the example? Is an apple a fruit, colours, breakfast, juice, an orange, birds, a garden or a face?* (a fruit) Point to 'fruit' in the text. Learners could cross out 'fruit' in the word box.

o   In pairs, learners find the other missing words and write them in the text.

> **Check answers:**
> **1** orange   **2** gardens   **3** birds   **4** juice   **5** colours

Optional extension:

Learners each draw a picture of an apple. They could give it a face and colour it. If possible, learners cut their apples out. Tell learners to put their funny apples in different places. Use 'on', for example: *Put the apple **on** your hand / nose / foot / your friend's head / your desk / the floor / your book.*

G Play the game! Food, names and animals.

Note: Large classes (over 20 learners): divide learners into groups of 3–4. Smaller classes: learners play in pairs.

o   Write the following table on the board:

	food	names	animals
B			
L			
M			
C			
F			
S			
E			
T			

o   Learners copy the table into their notebooks. Tell them they will need a whole page for this.

o   Ask: *Do you know a food that begins with the letter 'b'?* (banana, bean, bread, burger)

o   Learners write their choice of food that begins with 'b' next to B in the food column.

o   Learners continue working together, choosing a name and an animal that also begin with the letter 'b' first. They then complete the table choosing and then writing words that begin with the other letters.

o   The first group or pair to complete the table calls out *Stop!* Alternatively, you could set a time limit for each letter of one to two minutes.

o   Learners take turns to read out their words. For each correct answer that is correctly spelled, the group or pair receives two points. For words which are not correctly spelled, they get one point. At the end of the game, the points are counted. The group or pair with the most points are the winners.

Suggested answers:

B	banana	Ben	bird
L	lemon	Lucy	lizard
M	mango	May	monkey
C	cake	Charlie	crocodile
F	fruit	Fred	frog
S	sausage	Sam	snake
E	egg	Emma	elephant
T	tomato	Tom	tiger

29 We're in the toy shop today

Topics places, toys, colours, numbers

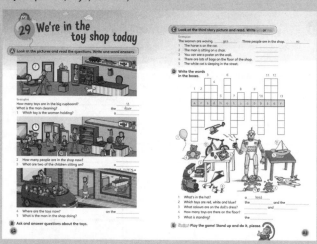

Equipment needed

○ A ball. See D.

(A) Look at the pictures and read the questions. Write one-word answers.

Reading & Writing Part 5

> **Starters tip**
>
> In Reading and Writing Part 5, candidates answer different questions that might begin with: *What … ?, Where … ?, Which … ?, Who … ?, What colour … ?, How many … ?* Make sure they understand what information each question is asking for.

○ Ask: *Do you like going to toy shops? Who do you go with? Do you play with some toys or games at home?* Learners answer.

Ask: *What's your favourite toy or game?* Learners answer the last question in pairs. Ask different learners: *What's your friend's favourite toy or game?* Learners could vote for the best toy or game at the moment.

○ Point to the first picture in **A**. Ask: *What's this?* (a toy shop) Learners work in pairs to find seven things in the picture that start with 'c'. Pairs put up their hands to show they can see the seven things.

> **Check answers:**
>
> car, cat, chair, clock, clothes, computer, crocodile

○ Ask questions: *What toys can you see?* (a plane, balls, a truck, a horse) *Is the shop open?* (no) *What colour is the cat?* (white) *What's on the floor between the man and the woman?* (a box of toys) *How many chairs can you see?* (two).

○ Learners look at the two example questions. Ask: *Are the answers right?* (yes). *How many toys are on the small cupboard?* (two) *What are they?* (a boat and a ball) *Is the floor in this toy shop dirty now?* (no)

○ Learners work on their own or in pairs and answer questions 1–5.

> **Check answers:**
>
> **1** ball **2** 11/eleven **3** horse **4** car **5** sleeping

○ Point to the man in the third picture. Say: *This is Mr Homes.* Yawn to teach 'tired'.

Say: *Let's tell this story now.*

Tell the story, stopping for different learners to add a word (in brackets here) before you continue.

This is Mr and Mrs Homes' toy (shop). In the morning, Mr Homes cleans the (floor) and Mrs Homes puts toys in the big (cupboard).

In the afternoon, Mrs Lime and her (children) come to the toy shop. Two of her children are playing on a (horse). One girl is sitting on a chair. She's playing with a (doll). Mr Homes is holding lots of (boxes). Mrs Lime has three big, blue (bags) with lots of toys in them.

It's the end of the day now. Mrs Lime and her children are in their (car). They have lots of toys! Mrs Homes is waving and saying (Goodbye) and (Thank you!) Behind her legs is the (cat). The cat's name is (learners choose!)

But Mr Homes isn't with Mrs Homes or the cat. He's on his chair. He's very tired. Shhhh! He's (sleeping)!

(B) Ask and answer questions about the toys.

○ In pairs, learners choose their favourite picture. Ask: *Who likes picture 1? Put up your hands. Who likes picture 2? And picture 3?* Learners could then go and sit with others in the class who like the same picture best.

Ask: *How many toys can you see in your favourite picture?* Learners count and answer.

○ Say to the whole class: *Now look at picture 2 and answer these questions.*

Write on the board:

Which toy is next to the window?

Which toys are the girls playing with?

Which toys are the boys playing with?

Which toys are in the cupboard?

Which toys are on the floor?

Which toys are in the mother's bags?

○ Learners work in pairs to find the answers in the picture. They write the answers in their notebooks. Walk round and help with vocabulary and spellings if necessary.

○ Read out the questions. Different pairs answer.

I'd like to

○ Say: *You are in a toy shop now. Close your eyes. Can you see lots of toys? Which toy is your favourite?* Learners open their eyes.

Write on the board: *I'd like to play with …*

Learners take turns to tell everyone else in the class what they want to play with in their imaginary toy shop.

For example:

Learner A: *I'd like to play with the toy train.*

Learner B: *I'd like to play with the computer game.*

Learner C: *I'd like to play with the toy cat.*

Class activity:

Children each find 3–4 pictures of exciting toys and bring them to school. They could find these online and print them or cut them out from catalogues or magazines. In groups, they create a collage of their toys and label them and give each toy a mark out of ten! The collages could be displayed on the classroom wall.

(C) Look at the third story picture and read. Write *yes* or *no*.

Reading & Writing Part 2

○ Tell learners to look at the last picture in **A** again. Say: *Now look at the sentences in C.* Read out the first example: *The women are waving.* Ask: *Is that correct?* (yes) Ask one learner to read out the second example: *Three people are in the shop?* Ask: *Is that correct?* (no) *How many people are in the shop in picture 3?* (one) *What's that person's name?* (Mr Homes).

○ Learners read sentences 1–5 and write *yes* or *no* answers.

> **Check answers:**
>
> **1** yes **2** yes **3** no **4** no **5** no

○ Point to the boxes on the floor in the third picture and say: *These aren't paper bags, they're paper …* (boxes)

Point to the cat and say: *This cat isn't sleeping. It's …* (standing)

D Write the words in the boxes.

o Point to the picture in **D.** Say: *This is a toy shop too.* Ask: *Which toys can you see in picture 1 in A and in this picture*? (boats, dolls, planes, trucks)

o Learners look at the crossword. Ask: *How many numbers can you see?* (13)
  In pairs, learners look at the number on each toy in the picture and write its word under the same number in the crossword, using the letters from 'a red helicopter' in the puzzle to help them.

> **Check answers:**
> **1** balloon **2** train **3** alien **4** teddy **5** hat **6** game **7** lorry
> **8** kite **9** doll **10** plane **11** boat **12** bike **13** robot

Note: Remind learners that 'lorry' and 'truck' mean the same thing. 'Truck' is used more in American English and 'lorry' in British English.

o Ask: *What colour is the balloon?* (yellow). Say: *1, 2, 3, 4, 5, 6, 7, 8, 9 … What number is next?* (ten) Say: *Look at the number ten on the plane.* Say: *1, 2, 3, 4, 5, 6, 7, 8, 9, 10 … What number is next?* (11) Ask different learners: *What next?* until the class has counted to 20.
  Name one of the things in the picture, for example: *kite.* Ask: *What number is on the kite?* (eight) Learners continue asking questions like this in pairs.

o Say: *Can you see a guitar in this picture?* (no) *Draw a guitar in your picture now.* Learners draw a guitar in the picture wherever they like. Ask three or four learners: *Where's your guitar?*
  Learners answer, for example: *My guitar is in front of the kite.*

o Point to the teddy in the picture. Say: *What's this toy? Young children like playing with this. It's got arms and legs, but it's not a doll.* (a teddy / teddy bear) *Let's put another teddy bear in this picture! It can hold the yellow balloon! Draw your teddy there now , next to the teddy in the picture.* Learners draw a teddy bear holding the yellow balloon.

Prepositions of place.

o Pick up the ball you have brought to the class. Put the ball in different positions in relation to your bag, or a learner's bag. Each time you place the ball, say a sentence about it, for example: *My ball is on my bag. My ball is … ?* (under Toni's bag).

o Continue until you have practised all these prepositions: behind, between, in, in front of, next to, on, under.

o Tell learners to put a pencil in different places, for example:
  Put your pencil behind your head, under your arm, on your nose, next to your ear, in your hand, between your feet, in front of your friend.

o Learners look at the toys and the bike in picture **D**. Ask them *Where … ?* questions, for example: *Where's the board game?* (on the table)

o Say these sentences about the toys and bike. Learners point to and name the object.
  1 *It's under the white table.* (the kite)
  2 *It's in the hat.* (the boat)
  3 *It's between the tables.* (the robot)
  4 *It's in front of the robot.* (the doll)
  5 *It's behind the white table.* (the bike)
  6 *It's in front of the brown table.* (the plane)

o Read the first question: *What's in the hat?* (a boat) Point to the example answer 'boat' on the line next to question 1.

o In pairs, learners write the answers to the other questions on the lines.

> **Check answers:**
> **2** kite, plane **3** pink, white **4** 6/six **5** robot

E Play the game! Stand up and do it, please.

o Write on the board: *Sit on the chair.* Ask learners to say this sentence.
  Learners: *Sit on the chair.*
  Teacher: *Pardon?*

o Write *please* on the end of the sentence on the board: *Sit on the chair, please.* Ask learners to say the sentence: *Sit on the chair, please.*

o Say: *I'm going to tell you to do different things. If I say 'please', do the action. If I don't say 'please', don't do it.*
  Suggestions: (Say *please* sometimes but not at the end of every sentence!) Learners who do the things when you haven't said *please* are out of the game!
  Stand between two chairs.
  Put your foot under a chair.
  Walk behind your teacher.
  Stand in front of your desk.
  Put your pen in your bag.
  Put your hand under your book.
  Put your hands on your ears.
  Put one hand under your nose.
  Put your schoolbag on your desk.
  Smile.
  Open your book.
  Put a pencil on your book.
  Pick up your pencil.
  Close your book.
  Clap your hands.

30 Monsters in the park

Topics the home, colours, names

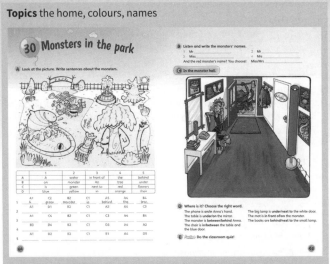

Equipment needed

o Colouring pens or pencils and A5 pieces of card or paper (two for each learner). See A.

o Scissors, photocopies of page 109 (one for each learner and one for yourself) and an envelope for each learner. See C.

A Look at the picture. Write sentences about the monsters.

o Learners look at the picture. Ask questions and encourage longer answers: *How many monsters can you see?* (I can see five monsters.) *Where are these monsters? Are they in a school?* (No, they aren't.) *Are they on a beach?* (No, they aren't.) *Are they at home?* (No, they aren't.) *Are they in a park?* (Yes, they are!)

o Say: *Find words to make sentences about these monsters. Look at the numbers, letters and the blue words under the picture.* To check understanding, point to the blue example sentence: A1 = *A*, C2 = *green*, B2 = *monster*, C1 = *is*, A5 = *behind*, A4 = *the*, B4 = *tree*

o In pairs, learners use the code to write sentences 2–5.

> **Check answers:**
> 2 A blue monster is in front of the flowers.
> 3 A red monster is next to the tree.
> 4 An orange monster is in the water.
> 5 A yellow monster is on the chair.

o Using their green, blue, red, orange and yellow pencils, learners colour the monsters in the picture.

Yes or *no*?

o Each learner makes two cards to hold up. One says *yes* and the other says *no*. Say: *Listen to sentences about these monsters. Show me the right answer.*
To check understanding, practise with one 'yes' and 'no' answer.
Say: *One of the monsters is red!* Pairs quickly decide if the answer is 'yes' or 'no' then show their 'yes' card.
Say: *The orange monster is in the tree!* Pairs show their 'no' card.
Say the following sentences about the monsters. Learners now work on their own, showing their 'yes' card if the sentence is right or their 'no' card if the sentence is wrong.

(Alternatively, learners could call out *yes/no* answers.)
Sentences:
1 *You can see a green monster behind the tree.* (yes)
2 *A pink monster is having a bath in the water.* (no)
3 *One of the monsters is purple.* (no)
4 *The yellow monster is sitting in the tree.* (no)
5 *An orange monster is swimming.* (yes)
6 *The blue monster has got some food and drink.* (yes)

o Ask: *Where are the monsters? What are the monsters doing?* Learners look for a minute at the coloured picture. They don't answer the questions but try to remember where the different monsters are and what they are doing.

o Learners close their books. Say the sentences 1–6 about the monsters again but in a different order. Each learner shows if the sentence is right or wrong by holding up their 'yes' or 'no' cards again. Every time a learner shows the correct answer, they get a point. The winners are the learners with the most points.
Note: If you have space in the classroom, instead of using the cards, you could ask learners to move to one side of the room for *yes* answers and the other side of the room for *no* answers.

Optional extension:
If your learners enjoy colouring and drawing, they could draw another monster in the picture and colour it and colour the rest of the picture too.

B Listen and write the monsters' names.

Note: To improve spelling, each learner could write words they find difficult on small cards. They could keep these in an envelope. On the front of their envelope, learners could write 'I'm good at spelling!' or 'Spelling is easy!'
Learners take out their cards and look at them from time to time. Ask learners to look at their cards and then turn them over and spell or write the words. They could then check their own spellings by looking at the words on the cards again.

o Write on the board: Mr   Mrs   Miss
Ask: *Which of these do we use for a man?* (Mr)
Which do we use for a woman? (Mrs, Miss)
Say: *I'm Mr/Mrs/Miss (Robinson).* Ask different learners: *What's your name?* (They answer, for example: *Miss/Mr Garcia*.) Learners then ask and answer each other in pairs.

o Say: *I'm going to tell you the monsters' names.* Learners listen and write the names next to numbers 1–4.
1 *Can you see the orange monster? His name's Mr Pink. That's funny!*
Mr Pink is in the water. You spell his name: P-I-N-K. P-I-N-K.
2 *There's a yellow monster with four legs. The yellow monster's name is Mr Enjoys. Yes! It's Mr Enjoys. E-N-J-O-Y-S. That's right. E-N-J-O-Y-S.*
3 *There's a funny monster in front of the house. That's Miss Bath. Yes! Her name's Miss Bath. B-A-T-H. Listen again. B-A-T-H.*
4 *And that green monster behind the tree is Mrs Duck. Mrs Duck is a funny name for this monster. You spell her name: D-U-C-K. D-U-C-K.*

o Point to the red monster in picture **A**. Learners decide if she's 'Mrs' or 'Miss', then choose a name for her and write it on the line.

o Ask different learners to say and spell the name they wrote for the red monster. Write the different names on the board.

o When you have written all their names, learners decide on the best name for her.

C In the monster hall.   Speaking Parts 1,2,3

> **Starters tip**
>
> In Speaking Part 1, candidates see eight object cards. They need to identify and place two cards in a big picture. In Part 3, they need to answer 12 questions about four other cards. Two of the cards are not used. Make sure learners fully understand what will happen in the test.

o   Give out a photocopy of page 109 and an envelope to each learner. Learners cut up the cards.

Say: *Find pictures of the piano, clock, radio, guitar, box, TV, chocolate and game. Put these eight pictures on your desk next to your book.*

Learners put the other pictures in their envelope.

Note: For the following activities, check learners are pointing to the correct part of the picture. Then check they are placing the correct object card in the right place. Walk round the classroom as you give the following instructions.

o   Point to the hall picture and say: *Look! Miss Bath, the blue monster, isn't in the park now. She's coming into the hall. The monsters live here with Anna. Miss Bath likes cleaning!*

1

o   Point to the table and say: *Here's the table.*

Ask learners: *Where's the mirror?* Learners point to the mirror. (They can say: *The mirror is here. / It's on the wall.*)

Ask: *Where are the lamps?* Learners point to the two lamps. (They can say: *Here and here. / One is on the (hall) table and one is next to the (bathroom) door.*)

o   Show learners the eight object pictures, one by one. Ask: *Which is the box?* Learners point to the box when they see it. Say: *I'm putting the box on the rug. You do that too!*

Learners put their box on the rug in their picture of the hall. Say: *Now put the box under the table.* Learners put the box under the table in their hall picture. (Learners leave the box card and the two following object cards on the picture.)

o   Show learners the other seven object pictures, one by one. Ask: *Which is the radio?* Learners point to the radio when you show the radio card. Say: *Pick up your radio. Put the radio on the bathroom door.* Learners put the radio card on the bathroom door.

o   Show the remaining five object pictures (the piano, guitar, TV, chocolate and game). Ask: *Which is the chocolate?* Learners point to the chocolate. Say: *Pick up your chocolate. Put the chocolate in front of the girl.* Learners put the chocolate card in front of the girl.

2

o   Point to the brown jacket in the hall picture. Ask: *What's this?* (a jacket)

What colour is it? (brown) How *many jackets are there?* (two)

o   Point to the girl in the picture. Ask: *What's the girl doing?* (talking/ phoning/smiling)

3

o   Point to the monster and say: *Tell me about this monster.* (She's blue. She's got a read hat. She's funny. She likes cleaning things. Her arms are very long.)

o   Hold up the small picture card of the piano. Ask: *What's this?* (a piano)

Can you play the piano? (yes/no) *What colour is your/this piano?* (black and white)

o   Hold up the small picture card of the television. Ask: *What's this?* (a TV/television) *Do you like watching TV?* (yes/no) *Where's the television in your house?* (in the living room / kitchen/bedroom, etc.)

o   Hold up the picture of the game. Ask: *What's this?* (a board game) *Do you play board games?* (yes/no) *Who do you play board games with?* (my friend/sister, etc.)

o   Hold up the picture of the guitar. Ask: *What's this?* (a guitar) *Can you play the guitar?* (yes/no) *What's your favourite song?*

o   Learners put all the object pictures back in the envelope with the others. You could collect the envelopes and keep them in a box for other activities. (See page 8 for ideas.)

D Where is it? Choose the right word.

o   Learners work in pairs. Say: *Look at the hall picture again. Look at the seven sentences and choose the right word.* Learners cross out the wrong word in each sentence.

Check answers by asking different pairs to read out one of their correct sentences.

The phone is **in** Anna's hand. The big lamp is **next to** the white door. The table is **under** the mirror. The mat is **in front of** the monster. The monster is **behind** Anna. The books are **next to** the small lamp. The chair is **between** the table and the blue door.

o   If your classroom has enough space, ask learners to gather together in a tight crowd. Write on the board: *next to   behind in front of   between*

Pointing to one or two of the prepositions on the board, ask each learner one or two of the following questions: *Who are you next to? Who is behind you? Who is in front of you? Who are you between?* Learners answer using their classmates' names.

E Do the classroom quiz!

o   Learners work in teams of 3–4. Each team needs a piece of paper and a pen or pencil.

o   Ask questions about the class and classroom. Teams whisper and write short answers (one or two words), for example: *What's on my desk?* Learners write: *books* or *your books* or *pens, books*. Teams write their answers anywhere on the paper. Answers shouldn't be numbered or ordered.

Questions:

What's in your bag?

What's on your desk?

How many children are in your class?

Is your teacher a man or a woman?

How many desks are in our classroom?

What can you see on the wall?

What colour is the board?

How many windows are there?

Is the door open or closed?

What colour is the floor?

Where are your crayons?

o   When you have asked all the questions, teams swap their answers. Ask the questions again one by one in a different order. After each question ask: *What's the answer?*

Teams quickly find the answer to your question (which will be anywhere on the page) and then put up their hands to tell you the answer. Most answers will be the same but accept any differences if they are correct.

31   Coming and going

Topics transport, colours

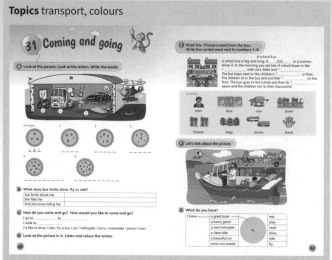

Movers words: *by* (prep), *town;* **Flyers word:** *wheel*

Equipment needed

o   Colouring pencils or pens. See D and G.

o   Three cards with questions on them. See C.

A   Look at the picture. Look at the letters. Write the words.

Reading & Writing Part 3

> **Starters tip**
>
> Candidates often lose marks in Reading and Writing because they do not check their spelling. Practise looking at words that are often misspelled (for example, *camera, clock*, etc.) and correcting them. In Reading and Writing Part 3, candidates should check that they have used all the jumbled letters in each of their answers.

o   Point to the car in the picture in **A** and ask: *What's this?* (a car) Point to the letters inside the wheel in the example and say: *c-a-r spells … ?* (car). Point to the word 'car' on the lines in the example.

Learners look at the numbered pictures and at the letters in the other wheels. They write the words on the lines. Remind learners to cross out the letters in the wheels as they use them.

Before you check answers, tell learners to check their spelling of all the words. Tell them to check that they have the same letters in their words as the letters in the wheels. They can look at their partner's answers to check that theirs are the same.

> **Check answers:**
>
> **1** bike   **2** plane   **3** lorry   **4** motorbike   **5** helicopter

o   Ask learners which word means the same as 'lorry' (truck). Learners write *truck* under 'lorry' in 3.

B   What does Sue Smile drive, fly or ride?

o   Point to the woman in the helicopter in the picture in **A** and say: *This is Sue Smile. She loves flying, riding and driving! What's she flying?* (a helicopter)

Say: *Today, Sue's flying a helicopter, but some days she flies her …* (point to the plane) (plane)
What does Sue drive? (a car, a lorry/truck)
What does she ride? (a bike, a motorbike)

Learners write *car* and *lorry/truck* in the box after 'Sue Smile drives her … '. They write *plane or helicopter* in the second box and *motorbike and bike* in the last box.

o   Point to the picture in **A** and ask questions: *What colour's the plane?* (pink) *What's green?* (the motorbike) *What's behind the plane?* (a/the car) *What colour's the truck?* (yellow)

C   How do you come and go? How would you like to come and go?

o   Ask different learners: *How do you come to school?* (by bus / by car / I walk) *How do you go home?* (by bus / by car / I walk) *How do you go to Madrid/Istanbul?* Say the name of a big city in your learners' country, for example: *How do you go to Madrid/Istanbul?* (I go by train/plane/bus/car.) Learners complete the first sentence by writing a place on the first line and the kind of transport on the second line.

Ask: *Where do you walk? Do you walk to school? Do you walk to the bookshop? To the bread shop?* Learners write the place they walk to on the line in the second sentence.

o   Say: *I can drive. But I can't fly a plane or a helicopter. I'd like to fly a helicopter! And you? What would you like to do? Choose! Circle the words for you!* Learners circle the verb and kind of transport in the third sentence.

Tell learners to practise saying their last sentence. They should try to remember it.

o   Give a learner a card with: *What would you like to drive?*

Give another learner a card with: *What would you like to fly?*

And a third learner a card with: *What would you like to ride?*

The three learners stand up and read out their question.

o   Everyone in the class stands up. Learners who would like to drive go to the person who asked the driving question and say: *I'd like to drive a bus/car/lorry/train.* Learners who would like to fly a helicopter or plane go and tell the person who asked the flying question. *I'd like to fly a helicopter/plane.* Learners who would like to ride a motorbike tell the person who asked the riding question. *I'd like to ride a motorbike.*

o   The three people who asked the questions say what they would like to do. They move groups if necessary. Learners form groups according to the kind of transport they would like to try.

Write on the board: *We'd like to … .*

Each group of learners then completes and says the sentence for them. For example: *We would like to drive a lorry.*

D   Look at the picture in A. Listen and colour the smiles.

o   Point to the woman in the picture in **A** and ask: *What's Sue's family name?* (Smile) *Can you find the seven smiles in the picture in A?* (on the wall, under the helicopter, in the picture, on the car, plane and lorry/truck, on the balloon)

Ask: *Which smile is blue?* (The smile on the balloon!)

Say: *Listen and colour five smiles!* Read out the sentences below twice, giving learners time to colour the smiles.

1   *Can you see the smile under the helicopter? Colour that smile green, please! Yes, green!*

2   *There's a smile on the plane. Can you make it black? Colour the smile on the plane black.*

3   *There's a smile on the car too! It's a really small smile. Make it red, please! A red smile on the car. That's right!*

4   *Now, find the big smile on the wall. It's behind the bike. Can you see it? Colour the smile on the wall yellow. Yes, yellow!*

5   *Right! The smile on the lorry. Colour the smile on the lorry pink. Make it pink! Thank you!*

> **Check answers:**
>
> **1** smile under helicopter – green   **2** smile on plane – black
> **3** smile on car – red   **4** smile on picture – yellow
> **5** smile on lorry – pink

E Read this. Choose a word from the box. Write the correct word next to numbers 1–5.

o Write on the board: 1 _ _ _ _ and _ _ _ _ 2 _ _ _ _ _
Say: *These are words for other things we go on.*

o Point to the lines next to 1 and ask: *How many lines can you see?* (four) Say: *There are four letters in this word.* You *can go on this on water, for example on the sea. What is it?* (a boat)
Ask a learner to write *b-o-a-t* on the lines.
Point to the lines after 'and' and ask: *How many lines can you see?* (four) Say: *There are four letters in this word. People can go on this on the sea too, but this is really big. What is it?* (a ship)
Ask a learner to write *s-h-i-p* on the lines.
Point to the lines next to 2 and ask: *How many letters are there in this word?* (five) Say: *This is very, very long. It stops in some towns. What is it?* (a train)
Ask another learner to write *t-r-a-i-n* on the lines.

o Point to the school bus in the picture. Ask: *What's this?* (a bus) *What can you see in the picture?* (**Suggestions:** a street, houses, children, schoolbags)

o Say: *This text is about a school bus.* Ask: *Is a bus big?* (yes) *Is a bus long?* (yes) *Can a child drive a school bus?* (no) *Who drives a school bus?* (a man or a woman) Read out the first and second sentences: *A school bus is big and long. A (man) or a woman drives it.* Point to the picture of the man and the word 'man' and say: *This is an example. Now you read the text and choose words from the box.*

o Learners choose words from the box and write them on the lines for 1–5.
Check learners' answers for number 1. Ask: *Do you see school buses in houses?* (no) *Do you see them in the street?* (yes) *Number 1 is 'street'.* Read out the last part of the sentence: *with cars, bikes and ...* Point to the words and pictures in the box and ask: *Which of these can you see on streets?* (lorries) *'Lorries' is the word for 2!*
Ask: *Where does the bus stop? Next to the children's ... ? 'Houses' is the correct word for 3!*
Mime carrying a schoolbag, sitting down and putting it on the floor. Ask: *What do children put on the bus floor?* (bags) *The answer for 4 is 'bags'!*
Read the next part of the text, pausing at the missing word: *The bus goes to the school and then its ... opens and the children run into their classrooms!*
Ask: *Does a cow open or close?* (no) *Does a door open and close?* (yes) *'door' is the answer for 5!*

o Point to the yellow bus in the picture in **E** and say: *What colour is this school bus?* (yellow) *Is it big or small? Who comes to school on the school bus?* (Learners who come to school on the bus stand up and answer questions.) Ask: *Is your school bus yellow? Is it big or small? How many children come to school in your bus?*

F Let's talk about the picture.

o Point to the picture and say: *Look at this. It's a beautiful day. The family are on a boat.*
Point to the car and say: *Here's the car. Where's the food?* (Learners point to the food and say: *Here's the food.*) Ask: *Where are the houses?* (Learners point to the houses and say: *Here are the houses.*)

o Point to one of the fish. Ask the questions below. Learners put up their hands to answer:
What's this? (a fish)
What colour is it? (yellow)
How many fish are there? (five)

o Point to the girl on the bike and ask: *What's the girl doing?* (riding [a bike])
Point to the boy and ask: *What's the boy doing?* (playing [with a toy train and lorry/truck])

o Point to your head and say: *What can I wear on my head?* (a hat) *I don't have a hat to wear today.*
Point to the woman in the picture and say: *The woman's wearing a hat. The woman has a hat to wear.* Write the second sentence on the board. Point to the man and say: *The man's wearing a hat. The man has a hat to wear.* Learners repeat the two sentences.
Point to the basket and ask: *What's this?* (orange juice) *What can the family drink?* (orange juice) Ask learners to make a sentence about the family and the juice like the sentence on the board. *The family has some orange juice to drink.* Ask: *Have you got some orange juice or water to drink today?* Learners answer.
Point to the girl on the bike and say: *The girl ...* (learners: has a bike to ride.)
Point to the boy on the boat and say: *The boy ...* (has a toy train and lorry/truck to play with.)

G What do you have?

o Say: *What can I read today? I know! I've got a great book! I have a great book to read!*
Look at G. Find the orange line between 'I have' and 'a great book' and 'to'. Draw an orange line between 'to' and 'read'. Learners draw the line with an orange pencil or pen. Say: *OK? Can you say my sentence? I have a great book to read!* Learners say the sentence.

o Point to the words in **G** and say: *You have lots of things! Make sentences about them!* In pairs, learners draw lines between 'to' in the yellow circle and the verbs to complete the sentences.
Check answers by asking different learners to say the whole sentence.
Sentences: *I have a funny game to play. I have a new helicopter to fly. I have a clean bike to ride. I have a beautiful car to drive. I have some nice sweets to eat.*
Divide learners into six groups. Give each group a number: 1–6.
Group 1 says the book sentence. Group 2 says the game sentence. Group 3 says the helicopter sentence. Group 4 says the bike sentence. Group 5 says the car sentence. Group 6 says the sweets sentence. Each group practises saying their sentence. Then, say a number, that group says their sentence. Do this quickly. Then, all the groups say their sentence at the same time!

32   Happy birthday!

Topics food and drink, clothes, colours

Movers words: *cups, week;* **Flyers words:** *letter, next*

Equipment needed

- Starters audio 32A.
- Colouring pencils or pens.
- Photocopies of page 115, one for each learner. See F.
- Ten small pieces of paper or card and some music. See 'Musical spelling'.

A ▶ Listen and colour.   Listening **Part 4**

> **Starters tip**
>
> In Listening Part 4, there are seven objects that are the same in the picture. For example, here, there are seven balloons. One balloon is already coloured as an example and five others need colouring. One of the balloons is not mentioned in the conversation and does not have to be coloured.

- Point to the picture and ask: *Where are the children?* (in a garden) *How many children can you see?* (six) *How many women can you see?* (one) *Whose birthday is it?* (the girl with the hat/present) *How many balloons can you see?* (seven)
- Say: *Listen to a boy and a woman. They're talking about the picture.* Play the example. Pause the audio. Ask: *Where's the blue balloon?* (in the tree)
- Play the rest of the conversation twice. Learners listen and colour the balloons.

> **Check answers:**
> 1 an orange balloon under the table
> 2 a green balloon on the girl's T-shirt
> 3 a red balloon in the boy's hand
> 4 a yellow balloon on the girl's hat
> 5 a pink balloon next to the window

Audioscript

Listen and look. There is one example.

Woman:	Can you see the balloon in the tree?
Boy:	Yes, I can.
Woman:	Colour it blue.
Boy:	The balloon in the tree?
Woman:	That's right!

Can you see the blue balloon in the tree? This is an example. Now you listen and colour.

1
Woman:	Look at the balloon under the table.
Boy:	Can I colour it?
Woman:	Yes. Colour it orange.
Boy:	The balloon under the table. OK. There!

2
Woman:	Find the balloon on the girl's T-shirt.
Boy:	Sorry? Which balloon?
Woman:	The one on the girl's T-shirt.
Boy:	Oh yes. I can see it now. Can I colour it green?
Woman:	My favourite colour! Yes! Do that now, please.

3
Woman:	Now, look at that boy with the balloon.
Boy:	I can see him. He's wearing shorts.
Woman:	That's right. Colour his balloon red.
Boy:	Great! I love that colour.

4
Woman:	And can you see the birthday girl's hat?
Boy:	Yes! That hat has got a balloon on it too!
Woman:	I know. Colour that balloon yellow, please.
Boy:	OK. Good! I've got that colour.

5
Woman:	And there's a balloon on the wall.
Boy:	Oh yes! It's really big.
Woman:	Yes, it is. Colour that balloon now, please.
Boy:	I'm colouring it pink. Is that OK?
Woman:	Yes! Thank you. Well done!

- Ask: *Which of the balloons did you NOT colour?* (The one on the boy's foot.) *Which of your colours did you NOT use?* (brown, grey, purple, black)

  Say: *Choose a colour for that balloon now!* In pairs, learners choose a colour then colour it. Ask 3–4 pairs: *What colour is your balloon?*
- Say: *I'm a balloon in this picture. Which balloon am I? Ask me questions!*

  Learners ask you questions to find out which balloon you are and everyone says what colour you are. For example:

  Learner A: *Are you in the boy's hand?*

  Teacher: *No, I'm not.*

  Learner B: *Are you in the tree?*

  Teacher: *Yes, I am.*

  All learners: *You're blue!*

  Teacher: *That's right! I'm a blue balloon!*
- In pairs, one learner chooses a balloon. The other learner asks questions to find out which balloon they are and says what colour they are.

B Listen and draw lines.

o Point to the three pictures in **B** and ask: *Which is the cake?* (Learners point to the cake.) Say: *Yes, that's right! Put the cake on the table! Draw a line from the cake to the table in A.* Learners draw the line.

o Ask: *Which is the horse?* (Learners point to the horse.) Say: *Put the horse next to the small table. Can you see it? It's in front of the house.* Learners draw a line from the horse to the small table next to the house.

o Ask: *Which is the jacket?* (Learners point to the jacket.) Say: *Put the jacket on the woman. Draw a line from the jacket to the woman.* Learners draw a line from the jacket to the woman.

C Answer the questions.

o Point to the questions under the cake. Read out the first question: *What's this?* (a cake/cake)
Ask different learners: *Do you like cake?* (yes/no) Everyone writes *yes* or *no* on the line.

o Learners look at the third question (*What do you eat for lunch?*) and think about their answer. Ask several learners this question. If necessary, ask more questions to help learners. *Do you like burgers? Rice?* Everyone writes their answers. For example: *chicken, carrots and rice.*

o Learners read the other questions about the jacket and horse and write their answers on the lines.

o In pairs, learners ask and answer the questions about the jacket and the horse.

o To check answers, ask several learners questions 2 and 3 about the jacket and the horse.

D Look at the picture in A. Read and write the words.

o Write on the board: 1 *You can see food and drink on this.*
Point to this sentence next to the crossword. Underline *food, drink* and *on* in the sentence on the board. Point to the picture in **A**. Ask: *Where is the food and drink?* (on the table)
Learners write *table* in the first line of boxes.

o Learners work in pairs. They read sentences 2–10 and write the words.

> **Check answers:**
> **2** garden **3** tree **4** shorts **5** window **6** hand **7** boys
> **8** cups **9** hat **10** shoes

o Point to the two words which appear in the completed crossword (from top to bottom). Ask: *Which two words can you read now?* (birthday cake)
Ask: *Where's the birthday cake?* (on the table)

o Write on the board: *Is it a … ? Is it some … ?*
Point to the present in the picture in **A** and say: *What's in this present? I know but you don't! Ask me questions!*
Learners try to guess the present by asking *Is it a/some … ?* questions.
For example:
Learner A: *Is it a computer game?*
Teacher: *No, it isn't!*
Learner B: *Is it a phone?*
Teacher: *No, it isn't!*
Learner C: *Is it some chocolates?*
Teacher: *Yes! There are some chocolates in this present!*
Learners could then play this game in pairs or small groups.

E Look at the pictures and write the words.

o Point to the picture of the skirt and ask: *What's this?* (a skirt) Point to the word 'skirt' on the line under the picture. Learners write the words for the other pictures.
Check answers by asking learners to spell the words. (1 camera, 2 ice cream, 3 shorts, 4 clothes, 5 basketball) Help learners with answers if necessary by miming holding a camera and taking a photo, eating an ice cream, playing basketball and pointing to

different clothes that learners are wearing.

o Point to the pictures and ask the three questions in **E**. Learners can answer using the words in **E** or think of other answers. For example: *What can you wear?* (a skirt, shorts, clothes) *What can you eat?* (ice cream, chocolate) *What can you play?* (basketball)
Write on the board: *What can you ....?* Tell pairs of learners to choose two other things from the pictures in **A** and **B** and to write a question about each using the words on the board.
Suggestions: *What can you wear?* (a hat / shoes/dress/T-shirt) *What can you ride?* (a horse) *What can you eat?* (a cake/burger/ sausage) *What can you open and close?* (a window / your eyes/mouth)

F Read about Sam and Jill. Write the words from E.

o Give out photocopies of page 115, one to each learner.

o Point to the first letter and to the boy. Say: *This is Sam. It's his birthday next week.* Read out: *I really like taking photos. It's fun!*
Point to the pictures in **E** and ask: *Does Sam want a skirt?* (No!) *Does Sam want a camera?* (Yes!)
Learners write *camera* on the first line.
Read out: *For my birthday, I'd like a new camera please, or some cool new ... for my sports lessons.*
Say: *Sam has sports lessons. Does he want a new skirt?* (no) *Some new shorts?* (yes)
Learners write *shorts* on the second line.
Read out the next two sentences: *For my party, I'd like to go to the park and play … I love that sport!* Point to the pictures in **E** and ask: *What can you play? Ice cream?* (no) *Can you play a skirt or clothes?* (no) *Can you play basketball?* (yes!)
Learners write *basketball* on the third line.
Ask: *Where does Sam want to play baseball?* (in the park)

o Learners read about Jill and choose words from **E** to write what she can make (ice cream), what she loves (clothes) and what she wants to get at the new shop (skirt).
Ask learners which party they would prefer to go to – Sam's or Jill's.

o Say: *It's your birthday.*
Write on the board: *What do you like?   What do you want for your birthday?   Where can you go?   What can you do?* Ask different learners the questions.

o Learners write a letter about their birthday on a piece of paper. They use Sam's and Jill's letters to help them. They write their name, a thing they like (a sport, hobby, clothes, etc.), a thing they want for their birthday, where they want to go and what they want to eat. They put their name at the end. They can add a photo or draw a picture of themselves in the box.

Musical spelling

o Give out one small piece of paper or card to ten different learners. Tell each learner to draw a different picture: a tablet, kiwi, crayon, ship, teddy, kite, boot, doll, poster, rug.

o Collect the cards. Learners sit or stand in a circle. (There should be about ten learners in the circle.)
Note: Large classes: Learners will need to make one set of picture cards for each group of ten learners. Learners will have to sit in different circles (ten learners in each circle).

o Give one learner a picture card. Play some music. Learners pass the picture card round the circle while the music is playing. Stop the music. The learner who has the card when the music stops has to say what they can see, and spell the word. For example: (the tablet picture) – *This is a tablet. T-A-B-L-E-T.*
If the learner doesn't know the word or doesn't say and spell it correctly, they continue passing round the same picture. If the learner says and spells the word correctly, they get a point.

o Learners play again, passing a different picture around their circle.

Optional extension:
Learners pass round the picture cards. When the music stops, the learner who has the card says what's on the card and what you can do with it, for example: *This is a (tablet). You can (play on/with it).*

33 On the beach

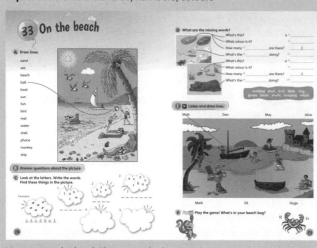

Movers word: *cloud;* Flyers word: *sky*

Equipment needed

o   Starters audio 33E.

Point to the picture. Speaking **Part 1**

o   Ask: *Do you like going to the beach?*

If learners live near a beach that they might visit, ask: *Who takes you to the beach? What do you do there? What do you wear to the beach?* Learners then answer the questions in closed pairs.

Learners continue working in pairs. Ask learners to imagine they are on the beach now. Ask: *What can you see at your beach? Write five things!*

Different pairs suggest one or two things. Write six or seven suggestions on the board, for example: *sand sea sun boats ice creams people birds*

Learners look at the picture in **A**. Ask: *Where are these people?* (on a beach) Point to the words on the board and ask: *How many of <u>these things</u> can you see <u>in this picture</u>?* Learners answer.

o   Point to the sun and say: *Here's the sun.* Ask: *Where's the ball?* Learners find the ball in the picture and point to it. Go round and check learners are all pointing to the ball. Ask: *Where are the shells?* Learners point to the shells and say, *'Here they are!'*

o   Ask volunteers to ask *Where's / Where are?* questions about the other things in the picture. The whole class points to the object.

o   Write on the board: *Where's the / Where are the … ?* Drill the question forms. Make sure learners pronounce 'Where's' as /weəz/

o   Learners continue in A and B pairs. Learner A asks: *Where's the … ?* Learner B points to the correct object in the picture then asks: *Where are the … ?* Learner A points to the correct objects in the picture.

Ⓐ Draw lines.

o   Learners look at the picture and words and draw lines between each word and the things in the picture. See the example (*ball*).

Check answers by asking different learners to come out to the board and to draw a picture for each word.

Ⓑ Answer questions about the picture. Speaking **Part 2**

o   Learners look at the picture. Ask *How many?* questions. Learners count the objects in the picture and answer.

How many fish/girls/boys/men/birds/boats/ships/shells/monkeys are there? (four fish, two girls, two boys, one man, three birds, two boats, one ship, eleven shells, one monkey)

In pairs, learners ask and answer 'How many?' questions.

o   After this, ask:

1   *What colour are the birds?* (blue [grey] and white)

2   *How many birds are there?* (three)

3   *What's the man doing?* (sleeping)

4   *What colour are the fish?* (orange)

5   *How many fish are there?* (four)

6   *What are the girls doing?* (playing [with a ball])

o   Repeat the questions with the whole class answering together.

Ⓒ Look at the letters. Write the words. Find these things in the picture.

o   Teach/revise 'cloud' by drawing one on the board.

o   Learners look at the letters in the first cloud. Ask: *What's this word?* (coconut). Say: *Point to the coconut in the picture.*

o   In pairs, learners look at the picture in **A** and at the letters. They decide what the jumbled words in clouds 1, 2 and 3 are and write the words on the lines.

> **Check answers:**
> 1 watch   2 foot   3 bananas

o   Say: *Find words for clouds 4 and 5 now.* Ask: *What's the word in cloud 2?* (foot). *How many letters are in 'foot'?* (four) *What's the word in cloud 3?* (bananas). *How many letters are in 'bananas'?* (seven). *Find two words for clouds 4 and 5. You choose. Your words can have four, five, six or seven letters in them.* Learners choose two other things in the beach picture and write their own letter word puzzles in the two empty clouds and add the correct number of lines for the two spellings.

Suggestions: beach, birds, boats, ship, faces, shorts, water, people, flowers, monkey, orange, phone, cloud.

o   Learners work in pairs. Ask: *What can you take to the beach?* Learners should ideally think of something they can't already see in picture A. They keep their word secret. If pairs need help, whisper a suggestion. For example: *kite, chair, camera, apple, bread, fruit, lemonade, watermelon.*

o   Using their chosen word, pairs create a jumbled letter puzzle in a cloud on a piece of paper.

o   Pairs take turns to come to the front of the class and copy their jumbled letter puzzles (in clouds) on the board. When they finish drawing their puzzle on the board, say: *Good! Great! Well done! Very good! Thank you!* or *Thanks!* In larger classes, pairs form groups of six or eight to show each other their puzzles.

o   The class solves the puzzles one at a time or work in pairs or small groups to solve all the puzzles. Check answers.

Optional extension:

In groups of 3–4, learners create five word puzzles for things they might **wear** to the beach on a cold day, for example: *dress, hat, jacket, jeans, shirt, shoes, socks, trousers.* Groups then come to the board, draw the word puzzles and the class tries to guess the answers.

D What are the missing words?

o Point to the first picture and to the incomplete questions and answers next to it. Say: *The ten words you need are in the water under this picture. Can you see them?*

o Point to the boat in picture 1 and ask: *What's this?* Say: *Find the word in the water.* Learners find 'boat' and write it on the line.

Ask the next question: *What colour is it?* Learners find 'green' and write it on the line.

Point to the next question and ask: *What's the answer to this question?* (2) *What's the word in the question? Look in the water!* Learners write 'boats' on the line.

Point to the bird and ask: *What's this?* Learners find 'bird' and write it on the line. Ask: *What's the bird doing?* Learners write 'walking' on the line.

o Check answers 1–5 (boat, green, boats, bird, walking).

o In pairs, learners find and write the words to complete the questions and answers for picture 2. Check answers by asking different pairs to read out their completed questions and answers.

Check answers:

6 shell **7** white **8** shells **9** dog **10** sleeping

E ▶ Listen and draw lines. Listening Part **1**

o Learners look at the picture. Ask: *Does this picture show the beach in the morning?* (no) *In the afternoon?* (no) *In the evening?* (yes) *How many people are in the picture?* (seven)

Option 1: Learners complete this task as a Listening Part 1.

o Learners look at the names and at the picture. Play the audio. Learners listen to the example then to the rest of the audio. They draw lines from five of the names to the correct people. Play the audio again. Learners check and complete their answers.

Option 2: Learners complete the task as test practice.

o Say: *You can see a line from the name Matt to a boy in the picture. This is the example. Which person is Matt? Listen!* Play the example. Ask again: *Which person is Matt?* (the boy in the boat)

o Play the rest of the audio. Learners listen and draw lines. Check answers by asking different learners: *Which girl is May/Jill/Alice? Which boy is Hugo/Dan?*

Check answers:

1 May and girl in coconut tree.   **2** Jill and girl looking at shells.
3 Hugo and boy running on sand with no shoes.   **4** Alice and girl in pink T-shirt sitting on chair.   **5** Dan and boy running into sea.

o Point to the boat in the sea and say: *Tell me about the boat.* Different learners say sentences about the boat.

Suggestions: *It's brown. I like this boat. A boy is in the boat. It's his father's boat. It's an old boat.*

Point to the shells and say: *Tell me about the shells.* Learners say sentences.

Suggestions: *They're on the sand/beach. There are two shells. They are very big. I like these shells. They're white.*

o In pairs, one learner points at things or people in the picture and says: *Tell me about the …* The other learner says sentences about the things or people.

Audioscript

Optional extension: Can you say it?

o Write on the board:

   1 *bouncing / Ben / likes / his / big blue ball / on this beautiful beach*
   2 *in the sea / on the sand / likes / Sue / swimming / and / sitting*

o In pairs, learners form two sentences using the words in each line.

   1 *Ben likes bouncing his big blue ball on this beautiful beach.*
   2 *Sue likes sitting on the sand and swimming in the sea.*

o Say the two tongue twisters. Learners listen and repeat.

F Play the game! What's in your beach bag?

o Learners suggest six things to take to the beach. Write their suggestions on the board. For example: *ball, bag, sunglasses, hat, mat, food, swimming costume, boat, water.*

o Each learner chooses and writes two of the things in their notebook.

o Say: *You have a beach bag!* Under their two things to take to the beach, learners draw and colour their bag. Ask different learners questions about their beach bags. For example: *What colour is your beach bag? Is it big or small? Is it new or old?*

o Learners now have two things to take to the beach and a beach bag. They then 'collect' the four missing things (from the list of six on the board) by walking around and asking other learners: *Do you have a ball? Have you got a hat?* If a classmate has the item, the learner can add it to their bag.

o Learners continue asking until they have collected all six things or until time runs out.

34 Let's go to the park

Topics animals, colours, sports and leisure

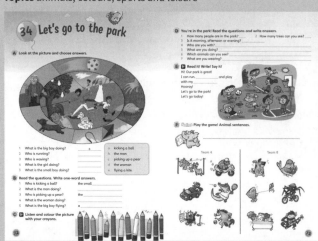

Equipment needed

- Starters audio 34C, 34E.
- Colouring pencils or pens.
- A photocopy of the sentences on page 116, made into flashcards. See F, 'More animal sentences'.

Ⓐ Look at the picture and choose answers.

- Point to the picture in the middle and say: *Look at this picture. These people are in a park.* Ask:
  How many people can you see? (five)
  How many boys can you see? (two; one big, one small)
  How many girls can you see? (one)
  How many women can you see? (one)

- Say: *Now, answer questions about the people.*
  Find the big boy. What's he doing? Point to the kite in the outside picture.
  Ask: *What's this?* (a kite) Say: *The big boy is …* (flying a kite)
  Ask questions about the other people in the picture. Learners point to the person then the second part of the picture to answer. Teach/revise vocabulary as necessary.
  What's the small boy doing? (kicking a ball)
  What's the girl doing? (picking up a pear)
  What's the woman doing? (waving to an old man)
  What's the man doing? (running with his dog)

- Point to and read out question 1: *What is the big boy doing?* (flying a kite) Point to this answer **e** *flying a kite* in the box and to the letter *e* on the line next to 1.
  Read out question 2: *Who is running?*
  Learners find this person (the man) in the picture and the answer in the box (b the man) and write *b* on the line in 2.
  Write up questions and answers 1 and 2 on the board.
  Point out that *who* talks about a person and *what* to an action.
  What is the big boy doing? (e flying a kite)
  Who is running? (b the man)

- Learners read questions 3–5 and write letters on the lines.

Check answers:
3 d   4 c   5 a

Ⓑ Read the questions. Write one-word answers.

- Read out question 1: *Who is kicking a ball?* and the first part of the answer: *the small* (boy). Learners write *boy* on the line.
  Learners read questions 2–5 and write answers. Remind them to write only one word.

Check answers:
2 running   3 girl   4 waving   5 kite

Ⓒ ▶ Listen and colour the picture with your crayons.

- Point to the crayons in C and ask: *How many crayons can you see?* (12) *What colours are the crayons?* (red, blue, yellow, orange, pink, white, purple) Ask different learners: *What's your favourite colour?*

- Say: *There are two animals in this park today. The man's running with his dog. The girl has a toy animal too.* Point to the zebra in the picture in **A** and ask: *What's this animal? Do you know?* Teach/revise: 'zebra'. Ask 2–3 learners: *What's this animal?* (It's a zebra.)

- Point to the people in the park and say: *This is a great picture but it's black and white! Let's add some colour! Have you got your colours?*
  Learners listen to the audio and colour the picture. Play the audio twice, pausing it between each question.

- Walk around the class and check learners have coloured the five things correctly (the boy's T-shirt yellow; the woman's dress purple; the man's jeans green; the pears on the tree pink; the zebra orange). Learners could then colour the rest of the picture.

Audioscript

Listen and colour.

1 Woman: Colour the boy's T-shirt for me, please.
  Boy: The boy's T-shirt? OK! What colour?
  Woman: Yellow.
  Boy: OK. I like that colour!

2 Boy: And can I colour the woman's dress?
  Woman: Yes, you can.
  Boy: Great. I'm colouring the woman's dress purple now.
  Woman: Very good.

3 Woman: Can you see the man?
  Boy: Yes. Can I colour his jeans?
  Woman: What colour?
  Boy: Green's a good colour for jeans.
  Woman: Yes it is!

4 Woman: Now, look at the tree. It's got a lot of fruit. Colour the pears, please.
  Boy: What colour? Can I colour the pears pink?
  Woman: Hmm … Yes!
  Boy: Thanks.

5 Woman: And now the zebra.
  Boy: Oh, look! It's a toy one!
  Woman: Yes, it is. Colour it orange.
  Boy: That's a funny colour for a zebra! But OK! There!
  Woman: What a nice picture! Well done!

D You're in the park! Read the questions and write answers.

○ Say: *Close your eyes! You're in the park!*
Read out the seven questions. Learners do not speak or write anything. They just imagine the park where they are and think of their answers.

1 *How many people are in the park?*
2 *How many trees can you see?*
3 *Is it morning, afternoon or evening?*
4 *Who are you with?*
5 *What are you doing?*
6 *Which animals can you see?*
7 *What are you wearing?*

○ In pairs or small groups, learners ask and answer the questions.

Optional extension:
Say: *Close your books! Who can tell me the seven questions?* Learners say the questions. You answer them. If they can't remember any of the questions, write the first word (the question word) on the board to help them.

E ▶ Read it! Write! Say it!

○ Ask different learners: *Do you like going to the park? What do you do in the park? Who do you go to the park with?*

○ Point to the picture in **E** and ask: *Where are these children?* (in a park) *What are they doing?* (running, playing, jumping)
Play the audio. Learners listen and write the words in the second and third sentences. (*jump, friends*)
Play the audio again, twice. The first time, learners listen and read. The second time, they read and say each sentence when they hear it. Then, the whole class says the sentences with you.

○ Divide learners into four groups.
Say to group one: *You say line 1.*
To group two, say: *You say lines 2 and 3.*
To all the groups, say: *Say: Hooray!*
To group three, say: *You say line five.*
To group four, say: *And you say line six.*
Groups say the lines in the correct order.
Groups then say the lines in different orders.
Finally, all the groups say their line at the same time.

Audioscript

Hi! Our park is great!
I can run, jump and play
with my friends!
Hooray!
Let's go to the park!
Let's go today!

F Play the game! Animal sentences.

○ Point to the elephant and ask: *What's this?* (an elephant)
What's the elephant doing? (drawing a picture)

○ Draw six lines on the board. Write *elephant* on the second line and *drawing a picture* on lines four, five and six so there's one word on each line and nothing on lines one or three.

○ Point to the line in front of *elephant* and ask: *What can I write here?* (The/An) Write *An* on the first line.
Point to the third line and ask: *What word do I write here?* (is) Write *is* on the third line.
Ask: *How many words are in this sentence?* (six)
Learners copy the sentence onto the line next to the elephant picture. (*An elephant is drawing a picture.*) Leave the sentence on the board.

○ Divide the class into two teams (A and B). Team A looks at the six pictures on the left, and team B looks at the six pictures on the right.
Larger classes: Form more A and B teams.
Explain that in their pictures, there are six different animals doing six different things. Say: *Write sentences about your six pictures.* Write on the board:
A .... is .... Say: *Write six sentences with six words!*

○ Learners in each team write the sentences in their notebooks. Do not check answers yet.

○ Point to the sentence on the board about the elephant. Say: *An elephant is drawing a picture.* Point to the words 'elephant', 'drawing', 'picture'. Explain that these are important words, so we say them more slowly and more loudly than 'An', 'is' and 'a'. Practise saying this sentence with learners.

○ Tell learners in team A that you are going to mime one of their sentences. (For example: *A crocodile is hitting a ball.*)
Mime hitting a ball with a tennis racket. A learner in team A writes the crocodile sentence on the board. Everyone in the team says the sentence. (A crocodile is hitting a ball.) Make sure learners stress 'crocodile', 'hitting' and 'ball'.

○ Repeat this with one of team B's sentences. (For example: *A dog is eating a banana.*)
For teams to gain a point, they need to say the sentence correctly and write the sentence correctly on the board.
The winning team is the one with the most points.

Suggested sentences
A
A goat is eating a shirt.
A frog is riding a motorbike.
A horse is bouncing a ball.
A duck is driving a car.
A cat is singing a song.
B
A bird is reading a book.
A spider is riding a bike.
A snake is having a bath.
A fish is flying a kite.
A monkey is playing the guitar.

Mime or draw more animal sentences!

○ Explain that the animals in **F** are doing different things now. One learner from team A comes to the front of the classroom. Show them a sentence from page 116. (For example: 'The cat is playing the piano'.)
The learner draws or mimes the animal and the action. (They can also make the sound the animal makes.)
If the other learners in team A say and write the correct sentence for this picture, the team gets a point.
Play the same guessing game several times, alternating between teams. The team with the most points wins the game.

○ You could end this activity by telling learners to look at the 12 pictures in **F** again and asking them questions about the animals. For example:
Which animal is eating a shirt? (the goat)
What's the goat doing? (eating)
What's the bird doing? (reading)
What's the bird reading? (a book)
What's the frog doing? (riding)
What's the frog riding? (a motorbike)
What's the fish doing? (flying a kite)
What colour is the kite? (pink and blue)

83

35   What, who and where?

Topics the home, possessions, colours

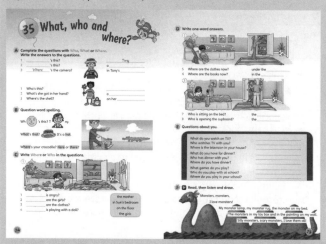

Equipment needed

- Colouring pencils or pens.
- Starters audio 35F.

A Complete the questions with *Who, What* or *Where*. Write the answers to the questions.

- Point to one of the learners near to you in the class and ask: *Who's this?* Learners say the name of the learner.

  Point to this learner's book and ask: *What's this?* ((It's his/her book.) *Where's the book?* (on his/her desk)

  Put the book on a chair. Ask: *Where's the book now?* (on the chair)

- Write on the board: Who   What   Where

  Say: *Look at the boy in A.* Point to the name on his hat and ask: *Who's this?* (Tony)

  Point to the word 'Who' on the board. Repeat the question: *Who's this?* Learners write *Who* on the line in question 1.

- Point to the camera in Tony's hand and to the word 'What' on the board. Ask: *What's this?* (a camera)

  Learners write *camera* on the line in 2.

  Point to the line in question 2 and to the question words.

  Say: *Who's this? A camera. Is that right?* (no!)

  Say: *What's this? A camera. Is that right?* (yes!)

  Learners write *What* on the line.

- Point to the word 'Where' on the board and read out question 3: *Where's the camera? In Tony's ...* (hand) Learners write *hand* on the line.

  In pairs, learners read out the questions and answers about Tony.

- Point to the girl and say: *Write the answers to the questions about this girl.*

Check answers:
1 Alex   **2** flower   **3** bag

- Learners work in pairs. Learner A points to Tony and asks the three questions. Learner B answers. Then, Learner B asks the questions about Alex and Learner A answers.

B Question word spelling.

Starters tip
Thinking of different ways to help learners remember a word's spelling, meaning and pronunciation can be very useful. Using word pictures like the ones here for 'Who' and 'What' and spelling patterns like: 'Where? Here or there?' can really support learning.

- Point to the round face (the 'O' in 'Who'). Say: *'Who' asks about a person.* Tell learners to think of this round face in the 'O' to remember that 'Who' asks about a person.

- Read out the second question and answer: *What's that? It's a hat.*

  Ask: *Can you see the word 'hat' in 'what' and 'that'? and in 'hat'.* Explain that a hat is a thing and that we use 'what' and 'that' to talk about a thing. Tell learners to think of a hat to remember that 'What' asks about a thing.

  Note: *What* can also ask about an activity. For example: *What's he doing?*

- Point to the picture of the boy and the crocodiles.

  Ask: *How many crocodiles are there?* (two) *Are the crocodiles next to the boy?* (one crocodile is but the other crocodile isn't)

  Write on the board: *where   here   there*

  Underline 'here' in all three words. Tell learners to remember these words together.

  Remind learners that 'here' talks about things that are near us, but 'there' is for things that are further away. And 'Where' is the question word to ask about the position of something or someone. All three words talk about place.

- Write on the board: *what   that   hat.* Point to each word and say it. Ask learners which word sounds different (what /wɒt/) Read out the second question and answer again. *What's that? It's a hat.* Learners repeat the sentences.

  Write on the board: *where   here   there*

  Say the words. Ask learners which word sounds different (here /hɪər/) Learners practise saying the questions.

  Your friend and your hat

  Learners copy the first two questions from **B** into their notebooks.

  Who's this?

  What's that?

  After the first question, learners write the name of a friend. The name should have the letter 'o' in it (for example, Paolo, Boris, Roberto). Learners use a different colour for the letter 'o'. They could also draw a small face in the letter 'o' to remind them that 'Who' always asks about a person or people.

  After the second question, learners draw their own hat or a hat they would like to have!

C Write *Where* or *Who* in the questions.

- Say: *Look at picture 1.* Point to the picture and say: *These girls are friends. Their names are Ann and Sue. Are the girls happy?* (yes)

  Point to the woman and say: *And this is Sue's mum. Is she happy?* (no)

  Who is angry – the girls or the mother? (the mother)

  Point to the line in question 1 and ask: *Which word do we write here? Is it 'Where is angry?' Or 'Who is angry?'* (Who) Learners write *Who* on the line in question 1.

  Point to the girls and ask: *Where are the girls?* (in Sue's bedroom)

  Point to and read out the answer to question 2: *in Sue's bedroom*

  Ask: *What's the question word for this answer: 'Where are the girls?' or 'Who are the girls?'* (Where)

  Learners write *Where* on the line in question 2.

- Say: *Look at the questions and answers for 3 and 4. Are they about a person or a place?* Learners write *Where* or *Who* on the lines.

Check answers:
3 Where   **4** Who

D Write one-word answers.

o Say: *Now, write the answers to questions 5 and 6. Write one word.* Learners look at picture 2 and complete the answers. Check answers by asking one learner to read out each question and a different learner to say the answer and to point to the clothes and the books.

> **Check answers:**
> **5** bed **6** cupboard

o Write on the board: *Where are the … now?* Say: *Ask a question about the toys with these words. (*Where are the toys now?) *Now, answer the question!* (in the cupboard) Ask more *Where are* questions with *socks, books, photos.*

Ask: *What's under your bed? Do you put your clothes on the floor? Do you have a big cupboard? What's in your cupboard? Where do you put your toys?*

After each question, pairs of learners tell each other their answers.

o Say: *Look at questions 5 and 6: Where are the clothes now? Where are the books now? What are the answers?* (under the bed, in the cupboard). *Look at questions 7 and 8. They start with 'Who'. These questions are about a …* (person). *Look at picture 3 and complete answers 7 and 8.*

> **Check answers:**
> **7** girls **8** mother/woman

Which picture?

o Tell learners that you are going to say a sentence. Say: *Look at picture 1 in C and look at picture 2 and picture 3 in D. Say which picture my sentences are about. Picture 1, 2 or 3?*

For example: *The mother is not in the room.* (picture 2)

1 *The girls are standing.* (picture 2)
2 *The mother is pointing.* (picture 1)
3 *One cupboard door is closed.* (picture 2)
4 *The clothes are on the floor.* (pictures 1 and 2)
5 *The books are in the cupboard.* (picture 2)
6 *The girls are playing with dolls.* (pictures 1 and 3)
7 *The cupboard doors are open.* (pictures 1 and 3)
8 *There are three pictures on the wall.* (pictures 1, 2, 3)

E Questions about you.

o Ask different learners: *What do you watch on TV?* Write the different programmes they watch on the board. All learners write their answer on the first line in **E**. You could ask if they watch any programmes in English.

o Ask different learners: *Who watches television with you?* (my family/ brother …)

All learners write their answer to this question on the second line.

o Ask different learners: *Where is the television in your house?* (in the living room / kitchen / my bedroom)

All learners write their answer on the third line.

o Write a sentence about yourself on the board, combining the three answers.

For example: *I watch (The Y Factor) with my family in the living room.*

Learners write a similar sentence about themselves in their notebooks.

Say your sentence again, making sure you stress the important words (the Y Factor, family, living room). Learners say their sentence to the people next to them.

o Learners write their answers to the other questions. Walk around and help them with any words they need for their answers. Then, they write their three answers about dinner in one sentence and another sentence with their three answers about games.

Suggestions: *I eat (chicken or eggs) for dinner with my (mum and dad) in the (kitchen). I play (ball games) with (my friends Pauline and Robert) in the (playground).*

o Learners sit in a circle. (With bigger groups make several circles). One learner at each side of the circle says their sentence about dinner to the person on their right: *I have chicken for dinner with my mum and dad in the kitchen.* The next person then says their own sentence to the person on their right. Continue round the circle like this until all the learners have said their sentence. (There will be two learners talking at the same time.)

Finish by everyone in the class saying their sentence at the same time!

F ▶ Read, then listen and draw.

o Point to the bed in the pictures in **D** and ask: *What's this?* (a bed) *What colour is it?* (purple and pink) *What's on the bed?* (flowers) Point to the pictures on the wall and ask: *What are these?* (pictures) *What's in the pictures?* (a doll/girl, a teddy bear, a butterfly) Point to the rug in the pictures in **D** and ask: *What's this?* (a rug) *What colour is it?* (pink and red)

o Say: *Now listen to a boy. His name's Tony. Tony's talking about* his *room!* Play the audio chant.

Audioscript

> *Listen and draw.*
> *Monsters, monsters,*
> *I love monsters!*
> *My monster lamp, my monster rug, the monster on my bed.*
> *The monsters in my toy box and in the painting on my wall.*
> *Silly monsters, scary monsters, I love them all!*

Ask: *What does Tony love?* (monsters) *Does Tony have lots of monsters?* (yes) *Where are the monsters?* (on his lamp, rug and bed, in his toy box and painting)

o Say: *Listen to some more sentences about Tony's bedroom.* Read out all the sentences. Learners listen.

Tony loves monsters. He's got lots of monsters in his bedroom.
He's got a big bed and there's a big monster on it.
On the wall next to his bed, there's a painting with two monsters in it.
And on the table next to his bed, he's got a monster lamp.
On the floor, there's a big monster rug
And in his toy box, he's got four monsters.

o Say: *Now look at page 100. Listen again and draw Tony's bedroom.* Read the sentences again, one at a time. Learners draw the monsters in Tony's bedroom on page 100. Give them time to draw between each sentence.

Read it again, with fewer pauses.

o Now, tell learners to colour the monsters in the room. Pause after each sentence to give learners time to colour the picture.

The two monsters in the picture on the wall are yellow.
Tony's monster lamp is blue.
The monster on his rug is purple.
The big monster on the bed is green.
Two of the monsters in his toy box are orange and two are pink.

o Learners show each other their pictures in pairs or small groups. The learner who is showing their picture reads out the sentences in **F** in the Student's Book.

o Play the audio with the monsters sentences again. Learners listen and read and say the sentences. Practise this a few times, then learners say the sentences without the audio.

Divide the class into three groups. Different groups say one of the sentences. Then, each group could say all the sentences. To make it more fun and exciting, get them to whisper the sentences:

Monsters, monsters,
I love monsters!
My monster lamp, my monster rug, the monster on my bed.
The monsters in my toy box and in the painting on my wall.
Silly monsters, scary monsters, I love them all!

36   Great games, great hobbies!

Topics sports and leisure, colours

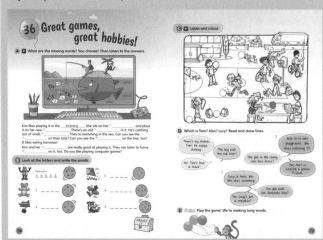

Movers words: *be good at, teeth;* Flyers word: *screen*

Equipment needed

- Starters audio 36A, 36C.
- Colouring pencils or pens. See C.

A ▶ What are the missing words? You choose! Then listen to the answers.

- Ask: *Who plays computer games?* Learners put up their hands. Write on the board: *What's the name of your favourite game? What can you see on the computer screen? Who do you play with? Where do you play?*
  In pairs, learners talk about computer games.
- Ask 3–4 learners about their favourite computer games. If learners agree that one computer game is a favourite, you might ask learners to draw something from the game on the board.
- Learners look at the picture in **A**. Say: *This is Kim's new computer game.* Point to the man in the game. Ask: *Is this a man or a woman?* (a man). *What's the man doing?* (fishing) *How many small fish are there?* (five). *What can you see on their tails?* (numbers). *Behind the man there's an animal. What is it?* (a monkey)
- Learners look at the example. Ask: *When does Kim play this game?* (in the evening). Look at the first gap together (Kim sits on her ….) Ask: *What's the missing word? Guess! What can Kim sit on?*
  Prompt answers if necessary (her bed, the sofa, a chair, an armchair). Say: *You choose an answer. Write it on the line.* In pairs, learners decide which answer to write next to 1.
  Say: *Now guess the other missing words.* Continuing in pairs, learners look at the picture, read the rest of the text and guess the missing words 2–8. Learners use pencils, not pens, to write their answers as they may want to change them.
- When pairs have finished, say: *Now listen and tick your right answers.* Play the audio. Learners tick their answers.
- Learners tell you any answers that are different. Say: *Well done!* to good alternative answers, for example: 1 bed, 2 phone, 5 lines, 7 brother, 8 songs/people.
- Learners suggest a name for the game. For example: *Big fish and small fish!*

Audioscript

Kim likes playing it in the evening. She sits on her **chair** and plays it on her new **computer**. There's an old **man** in it. He's catching lots of small **fish**. They're swimming in the sea. Can you see the **numbers** on their tails? Can you see the **monkey** on the tree, too? It likes eating bananas! Kim and her **dad** are really good at playing it. They can listen to funny **music** on it, too. Do you like playing computer games?

- Write on the board: *man He's fish They're monkey It*
  Say: *Find these words.* Learners find the words and draw circles round them. Show them that we can use 'He' to talk about the man, 'They' to talk about the fish and 'It' to talk about the monkey.

Optional extension:

Write on the board: *She It They He*

- Dictate four short sentences. Learners write them in their notebooks.
  Tom is playing.
  The children are drawing.
  My mum is great.
  The big fish is funny.
  Check answers by asking learners to help you with spellings as you write the sentences on the board.
- Point at the first sentence: *Tom is playing.*
  Ask: *Is Tom a boy's name or a girl's name?* (a boy's name)
  After *Tom is playing.* Write: *His favourite game is …*
  Point to the gap and ask: *What's Tom's favourite game? You choose!* Learners say for example, football. Add *football* to the sentence.
- Read the two sentences, pointing to 'Tom' at the beginning of the first sentence and 'His' at the beginning of the second sentence. Check again that learners understand when we talk about a boy, we can use his name or 'he'.
- Point to 'The children' in the second sentence and to the other pronouns on the board. Ask: *Which word do we need to talk about 'children'?* (They). Do the same with 'My mum' (She) and 'The big fish' (It).
  Say: *Now you write something more about these people and this animal.*
  In pairs, learners write a second sentence about the children, mum and the big fish in their notebooks. They begin each second sentence with the correct pronoun.
- Ask different pairs to read out one of their paired sentences, for example: *My mum is great. She likes computer games.*
- Point to your teeth and the teeth on the big fish and teach 'teeth'.
  Say: *Look at the computer screen. Listen to my sentences. Sit down for wrong sentences. Stand up for right sentences.* (Learners sit down between sentences.) Say:

The big fish has lots of teeth.	(Learners stand up.)
You can see a boat.	(Learners sit down.)
The monkey is behind the man.	(Learners stand up.)
The man is sleeping.	(Learners sit down.)
You can see the number 15.	(Learners stay sitting down.)

- Learners work in teams of 3–4. They look at the picture again and write four short sentences that are either right or wrong about the picture. For example: *Two fish are white. The big fish is under the man. The man is sleeping. You can see the number 10.*
- Two teams work together. Teams take turns to say their sentences and stand up for 'yes' answers or sit down for 'no' answers.

B Look at the letters and write the words.   Reading & Writing Part 3

> **Starters tip**
> In Reading and Writing Part 3, candidates complete spellings. They should carefully count the number of lines for each word and check their spellings have used all the letters.

- Learners look at the pictures. Ask: *What can you do with these six things?* (Play!)
- Look at the example together. Ask one learner: *What can you see in the picture?* (a robot) Ask: *Who can spell robot?* Learners look at the example answer and build the word by saying one letter each.
  Learner A: *r*
  Learner B: *o*
  Learner C: *b,* etc.

o Learners complete the five other words. Say: *Find the letters in the five balls!* Learners should cross off the letters as they use them. Say to five different learners: *Say and spell answer 1 / 2 / 3 / 4 / 5.*

Check answers:
1 bear **2** boat **3** kite **4** plane **5** monkey

o Ask: *Do you like these toys?* In pairs (or small groups in larger classes), learners give each toy a mark out of ten. You might suggest giving one mark for a toy they don't like, five for a toy that's OK and ten marks out of ten for a really great toy. Ask pairs for the marks for each toy and write them on the board to find the class's most popular toy.

📦 **Design a robot!**

o In pairs or on their own, learners design and draw a robot. In their robot picture, they name the robot and add a price if they want to.

o They say what the robot can do or what it is good at doing. For example: *This is the Super X Robot. It can walk and run and wave. It can pick up things and it can make burgers. It's very good at talking and fishing. It's good at playing football too.*

C ▶ **Listen and colour.**   Listening **4** (Part)

o Learners look at the picture. Point to the school building and say: *This is a school.* Point to the playground and say: *This is a … ?* (playground)

   If there is a playground at or near your school, ask: *What games do you like playing in the playground? Is your playground big or small? Who do you talk to in your playground?*

o Learners work in pairs. Ask: *What can you see in the picture of this playground? Find six things.* Ask different pairs for their words and write them on the board.

   Suggestions: playground, school, classroom, window, car, motorbike, lorry/truck, bike, street, boy, girl, dog, ball, crocodile, bag, book, kite, bird, table, pencils, trousers, T-shirts, skirts, socks, shoes, etc.

o Ask: *Are the children in the playground having fun?* (yes) *What are they doing?* (drawing, reading, playing with a kite, playing basketball)

o Ask: *How many balls are there in the picture?* (seven)
   Say: *One ball in the picture has a colour. Where is this ball? What colour is it?* (On the table. It's orange.)

o Play the example on the audio.

o Say: *Listen and colour five balls.*

o Play the audio. Learners listen and colour the five other balls.

Check answers:
colour dog's ball – yellow
colour ball kicked by girl – blue
colour ball behind boy – red
colour ball between bags – pink
colour ball held by boy – purple

Audioscript

Look at the picture. Listen and look. There is one example.
  Man: Can you see the ball on the table?
  Girl: Yes, I can.
  Man: Good. Colour the ball on the table orange.
  Girl: OK. I'm doing that now.
  Man: Great!
Can you see the orange ball on the table?
This is an example. Now you listen and colour.

1 Man: The dog's playing with a ball.
     Girl: Pardon?
     Man: The dog's playing with a ball.
     Girl: Oh yes! Can I colour it yellow?
     Man: Yes, you can.

2 Girl: One girl is kicking a ball. Look!
     Man: Oh, yes! You can choose the colour for that ball.
     Girl: OK! There! She's kicking a blue ball now!
     Man: Very good!

3 Girl: A boy is sitting on the ground. There's a ball behind him.
     Man: There's a ball behind the boy. That's right.
     Girl: Can I colour that ball red?
     Man: Yes, you can. Thank you.

4 Man: Now find the ball between the schoolbags please.
     Girl: Sorry?
     Man: Find the ball between the schoolbags.
     Girl: Oh … I can see it now. I'd like to colour that ball pink.
     Man: OK!

5 Man: Now, the ball in the boy's hand. Can you see it?
     Girl: Yes. He's holding it.
     Man: That's right. Colour that ball purple, please.
     Girl: OK! There! I love this picture now!
     Man: Me too!

o Learners finish colouring the picture of the playground. They choose their own colours to do this.

D **Which is Tom? Alex? Lucy? Read and draw lines.**

o Point to the playground picture and say: *We know three of these children's names. Their names are Tom, Alex and Lucy.*

o Learners read the mini-dialogues and draw a line from each of the three names to the correct child in the picture.

Check answers:
1 Tom has got black hair and is pushing a bike.
2 Alex is wearing a yellow T-shirt and is kicking the ball.
3 Lucy has got the crocodile and is carrying the bag.

o Ask: *What does Tom/Alex/Lucy like doing?*

Check answers:
Tom likes/enjoys fishing. Alex loves watching TV. Lucy likes swimming.

o Ask: *What are your hobbies?*
   Who likes flying kites? Drawing? Reading? Painting? Writing stories? Playing computer games? Climbing trees? Watching animals? Making clothes? Playing the piano? Taking photos?
   Teach new vocabulary as necessary, for example: collecting things, making models, doing puzzles, playing chess, cooking, etc.
   Learners could collect information about favourite hobbies in the class. To show the results, learners could create a labelled collage from cut-out magazine photos, printed internet pictures or their own 'children and their hobbies' drawings.

E **Play the game! We're making long words.**

o Ask: *Do you like playing word games?* Write the following words randomly on the board: *book, arm, cup, bike, play, basket, board, chair, case, room, ball, class, foot, motor, ball, room, ground, bath.*

o Learners copy these words into their notebooks.

o Learners work in pairs. Tell them to make nine new words by pairing up the words on the board.

o Learners put up their hands to show when they've finished. The first pair to do so are the winners.

Check answers:
bookcase, armchair, cupboard, motorbike, playground, basketball, football, classroom, bathroom

Note: See Unit 19D for 'armchair and cupboard' spelling activity.

37 Let's play

Topics sports and leisure, places

Movers words: *move, be good at*

Equipment needed

○ A5 pieces of card or paper (one per learner). See A.
○ A ball to demonstrate the verbs *throw, bounce*, etc. See B.
○ Starters audio 37D.

○ Write on the board: *ball   football   tennis ball*
Point to 'ball' and 'football' and say: *We can make new sports words with 'ball', like this.* Point to 'ball' and 'tennis'. Say: *We can put different words in front of 'ball', like this.*
Learners work in pairs. They copy *football* and *tennis ball* and write more words they can make using 'ball' in the same way.
Ask: *Who knows three words?* Pairs put up their hands. *Who knows five, six or seven words?* Pairs put up their hands. Check answers.
Suggestions at Starters level: *baseball, basketball, beach ball, football, hockey ball, table tennis ball, tennis ball*

Ⓐ Look and read. Put a tick or a cross in the box.
Reading & Writing Part 1

> **Starters tip**
> In Reading and Writing Part 1, the seven pictures are likely to come from different topic sets, so candidates might see, for example, an animal, a toy, an item of clothing, a piece of furniture, something to eat and a means of transport.

○ Draw a tick and a cross on the board. Point to the tick and ask: *Does this mean 'yes' (or 'that's right')?* (yes) Point to the cross and say: *And this means … ?* (no / that's wrong)

○ Learners look at the two examples in **A**. Point to the picture in the second example and say: *Can you see the cross? This sentence is wrong. These aren't bats, they're …* (horses). Point to the horses and ask: *Can you ride a horse?* Learners answer.

○ Learners put ticks or crosses in boxes for sentences 1–5.

> **Check answers:**
> 1✔ 2✘ 3✘ 4✔ 5✔

○ Ask: *What can you see in 2?* (a boat) *But the word is … ?* (goat) *What can you see in 3?* (T-shirts) *But the word is … ?* (jackets)
Write *boat/goat* and *T-shirt/jacket* on the board. Explain that these two were wrong for different reasons. The words *boat* and *goat* look almost the same. *T-shirts* and *jackets* are both clothes (see the tip).

Ⓑ What can you do with a ball? Write *a, e, i, o* or *u*.

○ Ask: *What can we do with a ball?* Take your ball and catch it, bounce it, hit it, kick it and throw it. As you do each of the actions, say: *Look! I'm catching/bouncing/hitting/kicking/throwing the ball!* If you don't have a ball, mime these actions.

○ Ask different learners to catch, bounce, hit, kick or throw the ball.
Note: If your school has a playground or sports hall with lots of balls, you could practise the verbs there for a few minutes.

○ Learners look at the words in **B**. Point to 'bounce'.
Ask: *What letters do we write here?* (o, u and e). Learners complete the word 'bounce'. In pairs, they complete the other four words.

> **Check answers:**
> catch, hit, kick, throw

○ Write on the board: *football   hockey   tennis   fishing   basketball*
○ Say: *Listen! Which sport am I talking about?* Point to the sports on the board. Ask these questions, pausing between each one for learners to choose their answer and write it in their notebooks.
In this sport, you run and kick a ball.
In this sport, you bounce, throw and catch a ball.
In these two sports, you run on grass and hit a ball.

> **Check answers:**
> football, basketball, hockey and tennis

Ask: *Do you run/throw/hit a ball / kick a ball in fishing?* (no)
Teach: *You sit and … ?* catch fish!
Note: In Britain and many parts of the world 'football' and 'soccer' are used to talk about the same sport. In American English, 'soccer' is the sport where players kick the ball and 'football' is where players carry, throw and kick the ball.

Ⓒ Write letters, sports and names!

○ Learners look at the five pictures. Ask:
Where are the people in picture a? (at the beach / in the sea)
Ask the same question about the other pictures (*in a garden / a playground / a park or sports centre / a living room*).

○ Read out sentence 1: *Alex is at the beach with his grandfather today.* Point to the beach in the picture and to the circled word, *beach*, in the sentence. Ask: *Which sport does Alex love?* Point to the example answer and ask: *He loves … ?* (swimming) Point to the small box at the beginning of the sentence about Alex. Say: *You can see the letter 'a' in this box. Which picture is Alex in?* (a).

○ Say: *Now read the sentences and look at pictures b, c, d and e. Write the correct letters in the boxes.* Learners write *b, c, d* or *e* in each box to show which picture the sentence is about.
Say: *Write the correct sports word in the sentences now.* Learners write answers on the lines.

> **Check answers:**
> **2** picture d – tennis   **3** picture e – football/soccer
> **4** picture c – basketball   **5** picture b – table tennis

○ Learners write the correct boy's or girl's name under each picture.

> **Check answers:**
> **a** Alex   **b** Mark   **c** Jill   **d** Anna   **e** Sue

Ⓓ ▶ Listen and tick the box.
Listening Part 3

> **Starters tip**
> In Listening Part 3, only one picture shows the correct answer but candidates hear something about all three pictures in each conversation. Remind them to listen very carefully!

○ Write on the board: *soccer   badminton   table tennis   swimming   baseball   hockey*
  Point to each of the sports words on the board and to the pictures in **D**, and ask: *How many pictures can you see of this sport?* Learners count the sports pictures and write the question numbers and letters.

> **Check answers:**
> soccer: (2) example C and 3B,   badminton: (1) 3C,
> table tennis: (1) 3A,   swimming: (1) 1C,   baseball: (2) 2A and 2C
> hockey: (2) 1B and 5A

○ Ask: *What sport can you see in picture 1A?* (horse riding) *and in 2B?* (basketball) *And what sport is the girl playing in 5B?* (tennis) *What sport can you see in picture 2B?* (basketball)

○ Point to the tennis racket in the girl's hand in picture 5b and ask: *What's this?* (a tennis racket) Then, point to the badminton racket in picture 3C and say: *And this is a ...* (badminton racket)
  Point to the baseball bat in picture 2C and say: *This isn't a racket, it's a bat. In baseball, you hit the ball with a bat.*
  If you have space in your classroom, tell learners to stand up and then say:
  Hit the tennis ball with your new tennis racket.
  And now, hit the baseball with your bat.
  Learners mime the sentences.

○ Learners look at the three pictures and question in the example. (Which is Ben's favourite sport?) Ask: *Which sports can you see in these three pictures?* (basketball, tennis, football/soccer)

○ Play the example on the audio. Say: *Ben doesn't like tennis or soccer. Ben's favourite sport is ...?* (basketball)

○ Learners listen to the rest of the audio twice and tick the boxes.

> **Check answers:**
> **1** B   **2** A   **3** C   **4** B   **5** C

Audioscript

Look at the pictures. Listen and tick the box. There is one example.
Which is Ben's favourite sport?
Woman: Do you like tennis, Ben?
Boy: No, I don't.
Woman: Do you like soccer, then?
Boy: No. I like basketball. That's my favourite sport!

One   *Which sport is Kim doing today?*
Girl: Do you have a swimming lesson today Kim?
Boy: No, we play hockey in our sports class today.
Girl: Great!
Boy: I'd like to ride my sister's horse. But I can't do that today.

Two   *What's Lucy doing?*
Boy: What's Lucy doing? Is she playing basketball?
Girl: No. She's playing baseball.
Boy: Is she hitting the ball?
Girl: No. She's throwing the ball.

Three   *What's Tom watching on TV?*
Woman: What are you watching on TV, Tom? Football?
Boy: No. I'm watching the badminton game.
Woman: OK. Would you like to play table tennis?
Boy: Not now, Mum.

Four   *Where's Dan?*
Man: So, where's Dan? Is he at the beach?
Girl: No. He's playing tennis in the park.
Man: The one behind Lime Street?
Girl: Yes, Dad.

Five   *Which girl is Sam?*
Boy: Look Mum! There's Sam! She's wearing a blue shirt.
Woman: The girl in the white skirt?
Boy: Not her. Sam's wearing black trousers.
Woman: Oh yes!

E Cool! OK! Great!, Yes, please! or No thanks!

○ Point to Jill's speech bubble. Say: *Let's play ... ?* (point to the basketball picture in **C**) Learners answer: *basketball!* Say: *Write basketball on the line.*
  Point to Mark's speech bubble. Say: *Do you want to play ... ?* (point to the table tennis picture in **C**). Learners answer: *table tennis!* Say: *Write table tennis on the line.*
  Point to Sue's speech bubble. Say: *Would you like to play ... ?* (point to the football picture in **C**) Learners answer: *football!* Say: *Write football on the line.*

○ Write on the board: *Cool! OK! Great!   Yes, please!   No, thanks!*

○ Ask one learner to read Jill's sentence. Answer: *Cool! OK! Great!* Ask two different learners to read out Mark and Sue's sentences. Answer: *Yes, please!* or *No, thanks!*

○ Say: *Stand up!* Learners stand up.
  Ask: *Do you want to play baseball now? Is your answer 'yes'? Then make a happy face, jump and say: 'Cool!', 'OK, great!' or 'Yes, please!' You choose.* Demonstrate smiling and jumping up and down once or twice while you say: *Yes, please!*
  Ask: *Is your answer 'no'? Then make a sad face, look at the floor and say, 'No, thanks!'* Demonstrate this response too, then ask the class the following questions. Learners respond with actions and *OK/yes* or *no* answers.
  Do you want to play baseball?
  Would you like to go horse riding?
  Do you want to go swimming?
  Would you like to play badminton?
  Do you want to play hockey?
  Would you like to go fishing?
  Do you want to ride your bikes?

I'm good at ...

○ Say: *I'm really good at running and I'm good at football. I'm not good at badminton and I'm not good at catching.* Ask one or two learners: *Are you good at running/football/badminton/catching?*

○ In pairs, learners choose, then write a list of six sports in this unit. Ask one pair: *Do you play tennis?* If learners have 'tennis' on their list, they answer *yes*. Ask: *Are you good at tennis?* Learners answer *yes* or *no*. Say: *For 'yes' answers, put a tick next to your sport. For 'no' answers, put a cross next to your sport.* Learners then add a tick or a cross next to each sport on their list.

○ Ask: *Who has hockey on their list? Who hasn't got hockey on their list?* Choose two learners who have hockey (learners A and C) and one who hasn't (learner B) to come to the front of the class. Support learners through the following role play:

Learner A: *Do you play hockey?*   Learner B: *No.*
Learner A: *Do you play hockey?*   Learner C: *Yes.*
Learner A: *Are you good at hockey?*   Learner C: *Yes! I'm really good at hockey!*

Learner A: *Let's play hockey!*   Learner C: *OK! Great!*

○ Learners now work on their own and move around asking and answering questions with other learners.

F Play the game. Let's move!

○ Tell learners to do the following actions, one at a time:
  jump, run, kick a ball, swim, bounce a ball, ride a bike, catch a ball, ride a horse, hit a ball, fish, play tennis, play hockey, play baseball.

○ After a while, tell learners to mime two, three and then a chain of actions. For example: Say: *Ride a bike and hit a ball. Ride a horse, fish and play tennis!* Say the actions slowly at first and then more quickly.

38 My favourites

Topics general revision

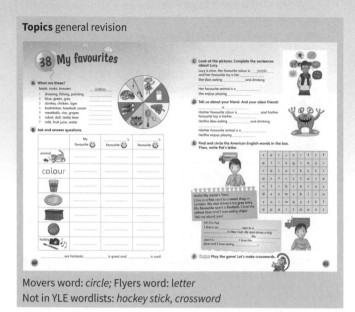

Movers word: *circle;* Flyers word: *letter*
Not in YLE wordlists: *hockey stick, crossword*

toys: alien, car, game, kite, monster, teddy bear, train, truck
sports: basketball, football, hockey, running, swimming, table tennis, tennis

Ⓐ What are these?

○ Write on the board: *boots, socks, trousers.* Ask: *Who's wearing boots today? Are you wearing socks? What colour are your socks? How many people are wearing trousers?* Say: *These are words for … ?* (clothes). Point to the word *clothes* on the first line in **A**.

○ Say: *Look at the three words on lines 1–7 now. These aren't clothes. What are they? Write words for 1–7 on the lines.*
Note: All the words they need are in the first column in B, in the singular form.

> **Check answers:**
> **1** hobbies **2** colours/colors **3** animals **4** sports
> **5** food(s) **6** toys **7** drinks

○ Point to the example again and ask: *Can you tell me more clothes words?* Different learners come to the board and write other clothes words.
Starters clothes words: cap, dress, hat, jacket, jeans, shirt, shoes, shorts, skirt, T-shirt.

○ Divide learners into teams of 4–5. Teams write as many hobbies, animals, colours, drinks, food, toys and sports words as possible in their notebooks. Give teams about five minutes to do this. They can use dictionaries if they want to.

○ Teams exchange notebooks and check each other's answers. Teams get a point for every correct word. (Correct spelling is needed). The winning team is the one with the most points.
Note: Learners may want to add other words to their lists, for example (sports) 'surfing', 'skateboarding', (food) 'yoghurt', 'pizza'. This is fine as long as they spell the words correctly. Teach any useful topic vocabulary that is not included in the Starters lists below.
Starters words:
hobbies: bird watching, playing games, listening to music, playing music, reading, singing, taking photos, writing
animals: bear, bee, bird, cat, crocodile, dog, duck, elephant, fish, frog, giraffe, goat, hippo, horse, jellyfish, lizard, monkey, mouse, polar bear, sheep, snake, spider, zebra
colours: black, brown, orange, pink, purple, red, white, yellow
drinks: lemonade
food: apple, banana, bean, bread, burger, cake, candy, chicken, chips, chocolate, coconut, egg, fish, fries, fruit, ice cream, lemon, lime, mango, meat, onion, orange, pea, pear, pineapple, potato, sausage, sweets, watermelon

Ⓑ Ask and answer questions.

○ Write your favourite animal and colour on the board. For example: *horse, yellow*
Say and write on the board: *I like dogs, but horses are my favourite animal. I like the colour blue, but yellow is my favourite.*

○ Point to the words in the first column in **B** and to the words 'My favourite' at the top of the second column. Say: *Write your favourite animal, colour, drink, food, toy, sport and hobby in the boxes under 'My favourite'.* Learners write the word for their favourite things in the second column.

○ Write on the board: …………'s your favourite …………?
My favourite animal is a horse.

○ Point to the lines in the question and ask: *Which words go here?* (*What, animal?*)
Write *What* and *animal* in the question on the board.
Ask: *Can you make this question with the word 'colour'?* (What's your favourite colour?)
The whole class ask and answer the questions about animals and colours together. (Each learner uses the word for *their* favourite animal and colour in the answer.) Learners then do this in pairs.

○ In pairs, learners write their partner's name at the top of the third column and ask and answer the questions about their favourite things. They write their partner's answers in the boxes below.

○ Learners then move and talk to a different person and write their name and answers in the last column.

○ Ask questions about the learners' favourite animals. Learners talk about their answers in pairs or small groups.
My favourite animal is a horse. A horse doesn't live in a zoo. Does your animal live in a zoo?
Is your animal big or small? What does it eat?
Do the same for food and sports:
Do you eat your favourite food for breakfast, for lunch or for dinner? Do you have that food on your birthday?
Where do you play your favourite sport? Who do you play with?

○ Point to the sentence under the table in **B** and say:
Horses are fantastic, basketball is great and music is cool!
Point to the first line in this sentence in **B** and say: *Write your favourite animals on this line!* Learners write their favourite animals. Point to the second line and say: *Write your favourite sport here.* Learners write. Point to the third line and ask: *Which hobby is cool? Write your cool hobby here!* Learners write.

○ Ask two or three different learners to read out their sentences. Then in pairs or groups of three, learners take turns to say their sentences individually. Then all the learners in the group/pair say their sentence at the same time. Then, everyone in the class says their sentence at the same time!

Ⓒ Look at the pictures. Complete the sentences about Lucy.

○ Point to the girl and say: *This is Lucy. She's nine years old.*

○ Point to the pictures in the circles around Lucy's head and shoulders.
Ask: *What can you see here?* (carrots, a goat, the colour purple, a hockey stick, orange juice, a monster) Point to the first two lines and ask: *What's Lucy's favourite colour?* (purple) Point to the word 'purple' on the line.

○ Say: *Lucy is nine. Her favourite colour is purple and her favourite toy is her … ?* (monster) Learners write *monster* on the line in this sentence.

○ Learners complete the other sentences with the words for the pictures in the circles.
○ Ask learners to say and spell the words. Write them on the board.

> **Check answers:**
> carrots, orange juice, goat, hockey

○ Different learners read out a sentence about Lucy.

D Tell us about your friend. And your alien friend!

○ Tell learners to look at the table in **B** again. They choose one of the names they wrote at the top of the third or fourth columns and write it in the first gap. Explain that they are going to complete a text about that person.
Ask: *How old is your friend?* Tell learners to write their friend's age in the second gap.
○ Learners write their friend's answers from **B** on the other lines. Remind them to circle 'He' and 'his' if they asked a boy or 'She' and 'her' if they asked a girl.
○ Learners show their texts to the person they wrote about.
○ Point to the alien picture and say: *This is your alien friend! What's its name? What are its favourite things?* Learners copy the sentences from **D** into their notebooks and complete them about their alien.
○ Pairs of learners talk about their alien to the rest of the class or to another pair. With bigger classes, do this in groups.

E Find and circle the American English words in the box. Then, write Pat's letter.

> **Starters tip**
> Both British and American words and spellings are accepted in the Reading and Writing. For example: *I live in a flat/apartment. My favourite/favorite colour/color is blue.* Make sure that learners are familiar with all the words on the Starters wordlist. (All the Starters words with British/US spellings are in the box in **E**.)

○ Write on the board: *lorry*. Point to Tom (the first boy) in **E**. Say: *This boy's British.* Point to the lorry behind Tom and ask: *What's this?* (a lorry) Say: *This is the word in British English.* Point to Pat (the second boy) Say: *This boy's American.* Point to the lorry behind Pat and ask: *What's the name for this in American English?* (truck) *Can you find the word 'truck' in the word search box?* Learners find the word and circle it. (It's in column 8.)
○ Write on the board: *rubber, flat, chips, shop, football, colour, favourite, sweets, grey*
Ask: *Can you find the American words for these British words?* In pairs, learners find the words in the word search box and circle them.

> **Check answers:**
>
> | s | o | c | c | e | r | f | l | f |
> | p | t | r | e | g | r | a | y | r |
> | c | o | l | o | r | k | v | t | i |
> | a | s | f | c | s | t | o | r | e |
> | n | e | r | a | s | e | r | u | s |
> | d | v | x | m | z | b | i | c | u |
> | y | a | i | w | q | y | t | k | f |
> | a | p | a | r | t | m | e | n | t |

○ Under the word *colour* on the board, write *color*. Under *favourite*, write *favorite* and under *grey*, write *gray*.
Point to the three pairs: *colour/color, favourite/favorite* and *grey/gray* and ask learners what the difference is.
If necessary explain that only the spelling is different. The meaning of the two words is the same.
○ Point to Tom, the boy with the UK map on his shirt and say: *This is Tom. He lives in England. He speaks British English.* Ask different learners to read out a sentence each from Tom's message. Ask: *What's next to Tom's flat?* (a sweet shop) *What's his favourite sport?* (football) *What does Tom love eating?* (chips)
○ Learners work in A and B pairs. Learner A says a British word; Learner B says the American word. Then Learner B says a British English word and Learner A says the American English word.
○ Point to the boy with the US map on his T-shirt and say: *This is Pat. He's American. Pat lives in a flat too, but he doesn't say 'flat'! Which word does Pat say?* (apartment) Learners write 'apartment' on the first line. Say: *Pat doesn't live next to a sweet shop! He's American, so he lives next to a ...* (candy store) *His dad doesn't drive a lorry, he drives a ...* (gray truck). Ask: *What colour is Pat's dad's truck? How does Pat spell that colour?* (gray) Learners write 'candy store' and 'gray truck' on the second and third lines.
Say: *Read Pat's letter.* Write words on the lines about Pat's favourite sport, colour and food. Learners write words on the lines. They can use the words that they circled in the wordbox to help them.

> **Check answers:**
> apartment, candy store, gray truck, favorite, soccer, color, fries

F Play the game! Let's make crosswords.

○ Write on the board (vertically):
h
o
b
b
i
e
s
○ Learners write words on the board to talk about hobbies around the word, using the different letters.
For example: fis**h**ing
ph**o**tos
ta**b**le tennis
basketball
draw**i**ng
enjoy
songs
○ Give different groups a topic (for example: sports, food and drink, home, school, family, clothes). They make crosswords. They could also cut pictures out of magazines or draw pictures or print them from their computer and make a collage around their crosswords.

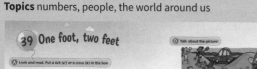

39   One foot, two feet

Topics numbers, people, the world around us

Movers words: numbers *21–26*

Equipment needed

- A5 pieces of card or paper (one per learner). See A.
- Two lists of words. See C ('Plural challenge').

A   Look and read. Put a tick or a cross in the box.

Reading & Writing Part 1

> **Starters tip**
>
> In Reading and Writing Part 1, two or three of the sentences are likely to be wrong. The picture might show something from the same lexical set, for example, a picture of a shoe (instead of a sock), something that has a similar spelling, for example, a horse (instead of a house) or there may not be an obvious connection, for example, a camera (instead of a boat). Activities like finding similar spellings and revising lexical sets will help.

- Learners look at the two examples in **A**. Point to the picture in the second example and say: *Can you see the cross? This sentence is wrong. They aren't men. These are … (girls).* Learners put ticks or crosses in boxes for sentences 1–5.

  > **Check answers:**
  > 1 ✗   2 ✔   3 ✗   4 ✗   5 ✔

- Say: *Let's look at the **wrong** answers.*
  Ask: *What can you see in 3?* (two hands) *Point to the feet in **B**.*

- Ask: *What can you see in 1?* (a chair) *But what's the word in 1?* (child)
  Write on the board:
  chair   child
  Point out that the first two letters are the same in these words but the rest of the spelling is different.

- Point to a chair in the classroom (or the picture of the chair in 1) and a child in the classroom (or the picture of a child in **B**) and say: *'Chair' and 'child' start with 'c-h'. Tell me words that start with 'ch'!*
  Starters words: *chicken, children, chips, chocolate, choose*

- Write on the board: *Charlie chooses chicken and chips and chocolate!* Point to the words as learners say them and then the complete sentence:
  Charlie.
  Charlie chooses.
  Charlie chooses chicken.
  Charlie chooses chicken and chips.
  Charlie chooses chicken and chips and chocolate.

- Ask: *What can you see in 3?* (hands) *But what's the word in 3?* (feet)
  Write on the board: *hands   feet*

Say: *These are parts of your … ?* (body) *Tell me words for parts of your body.* Learners answer.
Starters words: arm, ear, eye, face, hair, head, leg, mouth, nose

B   Complete the words.

- Point to one of the mice in the long line of pictures above **B** and **C** and say: *Look! It's a mouse!* Then point to both mice and say: *Look! There are two mice.*
  Point to the completed words 'mouse' and 'mice' in the example.

- In pairs, learners complete the missing singular and plural forms in the table using their wordlists or dictionaries if necessary.

  > **Check answers:** two feet, a man, ten women, a child, lots of fish, a sheep, six people.

- Write ***p e o p l e*** vertically on the board. Ask: *What's this word?* (people) Point to each letter in turn and ask learners to choose a name that begins with each letter. Add the chosen names next to the letters (see suggestions).

Tell me a girl's name. It begins with 'p'.	(Pat)
Tell me a boy's name. It begins with 'e'.	(Emil)
Tell me a boy's name. It begins with 'o'.	(Oliver)
Tell me a girl's name. It begins with 'p'.	(Poppy)
Tell me a girl's name. It begins with 'l'.	(Lucy)
Tell me a boy's name. It begins with 'e'.	(Erik)

- Learners look at the word picture. Ask: *How many people can you see in this word picture?* (five) *How many letters are there in 'people'?* (six) *Which person is making one letter with her head and one letter with her arms?* (Poppy)

- Check learners have colouring pencils. Say: *Listen and colour this word picture.* Pause between instructions to give learners time to colour. Use the names learners have chosen here.
  Colour (Pat's) hair. Make (Pat's) hair brown.
  Colour (Emil's) face. (Emil's) got a green face!
  Colour (Oliver's) hair. (Oliver's) got orange hair.
  Colour (Poppy's) face. Look at (Poppy's) pink face!
  And let's colour Poppy's arms. Make Poppy's arms blue.
  Colour (Erik's) hair. (Erik's) got yellow hair. Ask: *Can you see p, e, o, p, l and e in the word picture?*
  Learners look at each other's word pictures and then complete their colouring. Say: *You choose the colours.*

- Check learners' pronunciation of 'people' (/ˈpiːpəl/) and other /iː/ Starters words.
  Write on the board: *people, feet, sheep, tree, jeans, beans, Lucy, three, green, eating, cleaning, sleeping.* Point to and say each word.

- Learners work in groups of four to make a sentence that contains as many of these words as possible. To help learners, write one sentence in open class before they work on their own.

- Point to the word 'Lucy' on the board. Say: *Let's start our sentence with 'Lucy'. Which word can we put now? What does Lucy like doing?* Point to 'sleeping'. Say: *I think Lucy likes sleeping!*
  Write on the board: *Lucy likes sleeping.* Ask: *Where does Lucy like sleeping?* Point to the word 'tree'. Ask: *Does she like sleeping in the tree? Behind the tree? Under the tree? You choose!* Add learners' suggestion to the sentence. Ask: *What colour is a tree?* Point to the word 'green' if necessary. Add *green* to the sentence. Say: *Let's read our sentence now.* Point to each word as they say:
  Lucy likes sleeping under the green tree!

- Groups then write another sentence in their notebooks. Walk around and help if necessary. After checking sentences, choose a learner's sentence to drill, or one of the following:
  Three clean people are sleeping under the green tree.
  The sheep is cleaning its feet on Lucy's green jeans!
  Lucy's sheep are eating lots of clean green beans.

C Write yes or no.

o Learners look at the pictures above **B** and **C**. Point to the fish. Read out sentence 1: *There is one fish.*
Ask: *Is this right?* (No. There are two fish.)

o Learners read sentences 1–7 and write *yes* after the correct sentences and *no* if they are wrong.

> **Check answers:**
> **1** no **2** yes **3** no **4** yes **5** no **6** yes **7** no

o Learners correct the *no* sentences in their notebooks: **1** There **are two mice. 3** There **are two feet. 5** There **is one** sheep. **6** There **are lots of / five people**.

Optional extension: Plural challenge

o Divide the class into two teams. Give each team a list of ten words (see below). Each team writes the plural form for each word.
Team A: *foot, tomato, sentence, woman, bus, child, kiwi, rug, tablet, song*
Team B: *fish, class, favourite, skateboard, person, watch, classmate, potato, face, mouse*

o Team A says a singular word from their list then one person from that team writes the plural form on the board. Team B then does the same with a word from their list. Teams take turns to say the singular form and then write the plural form on the board. The winning team has the most correctly spelled plural words.

D Talk about the picture! Speaking Parts 1&2

Note: There are three sets of 'Where is/are' questions about the big picture in **D** here, but in Speaking Part 1, learners will only be asked one set of 'Where is/are' questions.

o Ask questions about picture **D**. Point to the picture and say:
Look at this. This is a park. The family are sitting and eating.

o Point to the sun and say: *Here's the sun. Where's the car?* (Learners say 'Here!' and point to the car.) *Where are the fish?* (Learners say 'Here!' and point to the fish.)
Stronger learners could practise prepositions by answering the questions *Where's the car? Where are the fish?* with full sentences.
It's behind the people / in the street. They're in the water!
Ask two more sets of questions for learners to answer in the same way:
Here's the tree. Where's the sheep? Where are the apples?
Here's the water. Where is the mother? Where are the children?
Point to the mice and say: *Tell me about the mice.*
Suggestions: *There are three mice. They're running. They're white. I don't like these mice. Cats like mice!*

o **Note:** In Speaking Part 2, learners will only be asked about one set of questions. Point to one of the pears in the tree. Ask:
What's this? (a pear) *What colour is it?* (yellow)
How many pears are there? (seven)
What's the bird doing? (singing)
Point to the chickens and say: *Tell me about the chickens.*
Suggestions: *There are three chickens. They're behind the family. Chickens make eggs. Some chickens can fly. They're funny.*
Point to the car and say: *Tell me about the car.*
Suggestions: *It's blue/purple. The door is closed. It's small. This car is great. It's on the street.*

o Point to one of the apples on the plate. Ask:
What's this? (an apple) *What colour is it?* (red) *How many apples are there?* (five) *What's the sheep doing?* (eating)

o Write on the board:
What's this? What colour is it? How many .... are there? What's the .... doing? Tell me about ...

o In pairs, learners write four other questions about the picture. Pairs work with other pairs and ask and answer the questions.
Suggestions: *What's this?* (a flower)
What colour is it? (white and pink)
How many flowers are there? (three)
What are the family doing? (eating)

Tell me about the dog/sheep/tree.
What's this? (a fish)
What colour is it? (green)
How many fish are there? (five)
What are the mice doing? (running)
What are the two boys doing? (playing)

E Make sentences about the picture in D.

o Point to the words in the table under the picture. Say:
One sheep is eating a flower. Where is the sheep?
(Learners point to the sheep and say: *Here!*)
What's the sheep eating? (a flower)

o In pairs, learners choose words from each column to make four more sentences about the picture. They use different colours to colour the boxes for each sentence.

> **Check answers:**
> *Two children are wearing blue T-shirts.*
> *Three mice are running behind the dog.*
> *Four people are eating some bread.*
> *Five fish are swimming in the water.*

F Look at the family and answer questions.

o Write these questions on the board or dictate them if you prefer.
1 *What is the bird doing now?*
2 *Who is playing badminton?*
3 *What are the man and woman cleaning?*
4 *Where are the mice now?*
5 *What are the fish doing now?*
6 *How many apples can you see?*
7 *What is the sheep doing now?*
8 *Which animals are eating bread?*

o Learners look at the picture in **F**. They work in small groups and write the answers as quickly as they can.

> **Check answers:**
> **1** flying **2** the / 2 / two girls **3** the car **4** in front of the dog
> **5** jumping **6** 1/one **7** sleeping **8** the (3/three) chickens

o Learners work in two groups: A and B. Group A looks at the picture in **D** and group B at the picture in **F**.
Say to everyone: *Listen to my sentences! Is the sentence right for your picture? Good! Stand up! But is this sentence wrong for your picture? OK! Sit down!*

o Say the following sentences. (Learners always sit down before you say the next sentence.)
1 *Five fish are swimming.* (Group A stands up.)
2 *Five fish are jumping.* (Group B stands up.)
3 *Two people are cleaning the car.* (Group B stands up.)
4 *A bird is singing.* (Group A stands up.)
5 *There are five apples.* (Group A stands up.)
6 *A bird is flying.* (Group B stands up.)
7 *Three chickens are eating bread.* (Group B stands up.)
8 *Four people are eating bread.* (Group A stands up.)
9 *A sheep is sleeping.* (Group B stands up.)
10 *The dog is running in front of the mice.* (Group A stands up.)

G Play the game! What's my word?

o Learners use the letters and numbers grid in the book or copy it into their notebooks.
Learners work in groups of 3–4 and quietly choose six words from this unit and 'spell' them on a piece of paper using the number code. For example 'birds' = 2, 9, 18, 4, 19. If you would like to make this puzzle task more difficult, learners could write their number coded words in reverse order, ie. 19, 4, 18, 9, 2.

o Groups work with other groups. Learners take turns to read out the numbers. Learners in the other group decipher the words.

40   Night and day

Topics time, numbers

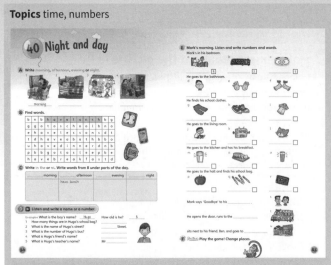

Movers words: *put on, wash, get up, When… ?*

Equipment needed

○ Starters audio 40D.

○ Scissors and photocopies of number matching game on page 117 (one per group of four learners). See D.

Starters tip

In the classroom, use the expressions *Hi!, Hello, Good morning, Good afternoon, Goodbye, Bye, See you* with learners so that they get used to hearing and saying them.

○ Write on the board: *m_rn_ng   _ft_rn_ _ n   _v_n_ng   n_ght*
Say: *These are parts of the day.* In pairs, learners copy and complete the four words in their notebooks (morning, afternoon, evening, night)
Talk with learners about when these parts of the day start and end.

○ Draw four clocks on the board showing seven, one, six and ten o'clock. If learners are more familiar with the 24-hour clock, write *07:00, 13:00, 19:00* and *22:00* on the clock faces.
Point to the time on each clock in turn and say: *When we see a person then, we can say Hi or Hello or we can say Good … ?* (morning / afternoon/evening). *We say Goodnight when we are going to bed.*
Point to the clocks in a random order. Each learner says *Good morning, Good afternoon, Good evening* or *Goodnight* (as appropriate) to their partner and to another learner sitting in front of them or behind them.

Ⓐ Write *morning, afternoon, evening* or *night*.

○ Teach/revise 'go to bed' and 'get up'. Ask: *Do you go to bed in the morning?* (no, in the evening) *Do you get up in the afternoon?* (no, in the morning) Point to picture 1. Learners look at the picture. Ask: *What's the girl doing? She's getting up.* Point to 'morning' under picture 1.

○ Point to the other pictures and ask: *What is this person doing?* (sleeping). *What are these children doing?* (going home at the end of school) *What are these people doing?* (watching TV). Learners write *afternoon, evening* or *night* under these three pictures.

Check answers:
2 night   **3** afternoon   **4** evening

Ⓑ Find words.

○ Point to the words 'have lunch' in the first line of letters in the word search box. Write *have lunch* on the board. Point out to learners that they can't see the space between 'have' and 'lunch' in the box.

○ Tell learners that there are eight other phrases in the word search box. Say: *Four start with 'have'. Three start with 'go to'. One starts with 'get'.*

○ Learners find eight phrases and write them in their notebooks. Say to different learners: *Come and write one of your answers on the board.*

Check answers:
Down: get up (column 1), go to bed (column 14)
Across: go to school (row 2), have lessons (row 3), have a bath (row 4), have dinner (row 5), go to sleep (row 6), have breakfast (row 7)

○ Learners choose one of the nine phrases on the board to mime.
Ask one confident learner to come to the front of the class and mime their phrase, for example 'have breakfast'. Other learners guess the phrase by asking questions, for example:
Is it 'have dinner'? No it isn't.
Is it 'have breakfast'? Yes, it is!
The learner who guesses correctly then comes to the front, crosses out the guessed answer and mimes another phrase. Continue until only one phrase remains. Learners all stand up and mime that last phrase.

○ Ask: *What colour is 'have lunch'?* (blue) Say: *Now colour all your 'have' answers blue too. Colour your 'go' answers pink and your 'get' answer yellow.* Learners colour the answers using blue, pink or yellow.
Say: *Some of the letters have no colour on them now. How many?* (15). *What are the letters?* (b, d and n). How many 'b's are there? (nine) And 'd's'? (three) And 'n's'? (three)

○ Write on the board: *b   d   n*
Learners work in pairs. Point to b, d and n in turn and say: *Find 15 words! Nine words start with 'b', three words start with 'd', and three words start with 'n'. Find your words on these two pages / in this unit. Go!* Pairs work quickly to write 15 words. Pairs put up their hands to show they have found all 15 words.
Check answers and spellings.
b, d and n words in this unit are: *day, dinner, door; night, name, number; bed, bath, breakfast, boy, bag, bus, bedroom, bathroom, Ben*

Ⓒ Write *in the* or *at*. Write words from B under parts of the day.

○ Write on the board: morning
            afternoon
            evening
            night

○ Draw a circle on the board. Inside the circle, write *in the* and *at*. Point to these words and ask: *Which words go in front of morning/ afternoon/evening/night?*
Ask four learners to add *in the* or *at* to *morning, afternoon, evening* and *night* on the board. Learners then copy *in the* (morning) *in the* (afternoon) *in the* (evening) *at* (night) on the lines in **C**.

○ Point to the example and say: *I have my lunch in the afternoon. Do you?* (yes) *And I have my breakfast in the morning. Do you?* (yes). *Write 'have my breakfast' under 'in the morning'.* Say: *I watch TV in the evening. Do you?* (yes/no). Learners who answer 'yes', write *watch TV* under 'in the evening'.

○ Ask a few learners to say something they do in the day. The class suggests where to write that activity. For example: run to school (in the morning)

○ Learners work in pairs, adding the words from **B** and their own ideas to the table. Walk around checking spelling and encouraging learners to ask for help with vocabulary if necessary. If available, learners could also use bilingual or digital dictionaries to find the words they need.

Ⓓ ▶ Listen and write a name or a number.
Listening Part 2

Starters tip

In Listening Part 2, answers are only a number or a name, which is spelt by the speaker. To prepare for this part, encourage learners to quickly check the questions before listening to the conversation so they know in advance which answers will be a number (1–20) and which answers will be a name (words from the Starters wordlist).

○ Say: *Look at this boy! What colour is his T-shirt?* (blue) *What can you see on his T-shirt?* (a sun, a happy face, a smiley). Learners look at the two examples. Ask: *What's his name?* (Hugo) *How do you spell Hugo?* (H-U-G-O). *How old is Hugo?* (He's 8). Ask: *Can you see the number 8 or the word 'eight' in this answer?* (the number).

Say: *Listen and write answers now. In number answers, write the number, not the word.* Play the audio twice. Learners write answers.

Check answers:
1 12   **2** New   **3** 17   **4** Sam   **5** Fish

○ Learners work in pairs. Ask: *How many things are there in Hugo's school bag?* (12) *What are these twelve things? You choose.* Ask: *Is there a pen?* (yes)

Learners decide on 11 other things and then draw them on a piece of paper. Pairs work with other pairs and take turns to ask and answer questions about their drawings: *Is there a pen? Is there an apple?*

Audioscript

Listen and write a name or a number.
There are two examples.
  Man: Good morning! Who's this?
  Girl: Hello! He's my brother. He's going to school.
  Man: Oh! What's his name?
  Girl: His name is Hugo. You spell Hugo, H-U-G-O.
  Man: How old is Hugo?
  Girl: He's eight years old.
  Man: Eight?
  Girl: Yes, that's right.
Can you see the answers? Now you listen and write a name or a number.
1 Girl: Hugo's got lots of things in his school bag.
  Man: Has he? How many things?
  Girl: Twelve!
  Man: Twelve! That IS a lot of things.
2 Man: And what's the name of Hugo's street?
  Girl: We live in New Street.
  Man: New Street? Do you spell that N-E-W?
  Girl: Yes! We like living there.
3 Girl: Hugo goes to school on a bus.
  Man: What number is his bus?
  Girl: He goes on the number seventeen bus.
  Man: The number seventeen bus. OK!
4 Girl: Hugo's got a funny friend at school.
  Man: Has he? What's Hugo's friend's name?
  Girl: His friend's name is Sam.
  Man: Sam?
  Girl: Yes. You spell that S-A-M.
5 Man: What's Hugo's teacher's name?
  Girl: His teacher's name is Mr Fish!
  Man: Mr Fish? Do you spell that F-I-S-H?
  Girl: Yes. He's a really nice teacher and Hugo is very happy in his class.
  Man: Fantastic!

Optional extension: Matching numbers game
Learners work in groups of four. Give each group a set of the matching numbers game on page 117. Learners cut up the game and place the cards face down on a table then take turns to look at two cards. They need to make a pair of a number and its word, for example: 8/eight. If they are successful, they keep the pair. If their pair doesn't match, they return the cards face down on the table. The winner is the player with the most matching pairs.

Ⓔ Tony's morning. Listen and write numbers and words.

○ Say: *Look at these pictures. How many pictures are there?* (21) *What can you see in the pictures?* Different learners describe each picture in one word. Write these on the board in a random order. Learners then write each word under its correct picture in **E**.

Check answers:
a) boy/bed   **b)** clock   **c)** eyes   **d)** face   **e)** hands   **f)** feet
g) trousers   **h)** shoes   **i)** shirt   **j)** baby   **k)** robot   **l)** cat
m) milk   **n)** bread   **o)** juice   **p)** apple   **q)** pencils   **r)** game
s) mum and dad   **t)** bus   **u)** school

○ Ask: *What's Tony's teacher's name?* (Mr Fish) Say: *Listen to Mr Fish. He's talking about Tony's morning.* Learners listen, but they do not write anything yet.
○ Read the story.

Tony's morning
It's the morning and Tony is in his bedroom. He opens his **eyes** and looks at the **clock** and he jumps out of **bed**.

He goes to the bathroom. He washes his **feet** and he washes his **face** and he washes his **hands**. He finds his school clothes and he puts on his **shirt**. He puts on his **trousers** and he puts on his **shoes**.

Tony goes to the living room. He plays with his new **robot**. He plays with his **baby brother**. And he plays with **his cat**. Tony's cat's name is Socks!

He goes to the kitchen and has his breakfast. He drinks some **orange juice**, he eats some **bread**. Tony drinks some **milk**, too.

He goes to the hall and finds his schoolbag. He puts an **apple** in his schoolbag. He finds his **game** and puts that in his bag. Tony puts his **pencils** in his bag, too.

Tony says 'Goodbye' to his **mum and dad**. He opens the door, runs to the **bus**, sits next to his friend, Ben, and goes to **school**.

○ Learners listen to the story a second time. Stop reading after 'bed'. Learners look at the numbers for pictures a,b and c (3, 2, 1). Ask: *What does Tony do in the morning? He opens his … ?* (eyes) Point to number 1. *He looks at the … ?* (clock) Point to number 2. *And he jumps out of … ?* (bed) Point to number 3.

Read the rest of the story. Learners listen and order each stage of Tony's morning in the same way.

Check answers:
face 2 / hands 3 / feet 1   trousers 2 / shoes 3 / shirt 1   baby 2 / robot 1 / cat 3   milk 3 / bread 2 / juice 1   apple 1 / pencils 3 / game 2   mum and dad 1 / bus 2 / school 3

○ Read the story a third time. This time learners mime the actions. Learners work in groups and plan their own school morning and mime it to other groups. Other groups guess what the actions are.

Answer questions about your day.

○ Ask different learners these questions. Write on the board:
Where do you have breakfast? Who do you have breakfast with? What do you have for breakfast?
○ Remove the word 'breakfast' from the three questions on the board. Write *lunch* instead. In pairs, learners ask and answer each other about their lunch. Do the same with *dinner*.

Ⓕ Play the game! Change places.

Play 'Change places' with learners using the verbs from this unit. See page 7 for how to play this game. For example: *Change places if you have breakfast in the morning.*

Suggested sentences:

Change places if you:	*walk to school.*
come to school by bus.	*listen to the radio in the car.*
have lunch at school.	*have music lessons.*
play football.	*go swimming.*
watch TV in the evening.	*drink water for lunch.*
go to sleep at night.	*learn English at this school!*

41   Trains, boats and planes

Topics transport, sports and leisure, the world around us

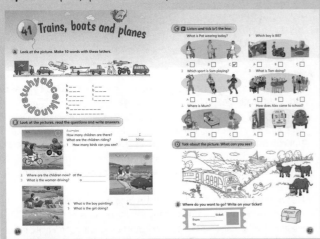

Movers word: *ticket*; Flyers word: *wheel*

Equipment needed

○   Starters audio 41C.

Ⓐ Make words with these letters.

○   Ask 4–5 learners: *How do you come to school? Do you walk to school in the morning?* Learners answer *yes* or *no*. Continue asking questions: *Do you come on the bus? On the train? In a plane? In a boat? Does your mum or dad drive you to school in their car?*

Write on the board: *How do you come to school?*

Learners ask and answer the question in pairs.

○   Point to the top picture in **A**. Ask: *What can you see here?*

(a lorry, a car, a helicopter, a boat, a truck, a bike, a plane, a motorbike, a bus)

○   Teach 'wheel'. Ask: *How many wheels has a motorbike/car/bus got? Has a helicopter/boat got wheels?* (no)

Say: *Look at the letter wheel. How many letters are in the letter wheel?* (16)

What colour are the letters? (purple)

○   Say: *Look at the letter wheel and the pictures and write the words.*

In pairs, learners use the letters to complete the words. They can use them as many times as they like. Learners use their dictionaries to check spellings if necessary.

> **Check answers:**
>
> bus, car, bike/boat, plane, truck/train, lorry, motorbike, helicopter.

○   Ask: *What can't you see in these pictures?* (a train or a ship)

○   Write on the board:

May's playing a great train game and I'm playing with my grey plane!

Learners copy the sentence in their notebooks.

○   Read the sentence, carefully pronouncing the /eɪ/ vowel sounds in the different spellings. Ask: *Which words have /eɪ/ in them?* Read the sentence again.

In pairs learners underline the /eɪ/ sounds in the sentence.

May's playing a great train game and I'm playing with my grey plane!

○   Say: *Listen! Mrs Shell is showing us the ship! Listen again! How many words are in the sentence? Mrs Shell is showing us the ship!* (7) Write the sentence on the board. Ask: *Who's showing us the ship?* (Mrs Shell) *What's Mrs Shell showing us?* (the ship)

○   The whole class, then pairs of learners, say the train and ship sentences.

Ⓑ Look at the pictures, read the questions and write answers.

Reading & Writing   Part 5

> **Starters tip**
>
> In Reading and Writing Part 5, candidates may need to answer a 'What/doing?' question. Answers must not be longer than one word, so they should write the present participle. For example: 'What's the bird doing?' 'Flying.'

○   Practise 'What/doing?' questions and answers. Point to the first picture and ask: *What are the birds doing?* (flying) Point to the second picture and ask: *What are the children and the woman doing?* (waving) Point to the third picture and ask: *What's the boy doing now?* (painting)

○   Learners look at the two examples. Ask: *How many children are there?* (two) *Is the answer a number or a word?* (a number) *The children are riding their … ?* (bikes) *Is the answer one word or two words?* (one word)

In this task, as in Reading and Writing Part 5, make sure learners write numbers (not words) and only one-word answers.

○   In pairs or on their own, learners write answers to 1–5.

> **Check answers:**
>
> **1** 2   **2** beach   **3** car   **4** boat   **5** swimming

Say more about the story!

○   Ask *Where's the … ?* questions. In pairs, learners listen and point to their pictures.

Look at picture 1. Where's the boat? Where's the motorbike? Where's the sun?

Look at picture 2. Where's the sea? Where's the lorry? Where's the woman?

Look at picture 3. Where's the sand? Where's the paint? Where's the girl?

○   In pairs, learners take turns to ask *Where's the … ?* questions and to point to the correct object, place or person in the picture.

○   Ask: *At the end of the story, is the girl happy? Is the boy happy?* Learners answer *yes* or *no*.

Ask: *Can you ride a bike? Drive a car? Do you like going to the beach? Do you like painting? Do you like swimming?* Learners answer *yes* or *no*.

Ⓒ ▶ Listen and tick the box.

Listening   Part 3

Option 1: Learners complete this task as a Listening Part 3.

○   Learners look at the pictures. Play the audio. Learners listen to the example then the five conversations. They tick the correct box (A, B or C). Play the audio a second time. Learners check and complete their answers.

Option 2: Learners complete the task as test practice.

○   Say: *Look at the example pictures.* Point to the girl and say: *This girl's name is Pat. What's Pat doing? Is she riding her bike?* (no) *Is Pat sitting on her bike?* (no) *Is Pat holding her bike?* (yes)

What's Pat wearing in picture A? A blue … ? (jacket) *a white … ?* (T-shirt) *and a yellow … ?* (skirt) In pairs, learners say what Pat is wearing in pictures B and C. (B: a blue dress; C: a white T-shirt, a yellow skirt)

Play the example on the audio. Ask: *Is Pat wearing a dress today?* (no) *Is she wearing a skirt?* (yes) *Is she wearing a jacket?* (no) *Which is the right answer?* (C)

Play the rest of the audio. Learners tick the correct boxes (A, B or C).

Play the audio a second time. Learners check and complete their answers.

○ Say: *Look at Pat in the example pictures again. Is Pat wearing a jacket in picture 1, 2 or 3?* (1) Ask different learners: *What are you wearing? Are you wearing a jacket?* Learners answer.

Audioscript

Look at the pictures. Listen and look. There is one example.
What's Pat wearing today?

Man:	Is Pat wearing her blue dress this morning?
Girl:	No, she's wearing a skirt today.
Man:	And is she wearing a jacket?
Girl:	No, she isn't.

Can you see the tick? Now you listen and tick the box.

One	*Which boy is Bill?*
Woman:	Is that Bill? The boy on that boat?
Girl:	No, Mum! Look! Bill's sitting on his dad's motorbike.
Woman:	Oh yes! And where's Bill's dad, then?
Girl:	He's on a plane!

Two	*Which sport is Sam playing?*
Girl:	Which sport is Sam doing now? Is he playing basketball?
Boy:	No. He's playing badminton.
Girl:	Does he like playing hockey?
Boy:	No, he doesn't play that sport.

Three	*What's Tom doing?*
Man:	What are Tom and his friends doing? Are they playing their guitars?
Girl:	Not today. They're singing.
Man:	Is Tom's teacher playing her piano, too?
Girl:	No she isn't.

Four	*Where's Mum?*
Girl:	I can't find Mum. Is she in the garden?
Man:	No, and she isn't in the kitchen.
Girl:	I know! She's sleeping in the bedroom, Dad.
Man:	Oh yes. Shhh!

Five:	*How does Alex come to school?*
Man:	Do you come to school on the bus, Alex?
Girl:	No, I don't.
Man:	Do you walk here, then?
Girl:	No. My dad drives me here in our car.

D Talk about the picture. What can you see?

Speaking Parts **1** & **2**

Note: In Part 1, learners are only asked two 'Where … ?' questions (and also to place two of the small object cards onto the big picture). In Part 2, they are only asked one set of 'What … ?/What colour … ? How many … ? What/doing … ?' questions plus a 'Tell me about …' question. In this task, they are asked two sets of questions about the picture for each part and are not asked about any object cards.

○ Point to the picture and say: *Look at this. A man is driving the train.*
Point to the kite and say: *Here's the kite.* Ask four more 'Where … ?' questions. Learners point to the correct part of the picture to answer.
Ask: *Where's the sea? Where are the flowers?*
Where's the boat? Where are the trees?

○ Point to the cow and ask: *What's this?* (a cow)
What colour is it? (brown)
How many cows are there? (three)
Point to the bird and ask: *What's the bird doing?* (flying)
Point to the train driver and say: *Tell me about this man.* (He's in the train. He's looking at the cows. He's old. He's driving. He's got a hat.)
Point to the flower and ask: *What's this?* (a flower)
What colour is it? (pink)

How many flowers are there? (two)
Point to the children and ask: *What are the children doing?* (running)
Point to the train and say: *Tell me about the train.* (It's long. It's white. I like this train. It's going to the beach. It's old. It's got lots of doors.)

○ Learners colour the remaining parts of the picture. Ask 4–5 learners: *What colour is your train/bird/kite? What colour are your trees?*

○ Learners work in A and B pairs. Say: *Look at the picture on page 100.*
Say: *Ask and answer the two 'What's this?' questions.* Say to A learners: *You ask the blue question.* Say to B learners: *You ask the orange question.*
Give learners time to ask and answer their questions then say: *Ask and answer questions about the fish and the cats now.* Say to A learners: *You ask about the fish.* Say to B learners: *You ask about the cats.*

○ Point to the girl in the picture. Ask:
What's the girl doing? (She's playing the piano. She's singing/smiling /sitting.)

○ Ask four pairs to ask and answer: 'What's / What are the … doing?' questions about the picture. For example:
What's the monkey doing? (drawing)
What's the boy doing? (singing)
What are the fish doing? (swimming)
What are the frogs doing? (singing)

E Where do you want to go? Write on your ticket!

○ Teach 'ticket'. Ask: *Do you get a ticket on the school bus?* (yes/no)
If learners answer *yes*, ask: *What colour is your school bus ticket?* Learners answer.

○ Learners look at the picture of the ticket. Ask: *What colour is this ticket?* (blue and white) *Is this ticket for the train? Boat? Plane? Bus? You choose!* In pairs, learners decide. Point to the line in front of the word 'ticket'. Say: *Write train, boat, plane or bus on the line.*
Ask: *Where are you now? You choose! Are you at school? In Africa? At the beach? In Park Street? You choose!* Tell learners to write where they are now after the word 'from'.
Ask: *Where do you want to go with your ticket? You choose!* Tell learners to decide where they want to go, for example: New York, London or another town or city in their country. Learners then write the place they want to go to on the line after the word 'to'.
Learners complete the ticket picture adding a price or a time or any other information they want in the pink square. They choose!

○ Learners show their ticket to others in the class and talk about it.

Suggestions:
This is my train ticket. I'm going from Istanbul to London now!
This is my boat ticket. I'm going from the North Pole to the South Pole now!
This is my plane ticket. I'm going from Paris to New York now!

Note: If learners need more support, before they add their own information, draw your completed ticket on the board, talk about it and then ask: *Would you like to come with me?*

🧳 **Travelling!**

○ Learners draw a picture of a train, boat or plane and write four or five short sentences under their picture. Prompt ideas by asking questions, for example: *What colour is it? Can you drive/ride it? Where do you go on it?*

○ **Suggestion:**
I love this train.
It's blue and red.
It stops in my town.
I take photos of it.
We go to my grandparents' house on this train.

42   About a phone

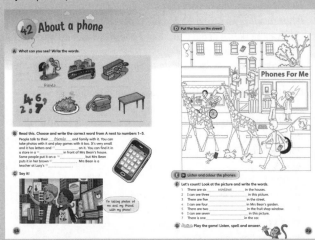

Equipment needed

- Colouring pencils or pens.
- A (non-transparent) bag with a watch inside. See B.
- Blank pieces of card or paper, 4cm square (two for each learner). See C.
- Starters audio 42E.

Ⓐ What can you see? Write the words.

- Ask: *What's the name of our school?* (for example, Leonard School) *Where is it?* (Rome) *Which street is it in?* (Panama) *Do your friends come to this school too?* (yes)

  Point to the first picture and ask: *How many children can you see?* (two)

  Say: *These two children are friends.* Point to the word 'friends' under the picture. Explain that the picture shows two friends, so this word has an 's' on the end.

  Point to the street picture and ask: *What's this?* (a street) *How many streets can you* see? (one) Learners write *street* on the line.

  Point to the third picture and ask: *What's this?* (a school) *How many schools can you see?* (one) *Do you write 'school' or 'schools'?* (school) Learners write *school* on the line under the picture.

- Learners write the word for the other four pictures. If there is one thing in the picture, they write the singular and if there is more than one, they write the plural.

  > **Check answers by asking learners to say and spell each word:**
  > numbers   chips/fries   bag/handbag   table

- Ask different learners: *Do you like eating chips?*
  Can you see a table in this room? Where's the table?
  What's your favourite number?
  Have you got a bag today? What's in your bag?

Ⓑ Read this. Choose and write the correct word from A next to numbers 1–5.

> **Starters tip**
>
> In Reading and Writing Part 4, learners have to choose the correct word to write in the text. Train learners to look carefully at the pictures. If they can see more than one object or person, its word will be plural. Learners should practise recognising the difference between singular and plural noun forms. It is also important that learners know the irregular plural forms like 'fish', 'men' and 'children'. Tell them to make sure they copy the correct form of the word into the text.

- Mime using a mobile phone. Point to the imaginary phone and ask: *What's this?* (a phone) *What colour is it?* (any colour)
- Point to the phone in **B**. Ask: *What colour is this phone?* (yellow and black)
- Say: *Read about this phone. Whose phone is it?* (Mrs Bean's) Learners read the text again and write one word from **A** for each gap.

  > **Check answers:**
  > **1** numbers   **2** street   **3** table   **4** bag   **5** school

- Read out the following sentences about the text. If learners think the sentences are correct, they stand up. If they think they are wrong, they sit down.
  *Mrs Bean's bag is brown. Her bag is **brown**.* (correct)
  *The phone shop is behind Mrs Bean's house. The shop's **behind** her house.* (wrong – it's in front of)
  *Mrs Bean's phone is blue. Her phone's **blue**.* (wrong – it's yellow)
  *Mrs Bean is a teacher. She's a **teacher**.* (correct)
- Write on the board: *What colour is it? What do you do with it? Is it big or small?*

  Show learners the bag with the watch in it. Explain that there is one thing in this bag. Learners ask you the questions on the board to guess what it is.
- Each learner thinks of another object that you can carry in a school bag. For example: a book, a pencil, ruler, book, rubber, an apple, sweets, juice.
- In groups of four, three learners ask the questions on the board and try to guess the object. The fourth learner answers. Repeat until all four learners have answered the questions.

Ⓒ Say it!

- Point to the boy with the phone and say: *Look at this. It's a picture of Dan and his friend Tom. What's on Tom's T-shirt?* (a zebra)
  Ask: *What's Dan holding?* (a phone) *What's he doing?* (taking a photo) *Where are they?* (in a street) *Are they happy?* (yes!)
- Point to and read out the sentence: *I'm taking photos of me and my friend with my phone!* Write on the board and say: *photos, friend, phone.* Point to the 'ph' in 'phone' and 'photo'. Explain that we write these words with 'ph' but we say them like an 'f'. (In your learners' first language they might write these words with an 'f' not 'ph'.)
- Say the whole sentence twice, (*I'm taking photos of me and my friend with my phone!*), then, say it in parts. Learners repeat each part:
  I'm taking photos
  of me and my friend
  with my phone

  Divide learners into A, B and C groups. Group A says the first part of the sentence, group B says the second and group C the third part, one after another.

  All three groups say their part of the sentence at the same time!
- The whole class says the whole sentence together.

Ⓓ Put the bus on the street!   Speaking Part 1

- Write on the board: *bus robot lizard cake*
  Ask learners to find these four things in pictures in their *Fun for Starters* book (bus: pages 45, 46, 47, 67, 85, 86, 87, robot: pages 19, 23, 42, 47, 63, 76, 90, lizard: pages 34, 35, 37, 47, 55, 94, cake: page 60, 68).

  Learners are going to draw a bus, a robot, a lizard and a cake next. Looking at these pictures will help them with ideas.
- Learners work in pairs. Give four blank cards to each pair of learners and ask them to make a set of four object cards (a bus, a robot's face, a lizard, a cake). Each learner draws two pictures.

o Point to the picture in **D** and say: *The phone store is behind the two children and in front of Mrs Bean's house. Where does Mrs Bean live?* (Learners point to the house behind the phone store).

Ask: *What can you see in the picture?* (the phone shop/store, a fruit shop/store, houses, a garden, flowers, windows, doors, the street, a tree, birds, giraffes, a woman, a man, a boy, a girl, a bike, a car)

o Read out the following questions. Pairs listen, hold up the correct object card and then put it in the correct part of the picture. They can do this in pairs.

Ask: *Which is the robot?* (Check that learners are holding up the robot card.)

Say: *Put the robot in Mrs Bean's garden.*

Which is the lizard? Put the lizard under the car.

Which is the bus? Put the bus between the two giraffes.

Which is the cake? Put the cake on the balloon.

o Check answers. Ask: *Where is the robot/lizard/bus/cake?* (in the garden / under the car / between the giraffes / on the balloon)

o Learners take the cards off the picture. Learner A tells learner B to put the robot, lizard, bus and cake in other places in the picture. Then Learner B tells A where to put the small pictures.

E ▶ **Listen and colour the phones.**　Listening **Part 4**

o Say: *There are lots of phones in this picture.* Ask: *How many phones are there?* (seven) *Where are the phones?* (on the bike, in the bird's mouth, in the girl's hand, in the woman's bag, in the tree, between the windows, on the phone store/shop door)

o Point to the phone in the bird's mouth. Ask: *What colour is this phone?* (orange)

o Check learners have a set of colouring pencils or pens.

o Play the audio twice. Learners listen and colour the phones.

Audioscript

Look at the picture. Listen and look. There is one example.
　　Man:　Can you see the birds?
　　Girl:　Yes. One of them has a phone in its mouth!
　　Man:　That's right.
　　Girl:　Can I colour it?
　　Man:　Yes. Colour the phone in the bird's mouth orange.
Can you see the orange phone in the bird's mouth? This is an example. Now you listen and colour.

1　Man:　Can you see the phone between the windows?
　　Girl:　The phone between the windows? Yes, I can.
　　Man:　Great! Colour that phone yellow, please.
　　Girl:　There! OK!

2　Man:　Now, can you see the phone on the man's bike?
　　Girl:　Sorry?
　　Man:　Find the phone on the man's bike. Colour that phone red.
　　Girl:　OK. I'm doing that now.

3　Girl:　Can I colour the phone in the girl's hand now?
　　Man:　Yes. You choose the colour for that phone.
　　Girl:　Great! Can I colour it blue?
　　Man:　Yes, you can!

4　Girl:　Can I colour the phone in the tree, too?
　　Man:　Yes! What colour?
　　Girl:　Can I colour it purple?
　　Man:　The phone in the tree! OK!

5　Girl:　There's a phone in the woman's bag too!
　　Man:　Oh, yes! Colour that phone brown, please.
　　Girl:　OK. I'm doing that now.
　　Man:　What a nice picture. Well done!

o Check answers by asking questions:
　What colour is the phone:　　between the windows? (yellow)
　　　　　　　　　　　　　　　on the man's bike? (red)
　　　　　　　　　　　　　　　in the girl's hand? (blue)
　　　　　　　　　　　　　　　in the tree? (purple)
　　　　　　　　　　　　　　　in the woman's bag? (brown)

o Ask: *Which phone hasn't got a colour?* (the phone on the phone shop door)

Say: *Colour that phone! You choose the colour!*

Ask different learners: *What colour is the phone on the door in your picture?*

Optional extension:

Learners draw and colour three more phones in the picture. They show each other their pictures and say where their three phones are.

For example: *There's a blue phone on the car door. There's a pink phone on the fruit shop. There's an orange phone under the giraffe.*

F **Let's count! Look at the picture and write the words.**

o Say: *Look at the picture again. How many doors can you see?* (three – the house door, the phone shop door and the car door) *How many windows can you see?* (six) Point to the word 'windows' on the line in 1.

Learners count things in the picture and write the words on the lines in sentences 2, 3 and 4.

> **Check answers:**
> **2** birds　**3** people　**4** chairs　**5** bananas　**6** phones
> **7** person/man

o Ask: *Where's the man?* (in the car) *What's the man doing?* (looking/ driving) *Where's the woman?* (next to the car) *What's the woman doing?* (walking)

o Write on the board: *Where's the … ?　What's the … …ing?*

Pairs of learners write these questions about two other things in the picture.

Two pairs work together. Pair A asks pair B their questions about the picture. Pair B answers. Then pair B asks and pair A answers.

G **Play the game! Listen, spell and answer.**

o Spell out the following jumbled words. (Do not read out the clues yet.) Learners listen and write the letters in their notebooks. Check that they have done this correctly by asking different learners to read out the letters.

o Read out the sentence about each word.

o In pairs, learners order the letters to make the right word. For example: r-t-a-w-e *You drink this.* (water)

Suggested words and clues:

1	r-o-d-o	*You open and close this.* (door)
2	b-r-e-z-a	*This animal is like a horse. It's black and white.* (zebra)
3	g-a-b	*You can carry things in this.* (bag)
4	a-r-c-s	*People drive these.* (cars)
5	k-e-b-i	*You can ride this.* (bike)
6	p-o-h-s	*You buy things here.* (shop)
7	d-e-a-h	*Your hair is on this.* (head)
8	b-d-s-i-r	*These can fly!* (birds)
9	t-r-f-i-u	*Apples and bananas are …* (fruit)
10	n-p-h-o-e	*Talk to your friend on this.* (phone)
11	r-e-p-p-a	*You write on this in books.* (paper)
12	h-t-o-s-r-s	*You wear these on your legs.* (shorts)
13	b-a-t-e-t-l	*This is like a small computer.* (tablet)
14	a-c-k-r-t-e	*You hit a tennis ball with this.* (racket)
15	e-r-b-a	*This is a big brown animal.* (bear)
16	e-i-p	*This has fruit or meat in it.* (pie)
17	t-a-b	*You can hit a ball with this!* (bat)
18	y-a-c-n-o-r-s	*You colour pictures with these.* (crayons)
19	h-i-j-l-l-s-f-y-e	*This animal lives in the sea.* (jellyfish)
20	k-a-d-b-s-e-a-o-t-r	*You ride on this but it isn't a bike.* (skateboard)

43 What are they saying?

Topics clothes, family and friends

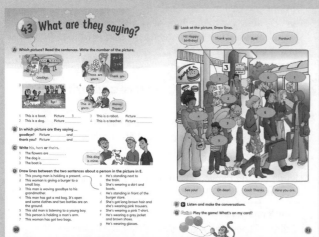

Movers words: *bottles, present*; Flyers words: *other, station*

Equipment needed

- O Starters audio 43F.
- O Colouring pencils or pens.
- O Photocopies of the sentences on page 118 (one for every three learners). See E and 'What's on my card?'
- O Photocopies of the sentences on page 119 (one for each group of learners, made into cards). See F.

A Which picture? Read the sentences. Write the number of the picture.

- O Read out sentence 1: *This is a boat.*
  Point to the pictures and say: *There's a boat in one of the pictures. Where's the boat?* (in picture 3) Point to the number 3 on the line in 1.
- O Learners read sentences 2–4. Ask: *Where is the dog, the robot and the teacher?* Learners find these in the pictures and write the correct number answer on the lines.

> **Check answers: 2** 4 **3** 1 **4** 2

- O Ask: *What other things can you see in the pictures?* Learners put up their hands to answer. They point to the things in the pictures and say: *This is a … or These are …*
  Suggestions (from the Starters wordlist)**: Picture 1:** bag, windows, door **Picture 2:** boy, woman, flowers, numbers, board, jacket **Picture 3:** people, sea, water, clothes **Picture 4:** man, boy

B In which picture are they saying … ?

- O Go out of the classroom and come back in again. Say: *Hello!* Do the same and say: *Hi!*
- O Say: *In two of these pictures, the people are saying goodbye. Which two pictures?* (1 and 3)
  Learners write 1 and 3 on the lines next to 'goodbye?'.
  Note: Explain: we can say 'Hello' or 'Hi' and 'Goodbye' or 'Bye'. They mean the same.
- O Say: *In two of these pictures, the people are saying 'thank you'. Which two pictures?* (2 and 4) Say: *The boy says: 'Hooray!' Does he like the dog?* (yes) *Is he happy?* (yes)
  Learners write 2 and 4 on the lines next to 'thank you?'
- O Learners work in pairs. They choose one of the pictures and role play the situation.

C Write *his, hers* or *theirs*.

- O Point to the boy and the teacher in **A** (picture 2). Ask: *What's the boy saying?* (These are yours.) Write this on the board: *These are yours.* Point to the word 'These' and ask: *What are 'these'? The boy, the teacher or the flowers?* (the flowers) Write: *These flowers are your flowers.* on the board under 'These are yours'.
  Point to the word 'yours' then to 'your flowers' in the second sentence. Explain that 'yours' tells us that these are 'your' flowers.
  Read out the father's sentence in picture 4: *This is yours.* Ask: *How many dogs is the father giving the boy?* (one) *We say 'This' for one dog or one thing. Is that right?* (yes)
- O Point to picture 2 and ask: *What's the boy giving his teacher?* (flowers) Say: *The teacher's got some flowers.*
  Write on the board: *They're ………… flowers.* Point to the line and ask: *Which word do I write here?* (her) Write on the board: *The flowers are …………* Point to the line and ask: *Which word do I write here?* (hers)
  Write on the board:
  These are   her flowers.
  These are   hers.
  Show learners that we can use just one word 'hers' to mean the same as 'her flowers'.
  Write on the board:
  This is   her T-shirt.   This is   … .
  Show learners that we can also use 'hers' here to mean the same as 'her T-shirt'. Learners write *hers* on the line in 1.
- O Write on the board:
  This is   his dog.   The dog is   his.
  Point to the word 'his' in the second sentence. Show learners that we can use just one word 'his' here to mean the same as 'his dog'. Learners write *his* on the line in 2.
- O Point to the boat in picture 3 in **A** and ask: *Who's in the boat?* (two men) *Whose boat is it? His or theirs?* (theirs) Make sure learners understand that we can use just one word 'theirs' to mean the same as 'their boat' here. Learners write *theirs* on the line in 3.
- O Point to the picture in **C** and ask: *What's the boy doing now?* (showing his dog to his friends) *What's he saying?* (This dog is mine.)
  Listen and colour.
- O Check learners have colouring pencils or pens.
  Say: *Look at picture 1. Which thing is not coloured?* (the robot)
  Say: *Listen and colour things in the pictures.*
- O Read out these sentences, giving learners time to colour between each one.
  1 *Can you see the boat? Colour the boat yellow. Yes, yellow!*
  2 *Find the robot and colour it red. Yes, a red robot!*
  3 *Do you like the dog? The dog is brown. Colour it brown, please.*
  4 *Now, colour the flowers with your favourite colour!*

D Draw lines between the two sentences about a person in the picture in E.

- O Teach/revise: *station* then ask questions about the picture in **E**:
  1 *Are these people in a park or at a station?* (at a station)
  2 *How many people are there in the picture?* (14)
  3 *Who's on the train?* (an old woman / a grandmother)
- O Point to sentences a–g in **D**. Ask:
  Which sentences are about a man? (a, c, f, g)
  Which sentences are about a woman? (b, d, e)
- O Point to and read sentence 1: *This young man is holding a present.*
  Ask: *Where's the young man with the present?* Learners point to the young man in the red sweater.
  Say: *Look at the second sentence about this man.*
  He's standing in front of the burger store.
  Ask: *Is this young man in front of the burger store?* (yes)

100

- Read sentence 2: *This woman is giving a burger to a small boy*. Ask: *Where is this woman?* Learners point to the woman with the burger in her hand.

  Point to sentence a. Ask: *Is she standing next to the train?* (no) *Has she got long brown hair and is she wearing pink trousers?* (yes) *Which is this sentence?* (d) Learners draw a line between 2 and d.
- Teach/revise: 'bottle'. Point to the two bottles on the ground at the front of the picture. Ask: *What are these?* (bottles) Learners read sentences 3–7 and draw lines between the sentences.

  > **Check answers: 3** a **4** f **5** g **6** b **7** e
- Read out sentences 1 and c: *This young man is holding a birthday present. He's standing in front of the burger store.*

  Ask: *Can you tell me more things about this man? What's he wearing?* (a red sweater and purple trousers) *What colour's his hair?* (brown/orange) *What's in his hand?* (a present) *What is the present? You choose!* Learners answer.

  Say: *Find the old man. Write two sentences about him. For example, Where is he? What's he wearing? What's he doing? How old is he? What's the boy saying to him? Is he the boy's grandfather? Friend?* Pairs of learners write two sentences about this man.

  Suggestions: *The man's in front of the young man with the present and the man in the orange and white T-shirt. He's wearing glasses, a yellow sweater, blue trousers and brown shoes. He's talking and listening to a small boy. The boy's saying 'This train isn't ours, Grandpa.'*

E Look at the picture. Draw lines.

> **Starters tip**
>
> Train learners to say 'hello' to the examiner at the start of the Speaking Test and to say 'goodbye' before they leave the room. This will help them create a good impression.

- Say: *Some of the people in the picture are talking.* Tell learners to look at the two people with the present. Ask: *What are they saying?*
- Learners follow the lines between the speech bubbles outside the picture to bubbles 1 and 2 inside the picture. (The man is saying *Hi! Happy birthday* and the woman is saying *Thank you*.)
- Learners look and draw lines from the other speech bubbles to the bubbles next to the people in the picture.

  > **Check answers:**
  >
  > **3** The old man: *Pardon?*
  > **4** The woman with the burger: *Here you are.*
  > **5** The boy taking the burger from the woman: *Cool! Thanks.*
  > **6, 7** The two people waving goodbye: *See you! / Bye!* (any order)
  > **8** The man and woman with the open red suitcase: *Oh dear!*

- Ask learners which other word we can say when we don't hear what a person says. (Sorry?)

  Listen carefully!
- Make groups of 8–10 learners. Each group stands in a line.

  Give one card from page 118 to the first learner in each line. The learner reads the card and whispers the words on it to the person behind them, who listens carefully.
- Each learner in the group whispers what they hear to the person behind them until the last person hears it and says it out loud. Usually, the sentence will have changed considerably!
- Say the first word from one of the expressions on the cards. The class says the second part of the expression:

Teacher	Learners
Oh	dear
Well	done
See	you (etc.)

  Learners continue this in pairs. Learner A says the first word. Learner B says the second part.

- Learners sit down. In pairs, they try to remember and then write down all the expressions in their notebooks. Ask different pairs to read out and reply to one of the expressions, for example:

  Learner A: *Well done!*   Learner B: *Thank you!*
  Learner C: *Don't worry!*   Learner D: *OK!*

F ▶ Listen and make the conversations.

> **Starters tip**
>
> Teach learners how to ask for repetition or clarification in English. This will make them more confident if they don't understand something during the Speaking Test. For example: *I don't understand. I don't know. Sorry? Pardon? Can you say that again, please?*

- Say: *Listen to Ben. He's doing his Starters Speaking Test.*
- Divide the class into groups of three. Give each group a set of the sentences for the first part of the Speaking Test. These have number 1 on them (see photocopiable page 119). The sentences should be cut into eight cards.

  Say: *Listen to the first part of Ben's Starters Speaking Test. Listen and put the sentences in the correct order.*

  Play the audio for 1 twice. Learners listen and put the sentences in the correct order.
- Give each group the ten cards for the second part of the Speaking Test. These cards have the number 2 on them. Learners read the questions and answers and put the cards in the order they think they will hear them.

  Say: *Listen to the last part of Ben's Starters Speaking Test.* Play the audio twice.
- Check answers by playing the audio again. Learners hold up the card for the sentences as they hear them. (see below)
- Ask: *Are Ben's answers good?* (yes)

  (He said *Good morning* and *Goodbye*. He asked for repetition: *Sorry? Pardon?* He asked for clarification: *I don't understand. What is 'lesson'?*)
- In pairs, learners role play the conversations.

Audioscript

1	Woman:	Hello, Ben. My name's Anne.
	Boy:	Good morning.
	Woman:	Now, Ben. How old are you?
	Boy:	Sorry?
	Woman:	Are you seven years old?
	Boy:	I don't understand.
	Woman:	Are you seven years old? Are you eight years old?
	Boy:	Oh! No. I'm nine years old.
2	Woman:	What's your favourite lesson?
	Boy:	What is 'lesson'?
	Woman:	What is your favourite class? Do you like reading?
	Boy:	Yes.
	Woman:	Is your teacher a man or a woman?
	Boy:	Pardon?
	Woman:	Is your teacher a woman?
	Boy:	No, a man.
	Woman:	OK. Thank you, Ben. Goodbye.
	Boy:	Bye!

G Play the game! What's on my card?

- Place the cards that learners used for the whispering activity in **E** face down on a table. Ask learners to tell you the expressions. (*Good evening., Well done!, Oh dear!*, etc.) Pick up one card and ask: *What's on my card?* Learners put up their hands to answer.

  For example: Victor: *Good evening?* Teacher: *no* Marie: *Well done?* Teacher: *no!* Richard: *Pardon?* Teacher: *You're right!*
- Learners play the game in groups. One learner picks up a card and reads it silently. The other learners in the group try to guess what's on the card.

44 About us

Topics general revision

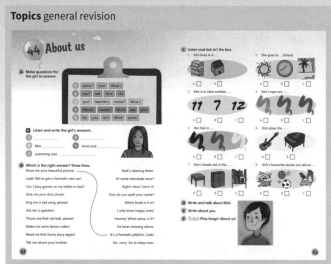

Movers words: *more, only*; Flyers word: *left*

Equipment needed

- Starters audio 44A.
- Photocopies of page 120 (one for every four learners) cut up. See D.
- Photocopies of the questions on page 121 (one for every ten learners) cut up. See 'Our class'.

A Make questions for the girl to answer.

- Point to the jumbled words in 1: *name?/your/What's*
  Ask: *Can you make the question?* (What's your name?)
  Write the question on the board.
  Point to the capital letter at the start of 'What' and to the question mark after 'name'. Remind learners that a question starts with a capital letter and ends with a question mark. Learners write the question in their notebooks.
- In pairs, learners make questions from the jumbled words in 2–5 and write them in their notebooks. (They will need to answer these in the listening task.)

> **Check answers:**
> **2** How old are you? **3** What's your teacher's name?
> **4** What are your friends' names? **5** What sports do you do?

- Write on the board: *What's your friend's name?* Point to the 's' and ask: *How many friends am I asking about – one or two?* (one)
  Write on the board: *What are your friends' names?* Ask: *Am I asking about one friend here?* (no)
  Explain that the verb 'are' and the apostrophe at the end of 'friends' (friends') show us that we are asking about more than one friend.
  Teach/revise: Miss, Mrs and Mr.
  Say: *My family name is (Garcia) Am I Miss, Mrs or Mr Garcia?* Learners answer.
  Make sure learners understand that we use 'Mr' before a family name to talk about a man and 'Mrs' and 'Miss' (and Ms) before a family name to talk about a woman. 'Mrs' usually means that a woman is married.
- In pairs, learners ask and answer the five questions. They do not write anything.

  ▶ **Listen and write the girl's answers.**

> **Starters tip**
> In Listening Part 2, all the words that candidates have to write are in the Starters wordlist. Words like 'Lime', 'Green' or 'Cross' might be a surname or the name of a street or school. In this listening, Kim's teacher's name is 'Miss Green'.

- Point to the picture of the girl in **A** and ask: *What's this girl's name? How old is she? Guess!* Write learners' suggestions on the board.
  Say: *Look at the five questions in your notebooks and listen to a man asking those questions. What are the girl's answers?* Learners listen, then whisper the answers they can remember to their partner.
- Say: *Now listen again and write the girl's answers in your notebooks.* Play the audio again. Learners listen and write the girl's answers. If necessary, play the audio a third time for learners to check their answers.

> **Check answers:**
> **1** Kim **2** 8/eight **3** Green **4** Nick **5** basketball

Audioscript

> *Listen and write.*
>
> **1** Man: Hello. Can I ask you some questions?
> Girl: Yes. OK.
> Man: What's your name?
> Girl: It's Kim. I'm Kim.
> Man: Do you spell that K-I-M?
> Girl: Yes. That's correct.
>
> **2** Man: So, how old are you, Kim?
> Girl: I'm eight.
> Man: Wow! You're eight years old?
> Girl: Yes!
>
> **3** Man: And what's your teacher's name?
> Girl: Miss Green. Her name's Miss Green.
> Man: Is that G-R-E-E-N?
> Girl: Yes that's right.
>
> **4** Man: And have you got friends in your class?
> Girl: Yes. I've got two friends.
> Man: What are their names?
> Girl: Anna is great. I like Nick too. He's a good friend.
> Man: Does Nick spell his name N-I-C-K?
> Girl: Yes, he does.
>
> **5** Man: Do you like sport, Kim?
> Girl: I love doing sport!
> Man: Which sport do you like doing?
> Girl: I like swimming, I like basketball too!
> Man: Basketball! That's great!

B Which is the right answer? Draw lines.

- Say to one learner: *Give me a pencil, please.*
  Say to another learner: *Find me a rubber, please.*
  Make sure learners understand the difference between *Find a rubber.* (I'm not asking you to give the rubber to me.) and *Find me a rubber.* (The rubber is for me.)
  Write on the board: *Find **me** a rubber. Find a rubber **for me**.*
  Explain (in learners' first language if necessary) that these two sentences mean the same.
  Note: We can use this **imperative + me + object** structure at Starters with the following verbs: ask, do, draw, find, get, give, make, read, show, sing, tell, throw and write.
- Point to and read out the first sentence: *Show me your beautiful picture.* Ask: *Can you see the line? It goes to the right answer. What's the answer?* (It's a fantastic jellyfish. Look!)
- Point to the two sentences that end with 'please' and explain that when we add 'please', the sentence sounds more polite. You could also explain that when we're talking to friends or families we don't always add the word please, but it's important to do that when we're talking to people that we don't know well.
- In pairs, learners find the right answers to the other sentences and draw lines. Check answers by asking different pairs to read out one sentence and its answer.

○ Write on the board: *Tell me about your family.*
Choose one learner to ask you to do this. Answer in simple short sentences, for example:
Learner: *Tell me about your family.*
Teacher: *I've got a sister. My father is a teacher. My Mum loves cats!*

○ In pairs, learners write three short sentences about their family in their notebooks.
Ask 3–4 learners to tell the class something about their own family or something about their partner's family. For example:
I love my Mum. My grandmother is really old. Maria's family lives in a big house. Maria's dad is very funny.

C Listen and tick the box.

○ Say: *Let's learn more about Kim. Read sentences 1–8 in C and look at the pictures.* Give learners time to read and look.
Read the story twice. Learners listen and tick the correct boxes.
Kim doesn't live in a house. She lives in a **flat** in London. She goes to **Clock** School. She's in class **eleven** now. Kim's got **brown** eyes and her hair is **brown** too.
You know that Kim likes swimming and playing basketball. Well, she can play the **guitar** too. She has guitar lessons in the evenings.
Kim reads **books**. She loves going to the bookshop and she has lots of books at home. Her books are in the **cupboard** in the dining room. She enjoys reading stories about **animals**. **Animals** are in her favourite stories.

○ Write the sentences on the board. Ask different learners to come to the board and write the missing words.
Kim lives in a … . She goes to … School. She's in class … . Kim's eyes and hair are … . Kim plays the … . Her books are in the … . Her favourite stories are about … .
Answers: flat. Clock. 11/eleven. brown. guitar. (dining room) cupboard. animals.

D Write and talk about Nick.

○ Point to the boy in the picture and say: *This is Nick. Nick is Kim's friend. Kim lives in a … . (flat) but Nick doesn't live in a flat.*
Write on the board: *Nick lives in a … .*
Point to the house in picture 1B. Ask a learner to come up and write *house* at the end of this sentence.

○ Point to the sentence on the board: *She goes to Clock School.* Say: *Nick's a boy. We don't say 'She'. What word do we say to talk about a boy?* (he)
Write on the board: *He goes to ………… School.* Point to the pictures of the sun and beach in B (question 2) and ask: *Which school does Nick go to? Does he go to 'Beach' School or 'Sun' School? You choose!* Learners copy the sentence *He goes to ………… School.* and write *Beach* or *Sun* in the gap.

○ Point to the picture of Nick and ask: *What colour are Nick's eyes?* (green) Write on the board: *His eyes are green.* Remind learners that we say 'his' to talk about a boy.

○ Learners write the sentences about Nick, choosing words for the sentences from the pictures in **C**. The sentences about Kim on the board will help them.

○ Say: *Kim goes to Clock School. Nick goes to Beach/Sun School.*
Underline the words 'house' and 'green' in the sentences about Nick on the board. Say: *Kim lives in a flat, but Nick lives in a house. Kim's eyes are brown, but Nick's eyes are … ?* (green) Point out that when we talk about differences, we can make them clear by stressing the word that expresses the difference (flat – **house**, brown – **green**).

○ Read out the sentences about Kim. Learners say their sentences about Nick. They stress the word that is different.
Learners continue reading out the sentences about Kim and saying their sentences about Nick in pairs.

E Write about you.

○ Say: *We know some things about Kim and Nick and their school and hobbies. Now, write about your school and hobbies.*
Give out photocopies of page 120 (one set of sentences to each learner).

○ Learners read the sentences and complete them.

○ Take the sentences from each learner and give everyone in the class another learner's sentences.
Note: Large classes: divide learners into groups of 4–5 at this point.

○ One learner reads out the sentences they were given, starting with the last sentence.
For example: *I like playing tennis and swimming.*

○ The other learners listen and decide who has written the sentence (The listening learners do not speak at this point). Then, the next sentence from the end is read out.
For example: *My classmates' names are Mary and Carol.* Continue like this until the final sentence (the learner's name). The learner who is reading out the sentences says: *My name's …* The other learners in the group guess who wrote these sentences.

F Play bingo! About us!

○ Give out a photocopy of the bingo card on page 121 to each learner.
Note: Large classes: give a bingo card to each pair of learners.

○ Explain the game to learners. Learners try to find a person who **has**, **does**, or **can do** each of the things in the bingo boxes.

○ Tell learners to read the things they need to find. First, they can write their own name in any box that is correct about them.

○ Write on the board in a square: *has a brother*.
Ask one learner: for example, *(Barbara), have you got a brother?* Barbara answers: *Yes, I have.* Write *Barbara* above *has a brother*.
Draw a square on the board. Inside the square, write: *walks to school.* Ask another learner: *(John), do you walk to school?* (John): *No, I don't.* Ask learners this question until someone answers *Yes!* Write their name above *walks to school.* Make sure that learners understand that they need to find someone who answers *yes* to the 'Have you?', 'Do you?' or 'Can you?' questions.

○ Learners move around, asking questions and writing names in the boxes. Stop when someone has got names in all their boxes (Bingo!) or after ten minutes.

45　Happy ending!

Topics general revision

Flyers words: *group, sound*; Not in YLE wordlists: *poem, crossword, dice, turn*

Equipment needed

o　One dice per 3–5 learners; a counter for each learner. See C.

o　Cards with different expressions on them. See C: 'The end'.

Ⓐ Look at the pictures. Write the words.

o　Point to the crossword and ask: *What words can you read?* (crossword and alphabet)

　　What letters can you see in the crossword? (a, b, c, d, e, f, g, h, i, j, k, l, m, n, o, p, q, r, s, t, u, w, y, z)

　　Point out that these letters are the first letters in the words in the crossword.

　　Ask: *Which letters of the alphabet are NOT here?* (v, x)

　　Say: *Let's do an alphabet crossword!*

o　Point to the pictures. Explain that the pictures are in alphabetical order.

　　Point to the apple and ask: *What's this?* (an apple)

　　Say: *Find the letter 'a' in the crossword.* Ask: *How do you spell apple?* (a-double p-l-e)

　　Point to the boxes under the letter 'a'. Learners write *p-p-l-e* in these boxes.

o　In pairs, learners write the words for the other pictures in the crossword.

> **Check answers:**
>
> **Across (top to bottom):** under, nine, grapes, kitchen, onion, tail, in, zoo, eleven, red, face, dress
>
> **Down (left to right):** lizard, watch, apple, head, skirt, bread, pear, coconut, jeans, question, mango, yellow

o　Ask different learners:

　　How many of the words are fruit words? (five)

　　Which are the fruit words? (apple, coconut, grapes, mango, pear)

　　Ask different learners: *What's your favourite fruit?*

　　How many of the words are clothes? (four)

　　What are these words? (dress, jeans, skirt, watch)

　　Ask different learners: *Are you wearing a dress / jeans / a skirt / a watch today?*

How many numbers are there? (two: nine and eleven)

Ask different learners: *What's your favourite number?*

Which colour words can you see? (red, yellow) *What colour is the apple?* (red) *What colour is the skirt?* (yellow) *What's your favourite colour? What colours are your clothes?*

Which words are about animals? (lizard, tail, zoo)

Ask different learners: *Which animals do you like?*

o　Point to the word 'question' in the crossword. Point out how the first letter of 'under' is the second letter of 'question'. The fifth letter of 'crossword' is the fourth letter of 'question'. The second letter of 'nine' is the sixth letter of 'question'.

　　Say: *Now, you make a crossword!* Write on the board: *fruit, clothes, number, colour, animal.* Learners write their words for these things so that they 'share' letters like the letters in 'question'.

　　Learners show each other their crosswords in small groups and talk about their favourite things.

Ⓑ Make word groups.

o　Point to the beans in picture 1 and ask: *What are these?* (beans)

　　Point to the word 'bean' in the first blue circle and say it. Learners repeat the word.

　　Point to the first wordbox and read out the first three words: *wall, clean, they.*

　　Say: *bean, wall. Do these two words sound the same?* (no)

　　Say: *bean, they – do these two words sound the same?*

　　Say: *bean, clean. Do these two words sound the same?* (yes)

　　Point to 'green' in the second wordbox.

　　Say: *bean, clean, green. Do these three words sound the same?* (yes)

　　Point to the word 'green' in the second wordbox. Point to these words in the first blue circle. Make sure learners see the that there is one word in each wordbox which sounds like the word in each of the blue circles.

o　Complete the other five blue circles in open class or with learners working in pairs. Check answers by asking different pairs to say the three words in one of the blue circles.

> **Answers:**
>
> day – they – say, right – kite – night, three – sea – bee, zoo – two – you, ball – wall – hall

o　Write on the board and say: *The green beans are clean.* Ask: *Which picture shows this sentence?* (Picture 1)

　　Drill this sentence with learners, stressing 'green', 'beans' and 'clean' to practise the /i:/ sound.

　　Change the sentence to: *Clean the green beans, please!*

o　Do the same with these sentences: *Fly your kite at night!* (Picture 2) *Don't throw your ball on the wall in the hall!* (Picture 3)

o　In pairs, learners write a sentence and draw a picture with 'three', 'bee' and 'sea'.

　　Suggestions: The three bees are next to the sea. / There are three bees flying to the sea.

C Play the circles game!

Note: The idea of this game is to revise Starters words from different topics.

○ Teach learners this language for the game:
Pick up the dice. Throw the dice. It's your turn.
Say the sentences. Learners listen and mime picking up and throwing the dice and pointing to a person.

○ Explain the game. The winner is the person who has correctly spelled words for the most stepping stone letters (a–z). On each stone, there's a clue. Learners have to read the clue and then think of a word that starts with the letter next to the stepping stone.
Note: Sometimes, there is more than one possible answer.
All the learners have a counter. They all put their counter where it says 'the start'. One learner throws the dice. The learner moves their counter that number of stones and reads and says and writes the word(s) starting with that letter. For example, the learner throws a four. They move their counter four circles to the (d) stones: 'children play with these'. They write the word (dolls) in their notebook.

○ Learners can move forwards or backwards. They always move the number of stones shown on the dice. If they get to a letter they already have a word for, they stay on that circle but do not write a word.

○ If they get to one of the three stones with 'go to', they go to that letter.

○ At the end of the game, learners exchange lists. Learners come to the board and write words for the different letters. Learners get a point for each correctly spelt word.

Suggested answers (from the Starters wordlist):

a	afternoon	m	monkey/mouse
b	baseball/badminton/basketball	n	night
c	chicken/crocodile/cat/cow	o	orange
d	dolls	p	pea/pear/pineapple/pie
e	egg	q	question
f	fish/frog	r	radio
g	grandfather/grandpa	s	swim
h	hair/hand/head	t	table tennis/tennis
i	ice cream	u	ugly
j	jacket	v	very
k	kick	w	walk
l	lemon/lime	y	young
		z	zoo

○ Point to the clue for 'z' (zoo): 'you see animals here'. Ask: *Where can you see animals? In a zoo or a … ? (park/garden/farm)*
Point to the clue for 'w' and say: *You do this with your feet. You walk with your feet.* (Mime kicking a ball) *You (kick) with your feet.* (mime running) Learners: *You run with your feet.* Ask learners to think of other things we do with our feet.
Suggestions: ride a bike, jump.
They mime the action. The other learners say what the action is. They could do the same with *hands*.
Suggestions: wave, carry, hold, throw, catch.

○ Say: *You can make and play a stepping stones game, now! Listen! Draw six stones like the ones in C!* Learners draw six stones in their notebooks.
Say: *Look at the pictures and crossword in A. Choose six words and write a sentence for your six stones.* Learners use the clues in **C** to help them. Working in pairs, learners write their clues inside their stones and write the first letter of the answer outside each stone.

○ Two pairs work together. They show each other their stones. The other pair says what the word is for each stone.

Make a poem.

○ Write on the board:
I like the colour
I like eating
I like
I don't like

○ Learners copy the sentences into their notebooks and complete them. Ask different learners to read out their sentences.

○ Write these four words on the board: *bread, cakes, red, snakes*.
In pairs or groups of three, learners make poems by completing the four sentences from the board with these words. Alternatively, learners choose the words to end each line of their poem. Each word can only be used once. They can also draw a picture for the poem or for each sentence of the poem. You could display the poems on the classroom walls or make them into a book.

○ Various combinations are possible. For example:
I like the colour red. I like eating bread. I like cakes. I don't like snakes!
I like the colour red. I like eating cakes. I like eating bread. I like snakes. I don't like cakes.

○ Learners practise reading their poems aloud. You could record some of them.

The end!

○ To celebrate the end of the book, give six learners/groups a card with one of these expressions on:
1 *Bye!*   2 *Goodbye!*   3 *That's the end!*   4 *Well done!*   5 *What now?*
6 *See you!*
Each group practises saying their expression. Then, say a number, that group says their words. Keep this quick. Continue like this, varying the order of the numbers.
After a couple of times, add actions. When groups say *Bye bye!*, *Goodbye!* or *See you!*, everyone waves. When groups say *That's the end!* or *Well done!*, everyone claps.
Finally, all the learners say their words at the same time!
Note: Learners/groups could swap cards so that they practise saying different expressions.

Starters tip

After completing this book, learners will be familiar with all parts of *Cambridge English: Starters*. It is a good idea to set a practice test at least once, so that candidates for Starters are confident that they can complete the test in the time allowed. You can use the practice test on page 126.

Tick a box.	Write four numbers.
Write a name.	Say the alphabet.
Listen and colour.	Look at the letters.
Read the questions.	Draw a bird.
Put a cross in the box.	Draw three lines.

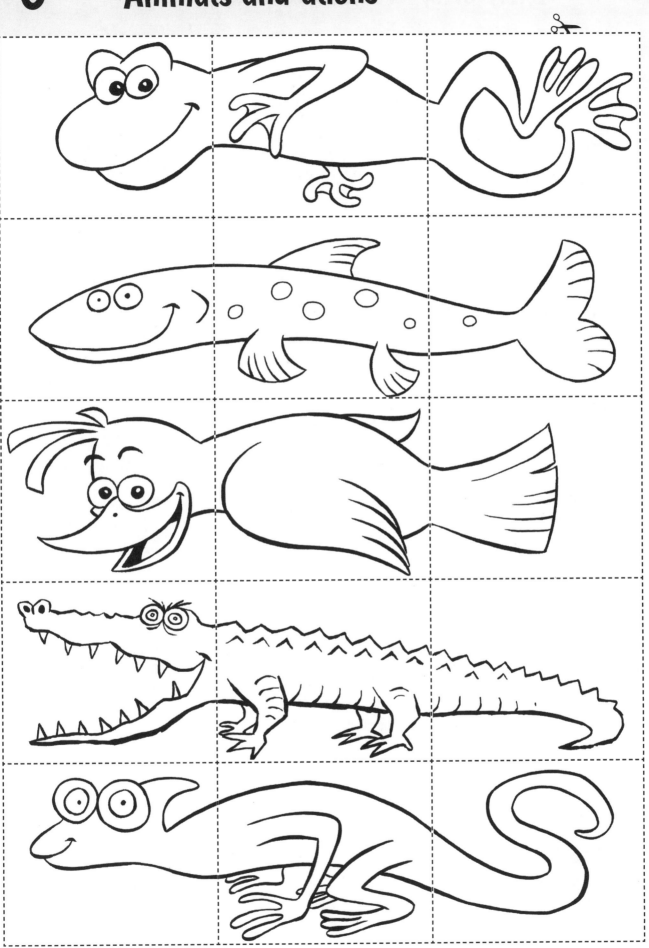

One, two, three animals

15 One, two, three animals

20 Ben and Kim live here!

Learner A

Write five questions.

> or dirty?   ~~or small?~~   or new?   or sad?   or closed?

1   Is your garden big _or small_?

2   Are the shops in your street open ....?

3   Is your street clean ....?

4   Are the children in this class happy ....?

5   Is our school old ....?

✂ -

20 Ben and Kim live here!

Learner B

Write five questions.

> or long?   or clean?   or old?   ~~or open?~~   or beautiful?

1   Is the window in your bathroom closed _or open_?

2   Is your school bus new ....?

3   Is the name of your street short ....?

4   Are the windows in our school dirty ....?

5   Are the flowers in your street ugly ....?

21   Play with us!

start, cross and stop	in the blue sky.	Wave at the train,	big and small	fly happy people
it's there again	at the boats and ships	in School Street.	here and there	And look …
Buses, bikes and motorbikes,	Helicopters and planes	on the railway line.	on the blue, blue sea.	trucks, lorries and cars

painting	running	counting
reading	listening	jumping
drawing	sleeping	eating
swimming	playing the piano	riding a bike
clapping	drinking	flying
playing the guitar	having a bath	riding a horse
opening the door	pointing	singing
watching TV	taking a photo	waving to a friend
smiling	driving a car	going to bed

27 Food I really like!

32   Happy birthday!

1

Hi Grandpa! I really like taking photos. It's fun!

For my birthday, I'd like a new ...., please, or some cool new .... for my sports lessons. Is that OK?

For my party, I'd like to go to the park and play .... I love that sport! Come and play with us! See you!

Sam

2

Hello Grandma!

Come and see us in our new house. The kitchen's great! I can make chocolate .... there now. Would you like some? It's fantastic!

Oh, and I love ....

I'd like a new red .... for my birthday, please. Can you take me to the shops?

Jill

A	B
The crocodile is playing badminton.	The cat is playing the piano.
The dog is cleaning a car.	The spider is flying a helicopter.
The snake is writing on a wall.	The horse is drinking water.
The goat is listening to music.	The bird is phoning a friend.
The duck is taking a photo.	The fish is watching TV.
The monkey is opening a sweet.	The frog is playing basketball.

40 Night and day

one	16	eight	7
20	four	11	thirteen
nineteen	1	sixteen	18
4	nine	8	eighteen
five	13	two	14
9	twenty	15	ten
twelve	19	eleven	6
5	three	2	seventeen
seven	3	fourteen	10
12	fifteen	17	six

43   What are they saying?

Hooray!	Cool!
Good evening.	I don't understand.
Here you are.	Can you say that again?
Happy birthday!	Pardon?
That's right.	Me too!
Yes please!	Well done!
See you!	Don't worry!
Let's go to the park!	Oh dear!

What are they saying?

1 Hello, Ben. My name's Anne.	**1** Good morning.
1 Now, Ben. How old are you?	**1** Sorry?
1 Are you seven years old?	**1** I don't understand.
1 Are you eight years old?	**1** Oh! No. I'm nine years old.
2 What's your favourite lesson?	**2** What is 'lesson'?
2 Do you like reading?	**2** Yes.
2 Is your teacher a man or a woman?	**2** Pardon?
2 Is your teacher a woman?	**2** No, a man.
2 OK. Thank you, Ben. Goodbye.	**2** Bye!

44 About us

My name's ....

I live in a ....

I'm .... years old.

My hair's ....

My eyes are ....

My teacher's name is
....

I'm in class number .... at
.... School.

My classmates' names are ....
and ....

I like .... and ....

My name's ....

I live in a ....

I'm .... years old.

My hair's ....

My eyes are ....

My teacher's name is ....

I'm in class number .... at
.... School.

My classmates' names are ....
and ....

I like .... and ....

My name's ....

I live in a ....

I'm .... years old.

My hair's ....

My eyes are ....

My teacher's name is ....

I'm in class number .... at
.... School.

My classmates' names are ....
and ....

I like .... and ....

My name's ....

I live in a ....

I'm .... years old.

My hair's ....

My eyes are ....

My teacher's name is ....

I'm in class number .... at
.... School.

My classmates' names are ....
and ....

I like .... and ....

B	I	N	G	O
lives in a house	can play soccer	doesn't like chocolate	wears glasses	can dance
walks to school	has a brother	can play the piano	loves sports	has a sister
enjoys writing stories	has a poster in their bedroom	can sing	has a skateboard	plays table tennis
goes home by car	lives in an apartment	has two sisters	likes peas	reads a lot
plays games on a tablet	has music lessons	likes trying new foods	phones their grandma	takes great photos

Listening

Part 1
5 questions

Listen and draw lines. There is one example.

Alice   Matt   Eva   Dan

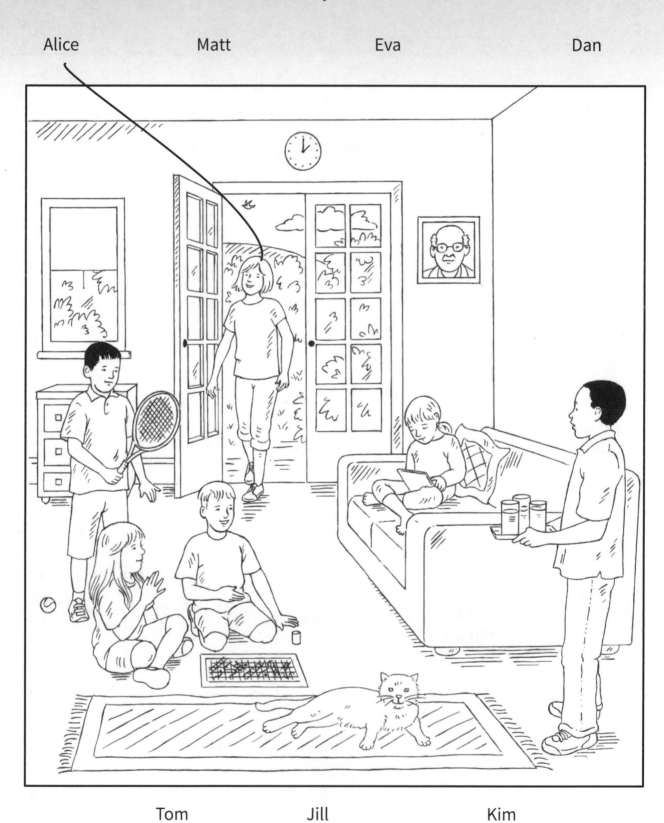

Tom   Jill   Kim

Listening

**Read the question. Listen and write a name or a number.
There are two examples.**

Examples

What is the boy's name? .... *Bill* ....

How old is he? .... *9* ....

Questions

1   Where does Bill live?   ....Street

2   What number is Bill's house?   ....

3   How many rooms are there in his house?   ....

4   What is Bill's sister's name?   ....

5   Who is Bill's friend?   ....

Listening

Part 3
5 questions

Listen and tick (✔) the box. There is one example.

Which boy is Nick?

A ✔

B ☐

C ☐

1 What can Tom do?

A ☐

B ☐

C ☐

2 What does Sam want for his birthday?

A ☐

B ☐

C ☐

Listening

3   What's in Kim's desk?

      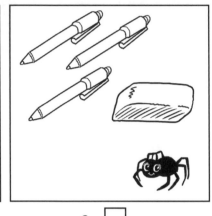

A ☐   B ☐   C ☐

4   What can Ben have for lunch?

A ☐   B ☐   C ☐

5   Which girl is May?

A ☐   B ☐   C ☐

Listening

Part 4

Listen and colour. There is one example.

Listening – Audioscript

Hello. This is the Starters Practice Listening Test.

Part 1

Look at Part One. Now look at the picture. Listen and look. There is one example.

Man:	Hi! I really like this picture. Who's that?
Woman:	That girl? She's next to the open door …
Man:	Yes. She's coming in from the garden.
Woman:	Oh, that's Alice.
Man:	Alice? What a nice name.

Can you see the line? This is an example.
Now you listen and draw lines.

One

Woman:	Can you see the boy with the drinks?
Man:	Yes! What's his name?
Woman:	His name's Tom. Tom's wearing his new jeans!
Man:	They're really cool!

Two

Man:	And who's that? The girl on the sofa?
Woman:	The one with the tablet in her hands?
Man:	Yes.
Woman:	Her name's Eva. Eva's reading a scary story.
Man:	Oh!

Three

Woman:	And there's Matt. He loves tennis.
Man:	Is he the boy with the tennis racket in his hand?
Woman:	That's right. That's Matt.
Man:	Does he play with his friends?
Woman:	Yes. At the park.

Four

Man:	And who's that? The person in the photo on the wall?
Woman:	That's the children's grandfather.
Man:	Oh! And what's his name?
Woman:	His name's Dan. It's a fantastic photo of Dan …
Man:	Yes, it is.

Five

Man:	And who's that child? The one on the floor?
Woman:	The girl with the board game … That's Jill.
Man:	She's got really long hair!
Woman:	Yes, she has. And she's having lots of fun!

Now listen to Part 1 again.
That is the end of Part 1.

Part 2

Read the question. Listen and write a name or a number. There are two examples.

Woman:	Hello. What's your name?
Boy:	Bill.
Woman:	How do you spell that?
Boy:	B-I-L-L. It's my birthday today.
Woman:	Happy birthday! How old are you?
Boy:	I'm nine today.
Woman:	Nine!

Can you see the answers? Now you listen and write a name or a number.

One

Woman:	Where do you live, Bill?
Boy:	I live in Ship Street.
Woman:	Do you spell that S-H-I-P?
Boy:	Yes, that's right. Ship Street.

Two

Woman:	What number is your house?
Boy:	Our house is number six.
Woman:	Six?
Boy:	Yes.

Three

Woman:	Do you live in a big house?
Boy:	Yes, I do. It's got ten rooms.
Woman:	How many rooms?
Boy:	Ten.

Four

Woman:	What's your sister's name?
Boy:	Her name's Lucy.
Woman:	Can you spell that?
Boy:	L-U-C-Y

Five

Woman:	And who do you play with?
Boy:	I play with my friend. His name's Mark.
Woman:	Mark? Does he spell his name M-A-R-K?
Boy:	Yes, that's right.

Now listen to Part 2 again.
That is the end of Part 2.

Part 3

Look at the pictures. Listen and look. There is one example.
Which boy is Nick?

Woman:	Do you walk to school, Nick?
Boy:	No, I don't.
Woman:	Do you go to school by car, then?
Boy:	No. I ride my bike to school.

Can you see the tick? Now you listen and tick the box.

One
What can Tom do?

Woman:	Can you ride a horse, Tom?
Boy:	No, I can't.
Woman:	Can you play basketball, then?
Boy:	Well, I can't play basketball, but I can play tennis.

Two
What does Sam want for his birthday?

Woman:	What do you want for your birthday, Sam?
Boy:	I don't know Grandma. I don't want crayons.
Woman:	Some new football boots?
Boy:	No thanks. I know! I'd like a new skateboard, please!

Three
What's in Kim's desk?

Man:	What have you got in your desk, Kim?
Girl:	My pens and an eraser.
Man:	And what's that?
Girl:	Oh no! It's a spider!

Four
What can Ben have for lunch?

Boy:	What can I have for lunch, Mum? Meatballs?
Woman:	Yes! You can have peas with those, too.
Boy:	Good! And have we got some apple pie?
Woman:	No, sorry! But you can have some ice cream.
Boy:	Great!

Five
Which girl is May?

Boy:	Can you see my friend, May, Dad?
Man:	May? Is she that girl? The one in the trousers?
Boy:	No. And she isn't wearing a dress today. She's wearing her new T-shirt and skirt.
Man:	Oh! I can see her now.

Now listen to Part 3 again.
That is the end of Part 3.

Part 4

Look at the picture. Listen and look. There is one example.

Woman:	Hello, Alex! Do you want to colour this picture?
Boy:	OK. Can I colour one of the helicopters?
Woman:	Yes. Colour the helicopter in the bag.
Boy:	The helicopter in the woman's bag?
Woman:	Yes. That's right. Colour it grey.

Can you see the helicopter in the bag? This helicopter is grey.
Now you listen and colour.

One

Woman:	Now, colour the helicopter on the boy's trousers.
Boy:	The helicopter on the boy's trousers. What colour?
Woman:	Make it yellow.
Boy:	Right. I'm doing that now.

Two

Boy:	Whose helicopter is <u>that</u>? Look! It's flying.
Woman:	Oh, yes. I don't know. Sorry!
Boy:	Can I colour the flying helicopter green, please?
Woman:	Yes, I love that colour.
Boy:	Me too!

Three

Woman:	Can you see the man? He's got a helicopter in his hands.
Boy:	Oh, yes! It's really cool!
Woman:	Yes, it is! Colour the man's helicopter red.
Boy:	Right! I can do that.
Woman:	Great!

Four

Boy:	There's an alien by the tree ... It's got a helicopter on its head!
Woman:	Oh, yes!
Boy:	Can I colour the helicopter on the alien's head orange, please?
Woman:	Yes, I love that colour.
Boy:	So do I!

Five

Woman:	Now look at the painting.
Boy:	Oh! There's a helicopter in it.
Woman:	Yes! Let's colour the helicopter in the painting now.
Boy:	OK. Can I colour it purple?
Woman:	Yes! Thank you.

Now listen to Part 4 again.
That is the end of the Starters Practice Listening Test.

Reading and Writing

Part 1
5 questions

Look and read. Put a tick (✔) or a cross (✗) in the box.
There are two examples.

Examples

These are babies.

This is an arm.

Questions

1

These are sausages.

2

This is a cow.

Reading and Writing

Part 1

3

This is a lorry.   [ ]

4

These are socks.   [ ]

5

These are guitars.   [ ]

Reading and Writing

Part 2
5 questions

Look and read. Write *yes* or *no*.

Examples

You can see four shells on the sand.   ....yes............

The two children are playing in the water.   ....no.............

Questions

1   The girl has got long black hair.   ....

2   The man is wearing a baseball cap.   ....

3   There are three kites in the picture.   ....

4   One of the birds is on the chair.   ....

5   A woman is sitting on the boat.   ....

Reading and Writing

Part 3
5 questions

Look at the pictures. Look at the letters. Write the words.

Example

<u>l</u> <u>a</u> <u>m</u> <u>p</u>

m p a l

Questions

1

_ _ _ _ _ _ _

d c p o
b u r a

2

_ _ _ _ _ _

r o i m
r r

3

_ _ _ _ _

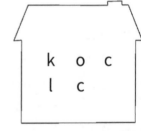

k o c
l c

4

_ _ _ _ _

e s h
u o

5

_ _ _ _ _ _

d w o i
n w

Reading and Writing

Part 4

5 questions

Read this. Choose a word from the box. Write the correct word next to numbers 1–5.
There is one example.

A dog

I have got four ....*legs*.............., two ears and a long (1) ....

at the end of my body.

I live with a family. I like eating (2) .... and I drink lots of

(3) .... I love playing with the people in the family. They take me

(4) .... in the evening. The children throw my ball and I run and catch

it in my (5) .... ! Oh! I don't like cats!

legs   park   computer   mouth

bed   tail   water   meat

Reading and Writing

Part 5
5 questions

Look at the pictures and read the questions. Write one-word answers.

Examples

Where are the people?   at the .... *zoo* ....

What is in the woman's bag?   some .... *fruit* ....

Questions

1   How many children are there?   ....

Reading and Writing

Part 5

2 What is the girl doing?   she's taking a ....

3 Where are the monkeys?   in the ....

4 Who has got the glasses now?   the ....

5 What is the boy holding?   a ....

Practice test

Practice Test

Answer key

Listening

Part 1 (5 marks)

Lines should be drawn between:

1   Tom and the boy with drinks, wearing jeans.
2   Eva and the girl on the sofa holding a tablet.
3   Matt and the boy who loves tennis holding a tennis racket.
4   Dan and the man in the photo on the wall.
5   Jill and the girl with long hair on the floor playing a board game

Part 2 (5 marks)

1   Ship
2   6/six
3   10/ten
4   Lucy
5   Mark

Part 3 (5 marks)

1   A
2   B
3   C
4   A
5   C

Part 4 (5 marks)

1   Colour helicopter on boy's trousers – yellow
2   Colour helicopter in the sky – green
3   Colour helicopter in the man's hands – red
4   Colour helicopter on monster's head – orange
5   Colour helicopter in the woman's picture – purple

Reading and Writing

Part 1 (5 marks)

1   ✗
2   ✔
3   ✗
4   ✗
5   ✔

Part 2 (5 marks)

1   yes
2   yes
3   no
4   no
5   yes

Part 3 (5 marks)

1   cupboard
2   mirror
3   clock
4   house
5   window

Part 4 (5 marks)

1   tail
2   meat
3   water
4   park
5   mouth

Part 5 (5 marks)

1   2/two
2   photo/picture
3   trees
4   monkey
5   banana

Speaking

Examiner's script

* Use child's name throughout the test

Part	Examiner does this:	Examiner says this:	Learner's minimal response:	Back-up questions:
1	(Usher brings candidate in.)	Hello. My name's (*Jane / Ms Smith*). What's your name?	Hello. (*name*)	Is your name (*child's name*)?
	Point to **Scene** card.	Look at this. This is a garden. The children are playing.		
	Point to book.	Here's the book. Where's the ice cream? Where are the flowers?	Points to ice cream. Points to flowers.	Is this the ice cream? Are these the flowers?
	Point to **Object** cards.	Now look at these. Which is the skirt?	Points to Object card.	Is this the skirt? (pointing to skirt)
	Put the skirt on the rug.	I'm putting the skirt on the rug.		
		Now you put the skirt next to the skateboard.	Puts the Object card in place.	Where's the skateboard? Next to the skateboard.
		Which is the frog?	Points to Object card.	Is this the frog? (pointing to the frog)
		Put the frog between the two boys.	Puts the Object card in place.	Where are the two boys? Between the two boys.
2	Remove **Object** cards and point to a bird in **Scene** picture.	Now, (child's name), what's this? What colour is it? How many birds are there?	bird grey two	Is it a bird? Is it white? Grey? Are there three? Two?
	Point to the **girl**.	What's this girl doing?	swimming	Is she swimming?
	Point to the **woman**.	Tell me about this woman.	She's wearing a hat. She's reading.	What's she wearing on her head? What's she doing?
		Thank you.		

Speaking
Examiner's script

Part	Examiner does this:	Examiner says this:	Learner's minimal response:	Back-up questions:
3	Pick out four **Object** cards			
3.1	Show **phone** card	What's this?	(a) phone	Is it a phone?
		Have you got a phone?	Yes/No	
		Is your/this phone old or new?	old	Is your/this phone old?
3.2	Show **pencils** card	What are these?	pencils	Are they pencils?
		Have you got some pencils?	Yes/No	
		What do you do with your pencils?	draw	Do you draw with your pencils?
3.3	Show **boots** card	What are these?	boots	Are they boots?
		Have you got a pair of boots?	Yes/No	
		What are you wearing on your feet today?	shoes	Are you wearing shoes?
3.4	Show **burger** card.	What's this?	(a) burger	Is it a burger?
		Do you like eating burgers?	Yes/No	
		What's your favourite food?	chocolate	Is it chocolate?
4	Put away all cards.	Now, (child's name), who lives in your home?	my family	Does your family live in your home?
		What do you like doing at home?	watching TV	Do you like watching TV?
		Which is your favourite room at home?	my bedroom	Do you like your bedroom?
		OK. Thank you, (*child's name*). Goodbye.	(Goodbye) *Leaves.*	

Speaking

Scene picture

Speaking

Object cards